Geographies of Affect in Contemporary Literature and Visual Culture

Spatial Practices

AN INTERDISCIPLINARY SERIES IN CULTURAL HISTORY,
GEOGRAPHY AND LITERATURE

General Editors

Christoph Ehland (*Paderborn University*)

Editorial Board

Christine Berberich (*University of Portsmouth*)
Jonathan Bordo (*Trent University*)
Oliver von Knebel Doeberitz (*University of Leipzig*)
Catrin Gersdorf (*University of Würzburg*)
Peter Merriman (*Aberystwyth University*)
Christoph Singer (*Paderborn University*)
Merle Tonnies (*Paderborn University*)
Cornelia Wächter (*Ruhr University Bochum*)

Advisory Board

Blake Fitzpartrick (*Ryerson University*)
Flavio Gregori (*Ca' Foscari University of Venice*)
Margaret Olin (*Yale University*)
Ralph Prodzik (*University of Würzburg*)
Andrew Sanders (*University of Durham*)
Mihaela Irimia (*University of Bucharest*)

Founding Editors

Robert Burden
Stephan Kohl

Former Series Editor

Chris Thurgar-Dawson

VOLUME 35

The titles published in this series are listed at *brill.com/spat*

Geographies of Affect in Contemporary Literature and Visual Culture

Central Europe and the West

Edited by

Ágnes Györke and Imola Bülgözdi

BRILL
RODOPI

LEIDEN | BOSTON

Cover illustration: Photos by Ágnes Györke and Imola Bülgözdi, editing by Fruzsina Papp and Dzsuliánó Takács.

Library of Congress Cataloging-in-Publication Data

Names: Györke, Ágnes, editor. | Bülgözdi, Imola, editor.
Title: Geographies of affect in contemporary literature and visual culture :
  Central Europe and the West / edited by Ágnes Györke and Imola Bülgözdi.
Description: Leiden ; Boston : Brill Rodopi, [2021] | Series: Spatial practices
  1871-689X ; volume 35 | Includes bibliographical references and index. |
  Summary: ""Eastern Europeans, while not 'other' as much as Asians or Africans,
  are also 'not quite' European; rather, they are semi-European, semi-developed,
  with semi- functioning states and semi-civilized manners" concludes Nataša
  Kovačević, in an attempt to summarize the main differences between Eastern
  and Western Europe, in her introduction to Narrating Post/Communism.
  The simple fact that Central European countries, with the exception of Germany
  and Austria, are at the same time also grouped under the term Eastern Europe
  due to their post- communist past, already hints at the complexity of this
  region's historical and cultural heritage"– Provided by publisher.
Identifiers: LCCN 2020045246 | ISBN 9789004440883 (hardback ;
  acid-free paper) | ISBN 9789004442559 (ebook)
Subjects: LCSH: Central European literature–20th century–History and criticism |
  Affect (Psychology) in literature. | Transnationalism in literature. | National
  characteristics, Central European. | Motion pictures–Hungary–History and
  criticism. | Cities and towns in literature. | Cities and towns in motion pictures.
Classification: LCC PN849.E87 G46 2021 | DDC 809/.894–dc23
LC record available at https://lccn.loc.gov/2020045246

Typeface for the Latin, Greek, and Cyrillic scripts: "Brill". See and download: brill.com/brill-typeface.

ISSN 1871-689X
ISBN 978-90-04-44088-3 (hardback)
ISBN 978-90-04-44255-9 (e-book)

Copyright 2021 by Koninklijke Brill NV, Leiden, The Netherlands.
Koninklijke Brill NV incorporates the imprints Brill, Brill Hes & De Graaf, Brill Nijhoff, Brill Rodopi, Brill Sense, Hotei Publishing, mentis Verlag, Verlag Ferdinand Schöningh and Wilhelm Fink Verlag.
All rights reserved. No part of this publication may be reproduced, translated, stored in a retrieval system, or transmitted in any form or by any means, electronic, mechanical, photocopying, recording or otherwise, without prior written permission from the publisher. Requests for re-use and/or translations must be addressed to Koninklijke Brill NV via brill.com or copyright.com.

This book is printed on acid-free paper and produced in a sustainable manner.

Contents

Acknowledgments IX
List of Figures X
Notes on Contributors XI

Introduction: Central and Eastern Europe and the West: Affective Relations 1
   Ágnes Györke and Imola Bülgözdi

PART 1
Edgy Feelings: Translocality, Trauma, and Disengagement

1 Impersonal Affect and Transpersonal Community in the Totaled City 21
   Pieter Vermeulen

2 Body, Trauma, Theatricality – Rereading Testimony in the Stage Performance of *Sea Lavender, or the Euphoria of Being* 35
   Miklós Takács

3 The City as a Lyric Archive of Affects in Lisa Robertson's *Occasional Work and Seven Walks* 53
   Katalin Pálinkás

PART 2
East-Central Europe as a Translocal Space: Gendering the "Periphery"

4 A Closet of One's Own: Places of Non-Hegemonic Masculinities and Rites of Retreat in Contemporary Hungarian Cinema 71
   György Kalmár

5 Young Mothers, Concrete Cages: Representations of Maternity in Hungarian Housing Films from the 1970s and 1980s 89
   Zsolt Győri

6   Queer Sex and the City: Affective Places of Queerness in Contemporary Hungarian Cinema   106
    Fanni Feldmann

PART 3
Translocality, Border Thinking and Restlessness

7   "They weren't even there yet and already the City was speaking to them" – The Translocal Experience as Fascination with the City in Toni Morrison's *Jazz*   125
    Imola Bülgözdi

8   "I again put on my veil" – Autobiographical Narrative, Feminism, and the Emergence of Border Thinking in Marjane Satrapi's *Persepolis* Books   139
    Márta Kőrösi

PART 4
Translocality and Transgression

9   "Whichever way you go, you are sure to get somewhere." Dysgeographic Mappings of Playable Loci and the "Compass" of Girlish Curiosity in Lewis Carroll's and China Miéville's Spatial Fantasies   163
    Anna Kérchy

10 Translocations of Desire: Urban Topographies of Love in Chimamanda Adichie's *Americanah*   181
    Jennifer Leetsch

PART 5
Criminal Affects: Crime and the City

11 Criminal Affects: Hard-boiled Discourse and the New Cultures of Fear in Patrick Neate's *City of Tiny Lights*   201
    Tamás Bényei

12 Inventing History: Katalin Baráth's Hungarian Middlebrow Detective Series   220
    Brigitta Hudácskó

   Index   235

Acknowledgments

The editors would like to thank the University of Debrecen for supporting the research project entitled "Gender, Translocality and the City" (RH/751/2015), which provided the theoretical framework this volume relies on. We are also grateful to the Hungarian Society for the Study of English (HUSSE) for supporting the first international conference the group organized in 2016, which helped to shape both the content of this book and its analytical approach, and to Károli Gáspár University's Faculty of Arts for assisting us in the final stages of revision (20659B800). The volume is the result of collaboration among thirteen scholars, eight of whom have been members of the Gender, Translocality and the City Research Group.

Our heartfelt thanks to Péter Csató for his professional commentary and linguistic revision of the manuscript, and to Fruzsina Papp for editing the cover image of the volume. We would also like to extend our gratitude to the Doctoral School of Literary and Cultural Studies at the University of Debrecen for the support we received.

Figures

2.1 The Symptoms' leaflet of the performance from "Tünet Együttes: Sóvirág"; *Csokonai Színház*; csokonaiszinhaz.hu, https://tinyurl.com/yb2uqfyb (Accessed 26 June 2020) 49
8.1 Satrapi in a liminal position (Satrapi, *Persepolis* 3) 142
8.2 Effect of the Islamic Revolution (Satrapi, *Persepolis* 3) 143
8.3 Adolescence (Satrapi, *Persepolis* 117) 144
8.4 Border position illustrated by Satrapi's self-portrait (Satrapi, *Persepolis* 6) 148
8.5 Women's public and private behaviour (Satrapi, *Persepolis* 2 151) 150
8.6 Donning the veil again (Satrapi, *Persepolis* 2 91) 154
8.7 Marriage as prison (Satrapi, *Persepolis* 2 163) 156

Notes on Contributors

Tamás Bényei
is Professor of English Literature at the Department of British Studies, of the University of Debrecen, Hungary. His main fields of interest are British fiction since the late 19th century, colonial and postcolonial literature, women's writing and crime fiction. He has published seven books in Hungarian and one in English. He has published essays in journals including EJES, *Commonwealth, Hungarian Journal of English and American Studies* and *Journal of the Fantastic in the Arts,* and in edited volumes published in the UK and the US.

Imola Bülgözdi
is an assistant professor teaching American Literature, Cultural Studies and Popular Culture at the Institute of English and American Studies, of the University of Debrecen, Hungary. She specializes in the literature of the American South, and her academic interests include novel-to-film adaptation, gender studies, and fantasy and science fiction. Her recent publications include "Space and Translocality: Revisiting Bradbury's Mars" (*Critical Insights: Ray Bradbury*, 2017), "Rock Opera and Resistance: Stephen the King as a Building Block of Minority Ethnic Identity in Transylvania and the United States" (with Zsófia O. Réti, *Popular Music History*, 2018) and "Spatiality in the Cyber-World of William Gibson" (*Cityscapes of the Future: Urban Spaces in Science Fiction*, 2018).

Fanni Feldmann
Ph. D. student of the Doctoral School of Literature and Cultural Studies at the University of Debrecen, researches the representation of sexual and gender identities in literature and film, primarily in Eastern European cinema. Her main interests are the psychological process of coming out, its visual representations and its interconnectedness with cultural, social and political contexts. Her most significant publications appeared in *Ekphrasis* (2017) and *Nemek és etnikumok terei a magyar filmben* (*Spaces of Genders and Ethnicities in Hungarian Film*, eds. Zsolt Győri and György Kalmár). She edited a volume of young researchers' essays in the Hatvani István Extramural College (University of Debrecen) entitled *(En)Gendered Lives* (2016).

Zsolt Győri
is an assistant professor at the University of Debrecen, Institute of English and American Studies. He has edited a collection of essays on British film history

(2010) and is the co-editor of three volumes dedicated to the relationship of body, subjectivity, ethnicity, gender, space, and power in Hungarian cinema (Debrecen University Press: 2013, 2015, 2018). His monograph in Hungarian, offering a critical introduction to Deleuzian film philosophy and analyses of selected films, appeared in 2014 (*Films, Auteurs, Critical-Clinical Readings*). He is the co-editor of *Travelling around Cultures: Collected Essays on Literature and Art* (Cambridge Scholars, 2016) and is the editor of the *Hungarian Journal of English and American Studies*.

Ágnes Györke
is Associate Professor of English at Károli Gáspár University, Budapest. Prior to this position, she was Lecturer and Senior Lecturer at the University of Debrecen's Institute of English and American Studies. Her academic interests include contemporary British and postcolonial literature, gender studies, diaspora and urban studies. She has published peer-reviewed articles about Salman Rushdie, Martin Amis, Tibor Fischer, Monica Ali, Buchi Emecheta, Doris Lessing and Géza Gárdonyi. Her book titled *Rushdie's Postmodern Nations: Midnight's Children, Shame and The Satanic Verses* was published by Debrecen University Press in 2012. She was a Visiting Scholar at Indiana University (2002–2003), the University of Bristol (January 2015), King's College London (June 2015), the University of Leeds (June 2016–October 2016; January 2018), and a Research Fellow at Central European University's Institute for Advanced Study (2012–2013). She is principal investigator of the "Cosmopolitan Ethics and the Modern City" research group based at Károli Gáspár University.

Brigitta Hudácskó
is a Junior Lecturer at the Department of British Studies at the University of Debrecen, Hungary. Her main research interests are recent television adaptations of Sherlock Holmes stories, crime fiction and crime drama, and popular culture. Her most recent publication concerns the portrayal of Captain Thomas Gregson in the television series *Elementary* in *Victorian Detectives in Contemporary Culture: Beyond Sherlock Holmes* (ed. Lucyna Krawczyk-Żywko. Basingstoke; London; New York: Palgrave Macmillan, 2017).

György Kalmár
is reader at the Department of British Studies of the Institute of English and American Studies, University of Debrecen (DE), Hungary, and guarantor at the Catholic University at Ruzomberok, Slovakia. He graduated at DE in 1997, where his majors were Hungarian and English. He worked as a postgraduate researcher and visiting scholar at the University of Oxford in Great

Britain and at the University of Indiana in Bloomington, USA. He gained a PhD in philosophy (2003) and one in English (2007) at DE. His main teaching and research areas include literary and cultural theory, contemporary European cinema, gender studies, and British literature. He has published extensively in the above mentioned fields. He is the author of over forty articles and five books, including *Formations of Masculinity in Postcommunist Hungarian Cinema* (Palgrave-Macmillan, 2017) and *Post-Crisis European Cinema: White Men in Off-Modern Landscapes* (Palgrave Macmillan, 2020).

Anna Kérchy

is Associate Professor of English Literature at the University of Szeged, Hungary. Her research areas include gender studies, the post-semiotics of embodied subjectivity, Victorian and postmodern fantastic imagination and intermedial dynamics, women's art and children's literature. She authored three monographs: *Alice in Transmedia Wonderland* (2016), *Body-Texts in the Novels of Angela Carter. Writing from a Corporeagraphic Point of View* (2008), and *Essays on Feminist Aesthetics, Narratology, and Body Studies* (in Hungarian, 2018). She (co)edited nine essay collections including *Posthumanism in Fantastic Fiction* (2018), *Feminist Interventions in Intermedial Studies* (2017), *Exploring the Cultural History of Continental European Freak Shows* (2012), *Postmodern Reinterpretations of Fairy Tales* (2011), and the forthcoming *Transmediating and Translating Children's Literature.*

Márta Kőrösi

graduated as a teacher of English language and literature from the University of Debrecen in 1998, and started working for the Institute of English and American Studies at UD in the same year. After moving to Budapest in 2002, she worked as an English teacher at King Sigismund College for a decade, while she completed the MA Programmeme in Gender Studies at Central European University in 2005, and started CEU's PhD Programme in Comparative Gender Studies three years later, obtaining her PhD degree in 2015. She has been doing research and teaching in the field of cultural studies, English language and literature, feminism and gender studies, autobiographical narrative, and is currently working on issues of post/humanism in narrative. She is now affiliated with the Liszt Ferenc Academy of Music in Budapest.

Jennifer Leetsch

works as a Post-Doctoral Researcher and Lecturer at the Department of English Literature and British Cultural Studies at Julius-Maximilians-University Würzburg, Germany. She is interested in the intersections of affect and space in contemporary diasporic women's writing and teaches seminars on migration, globalisation, and Black British literature. Her research foci include, amongst others: the interrelation of gender and disability, black life writing, and feminist ecocriticism. Her recent publications include peer-reviewed articles on the the poetics of travel in the works of M. G. Vassanji and Shailja Patel, the ocean imaginaries of refuge in Warsan Shire's poetry, and a chapter on Afro-European constructions of home/land in Helen Oyeyemi.

Katalin Pálinkás
independent researcher, holds a Ph.D. in comparative literature from Indiana University, Bloomington. She has taught courses at the Department of Comparative Literature, Indiana University and at the School of English and American Studies, Eötvös Loránd University, Budapest. Her main research areas are British Romanticism, women poets of the 18th and 19th centuries, lyric theory (with a special emphasis on temporality and suspension), and affect theory. Her publications include Hungarian translation of excerpts from Mary Wollstonecraft's writings, articles on Charlotte Smith's *Beachy Head* and on suspension in Wordsworth's "There was a Boy", and essays on women poets and on the history of the sonnet in the 1640–1830 volume of a forthcoming Hungarian history of English literature.

Miklós Takács
is an Assistant Professor at the Institute of Hungarian Literary and Cultural Studies, University of Debrecen. He also majored here in History and Hungarian Literature, and received his degree in 1999. He defended his doctoral dissertation in 2006 which was published in 2011 under the title *Ady, a korai Rilke és az "istenes vers"* (Ady, the Early Rilke and Their Religious Poetry) by Debrecen University Press. His wider field of interest being literary theory and contemporary literature, he is currently working on a monograph that focuses on the relationship of trauma and literature. His recent publication in English: *No Sound, No Picture? The Visual Narrativity of Trauma in W. G. Sebald's Novel* Austerlitz = *Text and Image in the 19th-20th Century Art of Central Europe*, eds. Katalin Keserü, Zsuzsanna Szegedy-Maszák, Budapest, Eötvös University Press, 2010, 149–158.

Pieter Vermeulen
is an assistant professor of American and Comparative Literature at the University of Leuven, Belgium. He is the author of *Romanticism After the Holocaust* (2010) and *Contemporary Literature and the End of the Novel: Creature, Affect, Form* (2015), and a co-editor of, most recently, *Institutions of World*

Literature: Writing, Translation, Markets (2015) and *Memory Unbound: Tracing the Dynamics of Memory Studies* (2017). He is currently writing a book for Routledge's Literature and Contemporary Thought Series entitled *Literature and the Anthropocene*.

INTRODUCTION

Central and Eastern Europe and the West: Affective Relations

Ágnes Györke and Imola Bülgözdi

"Eastern Europeans, while not 'other' as much as Asians or Africans, are also 'not quite' European; rather, they are semi-European, semi-developed, with semi-functioning states and semi-civilized manners" – concludes Nataša Kovačević, in an attempt to summarize the main differences between Eastern and Western Europe, in her introduction to *Narrating Post/Communism* (3). The simple fact that Central European countries, with the exception of Germany and Austria, are at the same time also grouped under the term Eastern Europe due to their post-communist past, already hints at the complexity of this region's historical and cultural heritage. Yet, Stefano Bottoni reminds us of the often overlooked fact that Eastern Europe did not exist as a political region before World War II, when the West-East conceptual relation turned from "unclear geographic boundaries into cognitive antipodes and the East came to play an exclusively negative role in the Western discursive field" (3); when Eastern Europe was imagined as an emphatically peripheral, or even non-European, space.[1] He also draws attention to the fact that many people, grouped under the umbrella term of Eastern European, "consider [this concept] little more than a historical and moral stigma," shedding light at various levels on the translocal experience in states of the former Soviet Bloc, where the consciousness of the forcible shared trajectory of Eastern Europe has been gradually fading since the fall of communism (1).

What is more, the presence of the emotionally charged German equivalent, Mitteleuropa[2] (Central Europe), extending from the Baltic Sea to the Mediterranean and the Black Sea, further complicates the question of regional

---

1 This fact is also reflected by Kovačević's definition, which pointedly lacks particulars while exclusively relying on comparison with a superior West. For a detailed analysis of the history of the concept of Eastern Europe see Stefano Bottoni's "Introduction: Reframing the Debated Concept of Eastern Europe" in *Long Awaited West: Eastern Europe since 1944*.
2 Friedrich Neumann's book *Mitteleuropa* was first published in Berlin in 1915 to be translated into English as *Central Europe* and published in London and New York in the subsequent two years respectively.

identification and the concomitant affects. This term, coined by pre-First World War German thinkers, originally referred to a hypothetical German-led political and economic alliance of German, Hungarian and Slavic peoples, to be later exploited by the Nazis to justify their territorial expansion (Bottoni 2). When Eastern Europe was politically and imaginatively constructed as a geopolitical space behind the Iron Curtain, Mitteleuropa ceased to exist (Lord 9), yet the notion resurfaced again in the 1980s when the crisis of communism became apparent in the region and dissident public intellectuals made the claim that Central Europe was markedly different from the East and "belonged to the Western sphere of civilization" (Bottoni 5). Eastern Europe, then, has not only turned into a cultural stigma, but also fails to capture the regional variations that have shaped the history of a large section of Europe since the times of the vast multinational Austro-Hungarian, Russian, and Ottoman Empires.

A number of recently coined terms offer new ways to engage with Eastern and Central Europe as a geopolitical space. The region is proclaimed to be a "borderline civilization" by Nataša Kovačević, who, two decades after the end of communism, still sees Eastern Europe caught in a limbo between the mutually exclusive categories of European and (ex-)communist (Kovačević 1–3). This legacy, however, is clearly based on centuries of divergent development: Omer Bartov and Eric D. Weitz call attention to the fact that this region is part of the "borderlands," or "shatterzones" of historical Empires, characterized by ethnic, social, and religious diversity and a turbulent history of shifting political influence (Bartov and Weitz 2013). Furthermore, Eastern Europe is often called a "periphery" in the cultural sense of the term, which nevertheless undermines conceptualizations of "core Europe," and reveals that the history of European modernity cannot be complete without the inclusion of these cultures (Colpani 2016). Though relying on the findings of these valuable contributions, we use the term "translocality" to re-think the significance of this region, which, as we argue, helps us include it on the map of Europe and reassert its significance in the global flow of ideas. Questioning both the binarism implied by the core-periphery opposition and West-centric theories of transnationalism, the translocal approach this volume takes calls attention to the role of locale, affect and difference in the re-conceptualization of Eastern and Central Europe, while it resolutely insists on the significance of a perspective that points beyond singular localities.

Our volume investigates the production of space in post-1945 translocal culture in a comparative theoretical framework, exploring the ways representations of space and emotion intersect in works of literature and film. Focusing on the emotional landscapes of cities and regions in the English-speaking world as well as in Central and Eastern Europe, the volume intends to open a productive intercultural exchange between the region and global urban studies. The contributions map both widely explored emotions, such as shame and fascination, for instance, and under-researched affective engagement, such as withdrawal in the post-1989 Hungarian cultural milieu. The volume also inquires into where Hungarian literature and visual culture can be located on the map of contemporary translocal studies, charting the ways in which emotional responses such as withdrawal and disengagement contribute to the current burgeoning research on affect and emotion.

1 Transnationalism and Translocality

Theories of transnationalism, which are often seen as precursors of translocal geographies, have failed to predict the revival of nationalism in the 21st century. Contrary to the assumptions of such scholars as Michael Hardt and Antonio Negri, who believed that the Western world had been transformed into a borderless Empire by the end of the 20th century, the past few decades have shown that the nation state has remained a significant factor in the cultural and political sphere. Hardt and Negri's influential book was written before the break-up of Yugoslavia and the war in Kosovo, as they themselves point out,[3] which signaled the revival of ethnic separatism in the region. Since the end of the 20th century, it has become more and more obvious that the nation state is far from being "on its last legs" (Appadurai 19): the emergence of dominant rightwing ideologies in Europe and the United States in the 21st century made it very clear that theories of transnationalism need to be reconsidered. Diana Mishkova and Balázs Trencsényi's introduction to *European Regions and Boundaries – A Conceptual History* (2017) draws attention to the complex processes that fell victim to transnational theories and have recently come under close scrutiny:

> Temporal terms – such as development, progress, conservatism, stagnation, or delay – acquired spatial embeddedness, and spatial terms – such as the East, the West, the North, the South, as well as centre, periphery, borderlands, or just "the lands beyond" – became historical terms. It was

---

[3] Although the authors acknowledge that they were unable to take recent events into account, they do not believe that the revival of ethnic nationalism challenges their argument: "This book was begun well after the end of the Persian Gulf War and completed before the beginning of the war in Kosovo. The reader should thus situate the argument at the midpoint between these two signal events in the construction of Empire" (xvii).

> this peculiar merging of cultural-historical and spatial imaginations that inspired a new symbolic map of Europe, whose taxonomic (and hierarchically graded) units cut across the administrative boundaries of empires and nation-states, as well as the cultural boundaries of religion.
>
> MISHKOVA and TRENCSÉNYI 3

Challenging transnational approaches, *Geographies of Affect* relies on a translocal theoretical framework, aiming to foreground the complex, often paradoxical, role localities play in the contemporary world. In other words, the volume investigates the significance of localities and subjectivities *within* the context of global flows. As Brickell and Datta put it, translocality is a "grounded" form of transnationalism (Brickell and Datta 10), which attempts to focus on the local without giving up its genuine interest in the global. This theoretical framework offers the opportunity to explore both diasporic literatures and other "peripheral" cultures, such as Hungarian, which is the local context several contributors and the editors of this volume work in. Some of the essays discuss cities in the context of diasporic cultural theory, which has been among the first to explore minority cultures in the context of intersectional differences: Avtar Brah, for instance, has convincingly demonstrated that diasporas cannot be mapped solely on the basis of nationality, ethnicity or location. Relying on new definitions of diaspora, a number of chapters explore specific local issues, ranging from cultural to social and psychological questions, within a global, meta-ethnic theoretical framework.

2   Affect and the Translocal Space

We believe that a translocal approach does not only foreground the significance of localities, but also *marks a shift towards affect.* These two aspects of global culture are not entirely independent of each other, of course; the local is the site where "contemporary diasporic social relations are constituted and *lived*" (Brah 199, emphasis added). This site is, by definition, more saturated with practices of everyday life, including affective interactions. Arjun Appadurai already used the term in 1996 to refer to "structures of feeling"[4] (Appadurai 181) as opposed to transnational flows, which shed light on the power relations that affect the production of localities, such as neighbourhoods, for instance.[5]

---

4 The term was coined by Raymond Williams in *Preface to Film* (1954), and he further developed it to problematize Antonio Gramsci's notion of hegemony.
5 "[T]ies of marriage, work, business, and leisure weave together various circulating populations with kinds of locals to create neighbourhoods that belong in one sense to particular

In his reading, localities are produced by global flows, primarily, the mass media, yet they also resist these transnational flows. As we hope to show in the volume, affect often appears in literary and visual narratives as an intricate site of this resistance.

The other major approach which has engaged with exploring the affective dimensions of the local is geography itself, no doubt inspired by the global movement of populations as well. Since the mid-20th century, psycho-geographers have attempted to map the impact of the geographical environment on the emotions of individuals. Pedestrian exploration of the urban landscape, influenced by much earlier works such as Walter Benjamin's *Arcades Project*, became a very widespread theme in the 1990s: Peter Ackroyd and Iain Sinclair, among other writers, popularized psychogeography in Britain and set new trends in the portrayal of urban and suburban spatialities. By the 1990s, cultural geography also became dissatisfied with the discipline's characteristic descriptive methodology and set out to "explore and understand the mental associations that places, things, and processes had for different cultural groups" (Jon Anderson 36). Leaving behind environmental determinism, it argued for the inclusion of the hitherto overlooked unintentional, unanticipated, and emotional moments of cultural life, complemented by a focus on the scale of the individual and the body, and asserting the importance of emotional and everyday experiences (43). This paradigm shift[6] resulted in the establishment of the constitutive co-ingredience of people and localities posited by cultural geography at a range of scales, which concept not only provides the foundation for the affective phenomena discussed in the volume, but also draws attention to the importance of place at the scale of the local in identity formation: as Crang puts it, "people do not simply locate themselves, they define themselves through a *sense of place*" (2, emphasis added).[7] Exploring the visions and sensory experiences of translocal subjects is especially revelatory, as the way they

---

nation-states, but that are from another point of view what we might call *translocalities*" (Appadurai 192, emphasis in the original).

6 Doreen Massey's pioneering geographical research (*Space, Place, and Gender*) on the local demonstrated how the processes associated with globalization in general, including the migration and mobility of people from their traditional locales, cross both geographical and cultural borders and transform the local itself.

7 John Anderson, as a social scientist, uses the term "place" to refer to concrete locations as opposed to the abstract notion of "space". However, some of the contributors in the volume (Katalin Pálinkás and Jennifer Leetsch, for instance) rely on Michel de Certeau's definition of these terms, who has defined space as *"practiced place"* (*The Practice of Everyday Life* 117, emphasis in the original), which refers to performative everyday localities that challenge hegemonic conceptions of place.

define themselves through the tangible and intangible attributes of specific locations often question the official rhetoric of nation states. "*Affect*," then, is significant in this volume at least in two senses. On the one hand, the focus on localities inevitably calls attention to sensations such as belonging or alienation, which mark the impact of the environment on the individual. On the other hand, affect also functions as a *site of resistance*, since localities often resist both national conditioning and transnational flows. As Jon Anderson points out, "[i]n many cases local and national senses of place are in conflict. The 'local interest' seeks to defend the ongoing composition of traces that is their locality, yet the 'national interest' often means that these places are redefined by traces imposed for the good of the nation" (Anderson 100). Therefore, it is often the case that local and national senses of place are experienced by the individual as conflicting due to local environments being redefined from above in the name of national interest (100). At the same time local resistance to the incursion of translocal migrants who do not blend in for any reason is also a well-documented phenomenon, leading to a re-evaluation of one's sense of belonging to a locality itself or a community centered around it.

Though aware of the conceptual differences between affect and emotion, the authors use these terms interchangeably in the volume. Many critics have shown that insisting on the terminological difference is not entirely helpful: Monica Greco and Paul Stenner, for instance, argue that the distinction "may actually obscure more than it clarifies at a conceptual level" (Greco and Stenner 11), while Teresa Brennan notes that "there is no reason to challenge the idea that emotions are basically synonymous with affects [...]" (Brennan 5–6). Others, such as Hardt, subsume emotions under affect (Hardt x). We prefer affect to emotion since the term evokes an embodied subject, in a world "mediated by feeling" (Thien 451), and foregrounds its interactions with the environment, which is the primary focus of this volume. The approach to affect which serves as a starting point for the majority of the essays is rooted in critical discourses of the emotions that have superseded the notion of the interiorized self.[8] Authors understand emotions as *social relations* (Joyce Davidson, Liz Bondi, Sara Ahmed, Carolyn Pedwell) rather than "properties encapsulated within the boundaries of individual subjects" (Pedwell 2014), recognizing that the role of the environment is central in this project: the mediated subject is no longer seen as an emotionally self-contained entity (Brennan 2), since there is no "secure distinction between the 'individual' and the 'environment'" (Brennan 6). In fact, exploring the

---

8 See Gregg and Seigworth, 8.

impact of localities on identity formation as well as the role emotions play in the transformation of conceptual designs into "practiced place" (de Certeau 117), is the twofold starting point of our investigation. This is exactly the point where *theories of affect* and the *translocal* intersect: the chapters in the volume foreground not only the role of the environment in the construction of identities but also the local characteristic features of emotional experiences that transform place into space.

3 Central and Eastern Europe and the West

The volume aims to put Central and Eastern Europe on the global map of literary and cultural studies, since this region is often overlooked by critics of global culture. Appadurai, for instance, recognized that 1989 marks a break in the genealogy of area studies,[9] but made no attempt to devote attention to the specificities of this region in his study. Perhaps his hasty prediction of the demise of the nation state is partly due to the fact that Central and Eastern Europe has remained a blind spot in his theory of global culture. In the 21st century we have seen the revival of nationalist ideologies both in this region and elsewhere in the world: Brexit marked a turning point in British history, as did the presidency of Donald Trump in the United States. Therefore, we believe these current events make the remapping of this region in a comparative, translocal framework inevitable.

Central and Eastern Europe has very often been seen and represented as an underdeveloped region compared to the West. Though the decades of communism after World War II obviously isolated these countries both in terms of economic and cultural development, the assumption that the region is lagging behind the West predate this period.[10] Omer Bartov and Eric D. Weitz argue that the territory extending from the Baltic to the Black Sea and to the Mediterranean, covering a considerable segment of Central and Eastern Europe, have been "borderlands" at the mercy of the power struggle of Prussia (later subsumed by the German Empire), and the Habsburg, Russian and Ottoman Empires for most of the nineteenth and twentieth centuries (1). This assumption helps understand the peculiar interaction of global, regional and local forces that led to the politically, economically, and socially divergent development of

---

9   He claimed that "the old way of doing area studies does not make sense in the world after 1989" (Appadurai 16).
10 On the role of orientalism in the invention of Eastern Europe see Wolff's *Inventing Eastern Europe*.

the region. The great ethnic and religious diversity and instability of the borderlands, further complicated by the emergence of nation states after World War I, itself followed by the upheaval caused by changing borders, genocide, forceful relocation, and foreign occupation at various points during the first half of the twentieth century,[11] has left its mark not simply on how the link between place and European/national/ethnic/personal identities is conceptualized, but also on the affects involved.

The centennial of the Treaty of Trianon[12] (June 1920), for instance, still makes emotions run high in Hungary and the surrounding states with significant ethnic Hungarian minorities, since "(t)o this day, Hungarians describe Trianon as an injustice done to the Hungarian nation. But for Romanians, it codified the unification of three territories into a larger Romanian state. For Czechs, Slovaks and Slavs in Transcarpathia, Trianon heralded their first incorporation into a Slavic state" (Stroschein 79). The intergenerational traumas of millions of Hungarians who were forced to live outside the borders of Hungary as minorities need to be acknowledged. The affects involved in the afterlife of this historical event can only be fully comprehended, however, in the light of the discourse of German and Hungarian national superiority in Central Europe, which gained prominence in the decades following 1880. As argued by Marius Turda, the narratives that presented these nations "as culturally superior and predestined to preside over other national groups [Romanians, Czechs, Slovaks, Croats, and Poles]" (2) mainly reflect the appropriation of Western European theories of race and superiority (9). It is the still-lingering effect of such discourses that bolster waves of nostalgia for a "Greater Hungary" and the rather predictable nationalistic backlash from the surrounding countries that were beneficiaries of the Treaty of Trianon.

The above-mentioned regional complexities of the multi-ethnic empires of the long nineteenth century set the stage for divergent development from the West due to the instability inherent in its borderland status long before the arrival of communism. In Austro-Hungary, early twentieth-century poets and writers self-consciously attempted to bridge this gap by adapting Western European standards and norms: the most innovative Hungarian literary journal was titled "*West*" (1908–1941), which expresses this orientation very clearly.

---

11   See Bartov and Weitz pp. 3–6.
12   Hungary, having fought for the Central Powers in WWI, lost approximately two-thirds of its territory to Czechoslovakia, Austria, Yugoslavia, and Romania, as well as about one-third of the Hungarian-speaking population, forced into the position of second-class citizens due to their ethnic origins in the newly founded nation states. See Stroschein for a detailed discussion of twentieth-century ethnic relations in Eastern Europe.

This approach, nevertheless, relies on the assumption that Hungary has fallen behind Western modernity, just like postcolonial countries. Western critical discourses attempting to institute their own standards as norms to follow need to be appropriated even today,[13] while scholars also have to be aware of the populist propaganda fostering nationalism in the region: the local specificities of Central and Eastern Europe need to be explored vis-à-vis the double bind of neoliberal and nationalist ideologies. Furthermore, there is still a considerable resistance in Hungary against theories such as gender studies, often stigmatized as an "ideology" upsetting the status quo. Relying on a translocal approach and taking gender into account, this volume hopes to make localities visible globally without compromising the specific characteristics and distinct cultural heritage of the region.[14]

4 Structure of the Volume

This volume, which intends to open a productive dialogue between the literary and cinematic works produced in the region and those in the Anglophone world, is the result of the collaboration of thirteen scholars from various countries ranging from Hungary to Belgium. We believe that the focus on the local in this global context, foregrounded by the translocal framework, helps us offer an innovative framework for the exploration of Central and Eastern

---

13   Though a number of critics use similar metaphors, such as translation (Kalmár) and intercultural exchange (Kiséry, Komáromy and Varga) to describe their own roles as mediators between Central and Eastern Europe and the Anglophone world, there is no agreement among Hungarian academics regarding the place of Hungary on the global map of cultural studies. According to György Kálmán C., "(i)n Central Europe today it can be said that the humanities – including comparative literature – have become a part of the globalized theoretical and academic universe" (Kálmán C. and Varga Z. 97). He also claims that "imported" Western theories such as deconstruction and gender studies have been "re-appropriated by the region's local intellectual and artistic traditions" (Kálmán C. and Varga Z. 98), which is, no doubt, true to some extent, yet it does not follow that these theories *themselves* have been appropriated as a result of a more visible inclusion of Central and Eastern Europe in Western academic networks.

14   The editors of the recently published *Postcolonial Europe? Essays on Post-Communist Literatures and Cultures* (Brill), Dobrota Pucherová and Róbert Gáfrik argue that Central and Eastern Europe is, in fact, a postcolonial region, which "should pay a major role in the current debates in postcolonial studies on European identity" (Pucherová and Gráfik 14). Acutely aware of the pressure of both the communist heritage and neoliberal domination, the editors raise serious issues regarding the cultural heritage of Central and Eastern Europe and express a profound need for a new paradigm for the study of the region in a global context.

Europe, with Hungary fulfilling the role of a case study, given the expertise of a number of our contributors. The chapters, each in their own distinct way, explore the affective dimensions of localities and provide new insights into the affective geographies of global cities, "sites for the accumulation, distribution and circulation of capital" (Barker 357), such as New York and London, still the world's two most influential cities as of 2018, according to A.T. Kearney's "Global Cities Report." Based on factors such as business activity, human capital, cultural experience, information exchange, innovation, political engagement, as well as personal well-being, the single Central European city to make the top twenty-five list is Vienna (7), which is discussed in detail below in Márta Kőrösi's essay " 'I again put on my veil' – Autobiographical Narrative, Feminism and the Emergence of Border Thinking in Marjane Satrapi's *Persepolis* Books." With Budapest ranked in sixty-second place, dropping sixteen places since 2014 (13), it is not far-fetched to claim that these scientific measures document the outcome of the post-World War II political divide and the continuing divergent development of post-socialist countries, which entails a diverse interaction of the local and the global as well as "new cartographic approaches, new forms of representation, and new ways of imagining our *place* in the universe" (Tally 41). The chapters focusing on Budapest and the Hungarian countryside investigate both personal histories of a "practical reconquest of a sense of place" (Jameson 51) as well as the representational techniques that link spatiality, politics, power, and affect, bringing to attention Central and Eastern Europe from the perspective of a global context. Hence, the focus on how narratives transform hegemonic notions of place into performative spatialities through affective engagement offers contributors the opportunity to explore the translocal aspects of this region and to challenge theories of globalization.

The section *Edgy Feelings: Translocality, Trauma and Disengagement* demonstrates how two contemporary novels, a theatrical performance which is based on the memoirs of a Hungarian Holocaust survivor, and experimental poetry are capable of surpassing personal emotion and creating a transpersonal affective community. The contributions offer the possibility to investigate this phenomenon from a more theoretically informed discussion of 21st-century urban experiences of translocality, and from the highly unique perspective of witnessing the live performance of non-agerian Éva Fahidi, whose re-enactment of her Auschwitz experiences not only brings to the audience a local version of the global trauma, but also sheds light on the physical embeddedness of the translocal experience. By highlighting forms of affective mobility, the authors also focus on the politically engaged nature of impersonal (also called transpersonal) affect, which supersedes established limits and offers possibilities for connection and community by means of emotive unsettlement.

Pieter Vermeulen's chapter, "Impersonal Affect and Transpersonal Community in the Totaled City," investigates the emergence of translocal connections through the affective dimensions of literature. Relying on the Deleuzian concept of affect, Vermeulen claims that Teju Cole's *Open City* and Ben Lerner's *10:04* move beyond codified emotions in order to intimate new forms of transpersonal communities in New York City and beyond. The tension between locatedness and drift, between fixity and flow, characterizes not only the novels' representation of cultural mobility, as Vermeulen points out, but also their engagement with emotion and affect. Literature, in fact, turns affect into emotion: by taking the reader to the edge of recognizable feelings, reading makes new and yet unimagined transpersonal communities possible.

"Body, Trauma, Theatricality – Rereading Testimony in the Stage Performance of *Sea Lavender, or the Euphoria of Being*" by Miklós Takács analyzes Fahidi's stage presence both as a unique Holocaust testimonial and a trauma performance, which not only testifies the trauma, but also her victory over the perpetrators. Staging the dehumanizing physical experience of the death camp draws the audience in as no ordinary testimonials can, opening up the position of the secondary witness in a translocal situation. Fahidi's victory results in intense positive emotions such as joy and euphoria, which are rarely experienced in connection with trauma, clearly marking affect as a site of utmost resistance. This is also available now in the recently released documentary *The Euphoria of Being* (2019, dir. Réka Szabó).

The transpersonal affects generated by the landscape of Vancouver in Lisa Robertson's Benjaminian project is in the focus of Katalin Pálinkás's chapter, "The City as a Lyric Archive of Affects in Lisa Robertson's *Occasional Work and Seven Walks*." It is Pálinkás's contention that by shifting the emphasis from depth to surfaces (fabric, colour, decoration, furnishing), Robertson renders collectively constructed urban experience in the course of random walks through the city and explores affects that appear to be freely circulating and residing in urban surfaces. Urban space thus resonates with an array of affects that are often generated by accretions of history, yet call for present change.

The next section, *East-Central Europe as a Translocal Space: Gendering the "Periphery"* focuses on gendered aspects of the late-socialist city and the new tendencies after the regime change, while investigating the emotional impact of the borders and boundaries instated by the system that link private and public in the East-Central European urban space. By delving into the affective dimensions associated with Budapest and the countryside, the three chapters provide a unique cross-section of the documentary and feature-film representations of a period of historical transition and dissatisfaction with conservative gender roles.

In "A Closet of One's Own: Places of Non-Hegemonic Masculinities and Rites of Retreat in Contemporary Hungarian Cinema," György Kalmár delineates the trajectory of the male protagonists of three contemporary Hungarian films presented at international film festivals: *Taxidermia* (Taxed 2006), *Delta* (2008), and *Land of Storms* (2014). This chapter presents a novel approach to post-communist Hungarian cinema by establishing the concept of the "return film," whose hopeful protagonist travels West only to return home in disappointment, which, in turn, results in a withdrawal from the open, public spaces of self-liberation, traditionally regarded as masculine, playing out the crisis of masculinity in translocal spatial terms.

Inquiry into the female perspective adopted by late state-socialist Hungarian filmmakers is a neglected area which refines the predominantly masculine experience of urban alienation and exposes the maternal claustrophobia resulting from the interaction between pronatalist policies and the spatiality of housing estates. In "Young Mothers, Concrete Cages: Representations of Maternity in Hungarian Housing Films from the 1970s and 1980s," Zsolt Győri points out that the Hungarian filmmakers' focus on the spatialization of conflicting conventional masculine and feminine values brings to the foreground the rather negative affects linked to maternity in the urban environment, which challenges the female emancipation advocated by the state, as well as signals the late state-socialist society's quest for a voice and space of its own.

In "Queer Sex and the City – Affective Places of Queerness in Contemporary Hungarian Cinema," Fanni Feldmann investigates the prevailing reductive conception of queerness in Hungarian mainstream cinema, and challenges the representation of the city as a place of shame via the analysis of two post-socialist documentaries which outline the birth of the queer community in Budapest. Thus, she uncovers the affective history of queering the city during state socialism, and demonstrates how affect and place-making are intertwined with the formation of the queer subculture.

In *Translocality, Border Thinking and Restlessness*, besides the effects of trauma, the construction of subjectivities is investigated in terms of other affective relations, such as mourning, nostalgia, and fascination. This section also sheds light on the possibilities offered to and the limitations encountered by the individual in the borderlands, both material and imaginary, whose central dilemma, the construction of a gendered subjectivity, plays itself out in translocal terms through the figure of the migrant, who bears traces of local and global histories. The fractured spatiality and politics of the borderlands also draw attention to the role of affect, disappointment and resulting disengagement, which account for the specific articulation of subjectivities in locations as diverse as the United States and the Islamic nation state.

The necessity of constructing a distinctly urban identity and its intertwining with gendered and racial urban violence serve as a backdrop to the characters' affective relation with Harlem, which forms the main enquiry in Imola Bülgözdi's " 'They weren't even there yet and already the City was speaking to them' – The Translocal Experience as Fascination with the City in Toni Morrison's *Jazz*." Mapping the urban world through the translocal experience of Southern African-American migrants, Harlem becomes a place of fascination, which encompasses attraction and desire but also fear and even terror, and is postulated as one of the most significant elements of the interface of urban structures and new subjectivities.

Disappointment with the West is a key factor in the construction of female subjectivity for the Iranian protagonist of the graphic novels discussed by Márta Kőrösi in " 'I again put on my veil' – Autobiographical Narrative, Feminism, and the Emergence of Border Thinking in Marjane Satrapis's Persepolis Books." Kőrösi focuses on the translocal female subject trying to locate herself outside the confines of both the domain of Western metaphysics, where she faces rejection due to cultural and ethnic othering in Vienna and Strasbourg, and the oppression experienced in the Islamic context in Tehran. The double critique that emerges as a result of the protagonist's translocal experience leads to a specific form of border thinking and a re-evaluation of feminism, Kőrösi argues, while her chapter highlights affect as a site of resistance in the face of both transnational flows and national conditioning.

Challenging white, masculine urban space from perspectives that produce alternative emotional and affective maps of the urban landscape is the overarching principle of the section *Marginalization and Reappropriation of the City*. The reimagining of the figure of Lewis Carroll's Alice as a curious female urban explorer in contemporary young adult (YA) fantasy, and the muted voices of postcolonial black women, challenge hegemonic portrayals of marginalized subjectivities, as well as surveillance and criminalization at various levels. The analysis of Miéville's *Un Lun Dun* (2007) supports the premise that affective relationships influence and, in turn, are influenced by urban space, emphasizing the possibility of empowerment in spatial terms, while Adichie's *Americanah* broadens the scope of the translocal experience to the scale of the global, while still focusing on how emotions, such as desire and the need to belong affect migrant space and subjectivity.

Anna Kérchy discusses how YA fantasy challenges and recycles the archetypal figures of the "lost little girl" associated in cautionary tales with the vice of curiosity, the nymph and the modernist bourgeois flaneuse in " 'Whichever way you go, you are sure to get somewhere.' Dysgeographic Mappings of Playable Loci and the 'Compass' of Girlish Curiosity in Lewis Carroll's and China Miéville's Spatial Fantasies." The challenge to masculine geographical discourse results in an affective re-appropriation of public places that facilitates a collective ludic interaction with our environment and affirms woman's creative and spatial agency. Jennifer Leetsch's contribution, entitled "Translocations of Desire: Urban Topographies of Love in Chimamanda Adichie's *Americanah*," explores the stages of settling down, travelling and homemaking as connected to affects, emotions and desire through the life of a Nigerian couple, whose divergent spatial narratives demonstrate the complexities of navigating the postcolonial world of late modernity. Her piece showcases how the narrative of romance that contains both the potentially destructive and reparative aspects of love (encompassing sexual encounters, desire, intimacy, and belonging) depends on and is at the same time implicated in the production of space and identities in cities as diverse as Philadelphia, Princeton, London, Newcastle and Lagos, resulting in situated knowledges which are able to reclaim and re-politicize, re-map and re-connect territories.

The section *Criminal Affects: Crime and the City* centres around the question of crime as a phenomenon closely associated with urban settings and the concomitant dynamics of fear and hate. The chapters analyze texts that feature unusual variants on the noir genre, playing both with the figure of the detective and the criminal and demonstrating the diminished relevance of the localized noir in a global world of crime, or simply discarding the traditional process of investigation due to a shift in favor of the exploration of the affective dimension, while, at the same time, providing insight into the less-than-straightforward national or ethnic identification of the characters. A recent development in Hungarian crime fiction saw an exciting interaction between the tropes of the traditional whodunit and the parallel investigation of the historical and geographical setting of the Austro-Hungarian Monarchy, retrospectively creating the missing middlebrow fiction from a female perspective.

Tamás Bényei's "Criminal Affects: Multicultural Noir and Terror in Patrick Neate's *City of Tiny Lights*" also revolves around the redrawing of London's cartography by an unusual private eye, a black British war veteran whose past encompasses experiences as varied as taking part in a militant Islamic organization and employment by the CIA. His "soldier identity" transforms the city into a war zone, while questioning his authority over a global city. The rise of the multicultural noir also attests to the ongoing reconceptualization of the genre, which becomes Patrick Neate's tool to probe into the legacy of colonialism and the British Empire. Besides these overarching translocal agendas, the analyses pivot around the spatial embeddedness of the main characters, whose affective maps, coloured by guilt, fear, and nostalgia, provide alternative visions of the city.

In "Inventing History: Katalin Baráth's Middlebrow Detective Series," Brigitta Hudácskó makes a convincing case for the significance of the figure of the home-grown detective, Veron Dávid, bookshop-keeper and feminist journalist, who is strongly reminiscent of a younger Miss Marple, while exploring the affective dimension relevant to the processes of committing, motivating and dealing with the aftermath of crime in early-twentieth century Budapest and the distinctly Hungarian and suffocatingly provincial countryside. The figure of the detective, in this case, instead of restoring order, questions social norms regarding gender and class, and explores the affective topography of the capital and the countryside via her transgressive mobility.

As attested by the twelve chapters in this volume, the translocal experience draws attention to the affective dimensions of localities. The more mobile populations become, the more accentuated this experience is for both those who travel and those who remain stationary. By taking into account the divergent affects generated by different locales, which bear traces of political, social, economic, and historical factors, this volume opens the door on Hungary as a specific articulation of the local and the global and also offers points of comparison with affects generated within global cities, in the hope that area studies and subsequent research into Central and Eastern European cultures will benefit from our findings.

Works Cited

Anderson, Jon. *Understanding Cultural Geography: Places and Traces.* London and New York: Routledge, 2015.

Ahmed, Sarah. *The Cultural Politics of Emotion.* Edinburgh: Edinburgh UP, 2004.

Appadurai, Arjun. *Modernity at Large: Cultural Dimensions of Globalization.* Minneapolis: U of Minnesota P, 1996.

"2018 Global Cities Report." *A.T. Kearney.* www.atkearney.com. Accessed: August 14, 2018. 1–15. Pdf.

Barker, Chris. *Cultural Studies – Theory and Practice.* London, Thousand Oaks and New Delhi: Sage, 2005.

Bartov, Omer and Eric D. Weitz. "Introduction: Coexistence and Violence in the German, Habsburg, Russian, and Ottoman Borderlands." *Shatterzone of Empires: Coexistence and Violence in the German, Habsburg, Russian, and Ottoman Borderlands.* Ed. Omer Bartov and Eric D. Weitz. Bloomington, IN.: Indiana UP, 2013. pp. 1–20.

Benjamin, Walter. *The Arcades Project*. Trans. Howard Eiland and Kevin McLaughlin. Cambridge, Mass.: Harvard UP, 1993.

Bottoni, Stefano. *Long Awaited West: Eastern Europe since 1944*. Translated by Sean Lambert, Bloomington, IN.: Indiana UP, 2017.

Brah, Avtar. *Cartographies of Diaspora: Contesting Identities*. London: Routledge, 1996.

Brennan, Teresa. *The Transmission of Affect*. Ithaca: Cornell UP, 2004.

Brickell, Katherine and Ayona Datta, eds. *Translocal Geographies: Spaces, Places, Connections*. Farnham: Ashgate, 2011.

Colpani, Gianmaria and Sandra Ponzanesi, ed. *Postcolonial Transitions in Europe: Context, Practices and Politics*. London: Rowman and Littlefield International, 2016.

Crang, Michael. *Cultural Geography*. London: Routledge, 1998.

Davidson, Joyce, Liz Bondi and Mick Smiths, eds. *Emotional Geographies*. Aldershot: Ashgate, 2005.

De Certeau, Michel. *The Practice of Everyday Life*. Berkeley: U of California P, 1984.

Greco, Monica and Paul Stenner. *Emotions: A Social Science Reader*. London: Routledge, 2008.

Gregg, Melissa and Gregory J. Seigworth. "An Inventory of Shimmers." *The Affect Theory Reader*. Ed. Melissa Gregg and Gregory J. Seigworth. Durham and London: Duke UP, 2010. pp. 1–25.

Hardt, Michael. "Foreword." *The Affective Turn – Theorizing the Social*. Ed. Patricia Ticineto Clough and Jean Halley. Durham and London: Duke UP, 2007.

Hardt, Michael and Antonio Negri. *Empire*. Cambridge, Mass.: Harvard UP, 2000.

Jameson, Frederic. *Postmodernism, or, the Cultural Logic of Late Capitalism*. Durham, NC: Duke UP, 1997.

Kalmár, György. *Formations of Masculinity in Post-Communist Hungarian Cinema: Labyrinthian Men*. London: Palgrave Macmillan, 2017.

Kálmán C., György and Zoltán Z. Varga, "Introduction to Comparative Studies in the Central European Context". *Hungarian Cultural Studies* 10 (2017): 96–105.

Kiséry, András, Zsolt Komáromy and Zsuzsanna Varga. *Worlds of Hungarian Writing: National Literature as Intercultural Exchange*. Madison: Fairleigh Dickinson UP, 2016.

Kovačević, Nataša. *Narrating Post/Communism: Colonial Discourse and Europe's Borderline Civilization*. New York: Routledge, 2008.

Lord, Christopher. *Central Europe: Core or Periphery?* Copenhagen: Copenhagen Business School Press, 2000.

Massey, Doreen. *Space, Place, and Gender*. Minnesota: U of Minnesota P, 1994.

Mishkova, Diana and Balázs Trencsényi. Introduction. *European Regions and Boundaries – A Conceptual History*. Ed. Diana Mishkova and Balázs Trencsényi. New York and Oxford: Berghahn Books, 2017. pp. 1–12.

Pedwell, Carolyn. *Affective Relations: The Transnational Politics of Empathy*. Basingstoke: Palgrave Macmillan, 2014.

Pucherová, Dobrota and Róbert Gáfrik. *Postcolonial Europe? Essays on Post-Communist Literatures and Cultures*. Leiden: Brill, 2015.

Stroschein, Sherrill. *Ethnic Struggle, Coexistence, and Democratization in Eastern Europe*. Cambridge: Cambridge UP, 2012.

Tally, Robert T., Jr. *Spatiality*. London and New York: Routledge, 2013.

The Euphoria of Being. Dir. Réka Szabó. Campfilm, 2019.

Thien, Deborah. "After or Beyond Feeling? A Consideration of Affect and Emotion in Geography." *Area*, vol. 37, no. 4 (Dec., 2005): 450–454.

Turda, Marius. *The Idea of National Superiority in Central Europe, 1880–1918*. Lewiston: The Edwin Mellen Press, 2004.

Williams, Raymond and Michael Orrom. *Preface to Film*. Michigan: U of Michigan P, 1954.

Wolff, Larry. *Inventing Eastern Europe: The Map of Civilization on the Mind of the Enlightenment*. Stanford: Stanford UP, 1994.

PART 1

Edgy Feelings: Translocality, Trauma, and Disengagement

∴

CHAPTER 1

Impersonal Affect and Transpersonal Community in the Totaled City

Pieter Vermeulen

Abstract

The relation between literature and mobility is not only a matter of representation, but also of affects and emotions. Drawing on recent work in affect studies, this chapter argues that literature can engage intractable, non-subjective, even impersonal affects in a way that can enrich existing approaches to translocality. It reads two recent New York novels, Teju Cole's *Open City* and Ben Lerner's *10:04*, and shows how these novels displace a subjective, personal form of emotion by a form of affective mobility that cuts across individuals, communities, and categories. In that way, the two novels illustrate the political potential of such literary affective mobility: they show how the novels' engagement with impersonal affect opens the way to an apprehension of a transpersonal community—a community that is not only made up of full-fledged persons, but also of less easily contained forces.

1   Introduction: Textual and Affective Mobility

Mobility and movement are never merely thematic features of literary works; as aesthetic and linguistic constructs, literary texts are themselves occasions of mobility—in the ways they travel through translation, in the ways they refract, repurpose, and remix other texts, and in the ways they affect, touch, and even upset their readers. The focus of this volume on translocality and feeling situates literary texts at the intersection of different forms of movement—as sites where physical, mental, and emotive dynamics interact. In this essay, I pursue the argument that contemporary literature directly engages with vectors of mobility, but refracts and recirculates them in unpredictable and intractable ways. Indeed, I argue that one reason to attend to literature in relation to feeling and translocality—a notion that has mostly been studied in fields such as anthropology, geography, or development studies, and not so much in literary studies—is that literature complicates certain assumptions we often bring to the study of physical and emotive movement.

Two of these assumptions are familiar. First, there is the prevalent idea that our globalized and digital world is marked by borderless and frictionless circulation and hyper-accelerated connectivity; this is an assumption that the paradigm of translocality, by highlighting the ineluctable locatedness of cultural activity, has worked hard to unsettle. Second, there is what literary critic Rachel Greenwald Smith has called "the affective hypothesis" underlying many discussions of emotion and literature: "the belief that literature is at its most meaningful when it represents and transmits the emotional specificity of personal experience" (*Affect and American Literature* 1). For Greenwald Smith, there is an unspoken consensus among readers, writers, and critics that "(w)e read works of literature because they allow us direct contact with individuals who are like us but not us; they allow us to feel what others feel; they provoke empathy" (1). Yet such intersubjective transfers do not exhaust the relation between literature and feeling; indeed, as I argue, literature is at least as much about feelings and intensities that *cannot* so easily be predicted, codified, and mapped; literature, that is, also generates and circulates what can be called "*im*personal" (Greenwald Smith's preferred term) or "*trans*personal" (novelist Ben Lerner's term, as we will see) affects—feelings and intensities that are *not* the properties of readers or characters, but that disrupt the boundaries between individuals and communities. This slightly complicates the focus in the translocality paradigm on the experiences of *human* subjects by underlining that personal trajectories are shot through with unsettling *non*personal forms of affective mobility. Such forms of emotive unsettlement are potentially productive: the power of literary affect to cut across the borders between established constituencies and groups (and even individuals) intimates possibilities for connection and community beyond settled limits. In this essay, I first elaborate my theoretical points about translocality and emotion; in the second half of the essay, I show how two recent New York novels, Teju Cole's *Open City* and Ben Lerner's *10:04*, move beyond customary emotional scenarios in order to intimate a sense of what Lerner calls "transpersonal" community—a connectedness cutting across entrenched divisions.

2   Translocality and the Dislocation of Emotion

So how exactly does translocality unsettle the fast and frictionless mobility that is sometimes celebrated under the rubric of globalization? The term "translocality" was coined to overcome the blind spots of popular theories of globalization and transnationalism; it "emerged from a concern over the disembedded understanding of transnational networks" (Brickell and Datta 3). The research paradigms of globalization and transnationalism tend to emphasize the interconnectedness and mobility afforded by global capitalism and international communication, but, so proponents of translocality argue, they often do so in an abstract and delocalized way; only *national* borders really figure as obstacles in these frameworks, and then only as limits to be crossed. What remains invisible is, first, the importance of *intra*national, or indeed "inter-regional or inter- and intra-urban" movement (Brickell and Datta 4), and second, the local contexts in which international flows are inevitably lived and experienced. By focusing so much on mobility and migration, the notion of globalization threatens to pre-empt an analytical focus on particular sites (such as cities) as overdetermined nodes in which different vectors, forces, and agents of mobility intersect in complex and contradictory ways. In contrast to globalization, translocality makes it possible to home in on "unevenness" and "specific limitations and blockages" (Freitag and von Oppen 1); it affords "an understanding of place-making as a process which depends on transnational as well as on more localized movements," as it "integrate(s) notions of fluidity and discontinuity associated with mobilities, movements and flows ... with notions of fixity, groundedness and situatedness" (Greiner and Sakdapolrak 376); it promotes a version of what has been called "grounded" or "rooted" transnationalism (Brickell and Datta 9).

This emphasis on how flows of mobility settle in particular places and, conversely, how particular sites can be analyzed through their participation in several overlapping and intersecting movements makes translocality a fruitful methodological lens through which to focus on formations like the city—as this volume does under the rubric of "urban space"—but also, I would argue, on literary works. If we want to understand the way literature engages in and is solicited by the social world, translocality invites us to study literary texts as what Clemens Greiner and Patrick Sakdapolrak have called "articulated moments in networks of social relations" (374). In *A Transnational Poetics*, Jahan Ramazani commends what he calls a "translocal poetics" for balancing local and more encompassing forces; in this way, "a *translocal poetics* [is] an alternative to understandings of the relation [of literature] to place as either rooted or rootless, local or universal" (xiii). "Neither localist nor universalist, neither nationalist nor vacantly globalist, a *translocal poetics*," Ramazani writes, "highlights the dialogic intersections ... of specific discourses, genres, techniques, and forms of diverse origins" (43). It invites us to consider literature without falling for "[c]elebratory discourses of hyper-mobility and nomadism," and to capture cultural movement in all its complexity and contradictoriness (M. Smith 189).

Scholarship on literature and space is underwritten by a conviction that literature at its best manages to *represent* cultural movement in complex, nuanced, and often surprising ways. Yet I want to stress that the tension between locatedness and drift, between fixity and flow, not only characterizes literature's representation of cultural mobility, but also its engagement with emotion and affect. In my book *Contemporary Literature and the End of the Novel*, I locate the ethical and political promise of contemporary literature in its manipulation of affect—which is, as I argue there, not quite the same as emotion. More specifically, recent innovations in the Anglophone novel disable the emotive scenarios through which novels traditionally operate—think of narrative suspense, anticipation of closure, significant and transformative plot events, or psychologically complex characters who invite empathy. Recent literary works such as those by Tom McCarthy, J.M. Coetzee, and Teju Cole deliberately frustrate readers' expectations of such emotions: instead of prompting significant emotional responses, they deliver flat cardboard characters, plots in which nothing happens, or experiences that fail to transform their characters. The result, for the reader, is a frustrated emotional experience. Yet crucially, such a frustrated emotional experience is not quite the same as an *un*emotional experience; instead, I argue in the book, readers are left with an awkward, uneasy sense of affective disorientation; such unpredictable and intractable affects, however, may paradoxically open promising avenues for new kinds of connection and attachment.

One way to describe this movement of feelings is in terms of the distinction between *affect* and *emotion*—a distinction that, I should underline, is never absolute, but that theorists of affect have begun to make under the influence of the work of (especially) the psychologist Silvan Tomkins and the philosopher Gilles Deleuze. While *affects* are non-cognitive and involuntary intensities that take place outside of consciousness, emotions like empathy, grief, or joy have a cognitive dimension, are part of a mental narrative sequence, and are therefore considered as belonging to individuals; they are supposed *to express* the individual's inner experiences. So, while affects, in the words of Brian Massumi, are non-subjective and non-semantic forces that are "narratively de-localized" and "disconnected from meaningful sequencing," their absorption as part of individual experience makes them "conventional, consensual," and "functional" (25, 28). When we recuperate bewildering *affects as emotional experiences*, the argument goes, these affects lose their radically nonsubjective character, and therefore also their potential to dissolve the self-contained interiority of the individual and to open it to new connections and recombinations.

Literary works that deliberately sabotage the production of recognizable and codified emotions—empathy, recognition, relief—make room for unrecognized and unowned affects that operate outside of "the subjective domain of consciously codified emotion" (Greenwald Smith, "Postmodern" 428). They disrupt the alliance between feeling and person, between emotion and individual, and make possible new and yet unimagined forms of connection. Affect, for Vilashini Cooppan, can never be fully captured, but "open[s] itself to potential liberations, escapes, and freedoms" (56); it is a dynamic principle that "passes through but also beyond personal feelings" (Terada 109) and that allows contemporary fiction to explore *im*personal feelings that more capriciously and less predictably circulate across the divisions that make up individuals and communities. Moving beyond predictable and recognizable emotion, contemporary literary texts release, in Rachel Greenwald Smith's words, "a wealth of feeling that is poised for connection, for recombination, attachment, and eventual codification" ("Postmodernism" 438).

An important qualification is in place here. It does *not* follow from the distinction between affect and emotion that we can imagine literature as a subjectless zone of pure, unmediated, and freely circulating affect (and however far-fetched the idea of such a zone may sound, it is often entertained by Deleuzian theory). As a *linguistic* construct, literature is by definition engaged with meaning, with cognition, and with the encoding of experience—with the processes, that is, that turn affect into emotion. Yet crucially, literature is not only a linguistic construct—it is also an *aesthetic* operation that tends to undo the stability and meaning it *also* generates. Like all works of culture, literary works are "linguistically based and therefore inevitably codifying" (Greenwald Smith, "Postmodernism" 431), *even if, as aesthetic formations*, they simultaneously generate affects that cut across these codifications. Tracking the emotive dynamics of literary texts is then a matter of tracing the movement between coding and decoding, between emotion and affect, and between the personal and the impersonal—a movement, or so I argue, that is staged quite deliberately in some of the most interesting contemporary fiction. Ultimately, this is why translocality and affect can enrich one another: both paradigms invite us to attend to the movements between fixity and flow and between personal possession and impersonal dispossession in all their contradiction and complexity; they make it possible to see how literature stages the restless dynamic between emotion and affect in order to intimate possibilities of transpersonal connection, recombination, and attachment.

In the rest of this essay, I bring this perspective to bear on two critically acclaimed recent New York novels—Teju Cole's *Open City* from 2011 and Ben Lerner's *10:04* from 2014. For all their differences, the two novels, I argue, evoke city life in ways that undermine the reader's conventional empathy and replace it with more awkward and uncomfortable affects that yet intimate new possibilities for connection and attachment. While my reading of *Open City* mainly focuses on how its literary strategies sabotage emotional codifications in order to generate an unruly affective dynamic, the discussion of *10:04* shows how that novel more decidedly mobilizes unpredictable affects for the intimation of a transpersonal community, however provisional. Cumulatively, the readings of the two novels do not present a progressive narrative from personal emotion over impersonal affect to transpersonal community; instead, they show that the movements between the personal, the impersonal, and the transpersonal makes up the force field in which these and other significant contemporary fictions operate.

3   *Open City*: Toward Impersonal Affect[1]

On a superficial reading, *Open City* presents itself as a celebration of intercultural connectedness and mobility. The story is told from the perspective of Julius, an extremely erudite, artistic, and sophisticated young psychiatrist with Nigerian and German roots. Julius's meandering thoughts are loosely organized by two narrative devices: first, his compulsive habit of walking the streets and traveling the public transport systems of New York and Brussels, which generates a number of intense aesthetic experiences as well as a series of encounters with a whole catalogue of storytellers; and second, Julius's memories, which connect the narrative present and the stories of Julius's interlocutors to his and his family's Nigerian and German pasts. *Open City* is clearly anchored in a particular metropolitan location, and it imaginatively opens up that locale by overlaying urban experience with a multiplicity of stories, contexts, and memories. With Julius as the reader's guide, it displays the complexity and contradictoriness of contemporary metropolitan life.

Readers encounter this multilayered experience through the perspective of the novel's extremely self-conscious first-person narrator, who painstakingly captures and filters the events and encounters that make up his everyday life. In the eyes of many critics, Julius's wanderings and ruminations build a perspective that is both intimate and detached, engaged as well as estranged. The many celebratory reviews of the novel did not fail to recognize Julius as an exemplary *flâneur* (see Foden; Messud; Wood). Famously theorized by Charles Baudelaire and Walter Benjamin, the nineteenth-century *flâneur* was

---

[1]   My discussion of *Open City* draws on an earlier essay on the book. See Vermeulen, "Flights of Memory."

a leisurely wanderer who was acutely attentive to the spectacle provided by the processes of commodification and urbanization that surrounded him. An aesthete who uniquely manages to engage with the realities of the modern city *without* fully surrendering to them, the *flâneur* emerges from Baudelaire's and Benjamin's work as a dialectical figure "who presented himself as open to everything but who actually saved himself from the chaos of randomness through his pretensions to epistemological control" (Rabinovitz 7).[2] In this way, the *flâneur* anticipates a cosmopolitan ethos that thrives on intercultural curiosity and the virtues of the aesthetic.

Thus, on the face of it, the novel's controlled and extremely self-conscious perspective affords the reader access to a translocal urban experience. Yet, as the novel progresses, it becomes increasingly apparent that Julius' ratiocinations and self-consciousness also function as a strategy for emotional neutralization. Indeed, this neutralization is so successful that it becomes fairly uncanny, as readers begin to note that for all his intercultural encounters and aesthetic experiences, Julius fails to be touched or transformed by what he encounters. It becomes apparent that, rather than cultivating a sophisticated and reserved distance from the world, Julius suffers from a more drastic dissociation from it, and this makes it increasingly hard for readers to empathize with him. This dissociative disorder manifests itself in Julius' compulsive walking—in which he often only belatedly realizes where he ended up or how he got there. Near the end of the novel, readers, who have only had access to Julius' mind, also discover that this mind is highly unreliable, as they learn that he has seemingly forgotten that he raped the sister of one of his friends years before. This revelation—for the reader, but also, disturbingly, for Julius himself—comes when the girl confronts him after a party in New York. Importantly, this confrontation is the only passage in the book that breaks with the novel's customary rhythm—its casually chronological flow punctuated by frequent excursions into Julius's or his interlocutors' pasts; it is the only sequence, in other words, that ruptures the composure of the *flâneur* that the rest of the novel seems to sustain. To make matters worse, Julius fails to muster any reaction to the girl's accusation. Rather than speaking, he imaginatively converts the river, at which the girl had been staring during her monologue, into an aesthetic spectacle: "the river gleamed like aluminium roofing" (246). Here, what seemed like the novel's studied affectless tone turns into something more sinister; what seemed like emotional neutralization generates an awkward and disturbing affect.

---

2 For critical takes on the figure of the *flâneur*, see Buck-Morss and Wilson.

As I have argued at greater length elsewhere (Vermeulen, "Flights of Memory"), the combination of compulsive walking and a failure of memory has a name: the American Psychiatric Association's *Diagnostic and Statistical Manual* calls it a "dissociative fugue." This condition is characterized by "sudden, unexpected travel away from home or one's customary place of daily activities," and often goes hand in hand with "confusion about personal identity" (523). Ian Hacking, who has devoted a book to the history of this pathology, characterizes it as "impulsive uncontrolled traveling, with confused memories" (77). Julius's amnesia, his compulsive walking, and his dissociation from the stories and memories he encounters—as well as, we can add, the novel's thematic engagement with musical fugues from its very first pages—all point in the direction of this phenomenon.

The figure of the *fugueur* emerged in the late nineteenth century as the dark counterpart of the *flâneur*. While the *flâneur* was part of an emerging discourse that exalted mobility and tourism as "exceptional, admired travel, a heightened form of travel," the *fugueur*'s "ambulatory automatism" served as the shadow side of this new-won mobility (Hacking 52). It was associated with *vagabondage* and the unbearable boredom of modern life. And while *flâneurs* take an acute interest in the world around them in order to enrich the self, *fugueurs*' compulsive escape form their normal lives is "less a voyage of self-discovery than an attempt to eliminate self" (30). By showing how easily the *flâneur* shades into the *fugueur*, I argue, *Open City* transforms the translocality of the metropolis from an emotional experience that readers are invited to share into an awkward, strange, unnamable unease, a negative affect that readers cannot immediately understand or absorb. Near the end of the novel, Julius disappears as a figure the reader can empathize with; what is left is the bitter aftertaste of a novel that has deliberately sabotaged the celebration of emotive and imaginative mobility it seemed to invite readers to share.

How can we understand these *im*personal affects that the novel releases in the place of the strong emotional experience that the reader is denied? I have argued that even minor or negative affects—what Sianne Ngai has influentially studied as "ugly feelings"—have the potential to generate new associations and connections due to the very fact that they don't belong to any one person and that they don't coincide with any existing collectivity. They are, to cite Rachel Greenwald Smith's words again, "poised for connection, for recombination, attachment, and eventual codification" ("Postmodernism" 438). *Open City* begins to intimate such larger connections by gradually changing its imagining of the metropolitan locale; rather than only a site of aesthetic transport and intercultural encounter, New York becomes part of a much vaster canvas. One strategy the novel uses is unearthing different layers of the history of—colonial, imperial, racial—violence that are (barely) buried under the surfaces of post-9/11 New York; another one is connecting New York to global contexts that overdetermine the lived experience of the city. Yet, near the end of the novel, the city's remit is expanded even further. The occasion is Julius locking himself out of Carnegie Hall; he finds himself "on a flimsy fire escape," and he is surprised to see the stars, as he had not expected to see them "with the light pollution perpetually wreathing the city":

> [the stars'] true nature was their persisting visual echo of something that was already in the past. In the *unfathomable* ages it took for light to cross such distances, the light source itself had in some cases long been extinguished, its dark remains stretched away from us at *ever greater speed* … in the dark spaces between the dead, shining stars, were stars I could not see, stars that still existed, and were giving out light that hadn't reached me yet, stars now living and giving out light but present to me only as blank interstices. (256; my emphases)

The novel's deliverance from codified emotion makes possible a connectedness to a much larger scale—to "unfathomable," "ever greater" cosmic dimensions. This signals a form of connection that does not stop at the limits of human life, but also implicates decidedly nonhuman forces. It is here, I argue, by bending the translocal investments of the novel through the power of impersonal affects, that *Open City* delineates the possibility of a community that might be more appropriate to a present in which climate change, species extinction, resource depletion, and mass pollution—all phenomena that are studied under the increasingly popular rubric of the Anthropocene—invite us to imagine forms of connectedness that do not stop at the borders of human life.

4   *10:04*: Toward Transpersonal Community[3]

In this final section, I take up the question of translocality and feeling in another recent high-profile New York novel—Ben Lerner's *10:04*. The (at least) semi-autobiographical novel recounts the life of the narrator, also called Ben, an early-twenty-first-century man, New Yorker, and writer. At the novel's opening, he finds himself overwhelmed by anxieties and commitments. He has just

---

3 My discussion of *10:04* draws on a more extensive reading of the novel. See Vermeulen, "How Should a Person Be (Transpersonal)?"

signed a contract for a novel on the basis of "an earnest if indefinite proposal"; he is diagnosed with a heart condition that gives him "a statistically significant" chance of sudden death; his best friend Alex has engaged his services as a sperm donor, without really resolving the issue of his paternal involvement (4–6); and to make matters worse, he is also a particularly self-conscious contributor to anthropogenic climate changes, who imagines the future "underwater" and "wrecked by dramatically changing weather patterns" (40, 14). From the outset, then, *10:04*'s New York, like *Open City*'s New York at the end of the novel, is made up of the incongruent interactions of vastly different scales and rhythms: the minute details in which the nervous, intense, careful, and hyper-self-conscious narrator registers his feelings, thoughts, and experiences; the vast, planetary scale of climate change and energy depletion that makes itself felt in New York through hurricanes and black-outs; and the mundane details of a not very exceptional life of friendship and work, desire and doubt.

For *10:04*, the future is first of all a site of insecurity, anxiety, and concern; the text invests most of its experimental energy in imagining literature and art as things that can prefigure a less constraining future—as, in the novel's own words, provisional "forms of collectivity that can serve as figures of [community's] real possibility," as "the stuff out of which we build a social world" (116). The novel allows literature and art to access what it calls "the transpersonal" by breaking with traditional regimes of narration, meaning-making, and emotional codification. In the same way that the novel presents New York as shot through by dimensions and scales that render it newly vulnerable and vibrant in equal measure, its *formal* innovations break with the traditional protocols through which literary fiction constructs meaning and emotion. In the terms I have been using, this means that *10:04* sabotages personal emotion in order to open itself up to *im*personal affects that, to the extent that they are not owned by either character or reader, remain "poised for connection, for recombination, attachment, and eventual codification" (Greenwald Smith, "Postmodern" 438)—in, or so *10:04* hopes, a future *trans*personal community, that is to say, a community not founded on intersubjective encounters *between* discrete persons, but in affective engagement that cut across the borders of the individual.

So, what does it mean, exactly, to break with the notion of the person and the emotional scenarios it promotes? I want to highlight two ways in which *10:04* challenges the traditional emotive operations of the novel genre: its manipulation of characterization and its destabilization of fictionality. The first element that pre-empts the reader's strong emotional identification with Ben, the novel's narrator, is that he is simply too specific to serve as a character and to leave the reader room for imagination. Indeed, Ben's very specificity, his proximity to the book's author, in a sense makes him less of a character. As Catherine

Gallagher has argued, a traditional fictional character never simply refers to an individual, but can instead refer to "a whole class of people in general" rather than to "persons in particular" (342). A character, Gallagher notes, is "at once utterly finished and also necessarily incomplete": it is "utterly finished" in that it is fully determined by the "finite set of sentences" by which it is described; yet because it is not exhaustively captured by that set, it is also "necessarily incomplete," and so invites readers to imaginatively complete them (358). Unlike real people, literary characters grant us full access to intimate thoughts, feelings, and motivations, and this unreal access allows readers to imagine familiarity and intimacy with them. This explains literary characters' "peculiar affective force" (Gallagher 356); it explains that readers engage with characters as more than just sums of textual features. The problem with Lerner's main character is that he is and is not the writer himself, and that he is, in a sense, too close to the real Ben Lerner to require imaginative completion or allow for fantasies of transparency and intimacy. If traditional fictional characters are, for Gallagher, "enticingly unoccupied" as they bracket reference to particular individuals (351), Lerner's narrator is, we could say, *annoyingly occupied* by the identity of the actual Ben Lerner (it is hardly possible for the reader *not* to notice the echoes between narrator and author), without, however, fully coinciding with him. There is neither a traditional character nor a real-life person to identify with, which means the novel invites the reader to engage in more awkward and open-ended affective work.

A second formal decision that hinders the reader's traditional emotional investment is the work's self-conscious self-positioning on the brink of fiction and nonfiction. *10:04* imagines itself as a text where "the distinction between fiction and nonfiction d[oes]n't obtain"; it is a place "on the very edge of fiction" (237); in this place, "the correspondence between text and world [is] less important than … what possibilities of feeling [are] opened up in the present tense of reading" (171). Remarkably, *10:04* uses several metafictional elements that are familiar from postmodern fiction, but they are deployed to heighten rather than to subvert the reality of what it describes. The proximity between author and narrator, the explicit reflections on writing, and the inclusion of essays, stories, and poems by the real Ben Lerner as part of the narrator's stream of consciousness emphatically do *not* serve to expose fiction as pure artifice or expose reality as an imaginative construct; instead, and in marked contrast to postmodern versions of metafiction, they serve to position reading, writing, and living on the same plane—a plane on which they are all equally real; the process of writing literature is part of the reality that is being written, and the reader is intermittently addressed as if they were participating in the construction of that new reality. A good example is a moment when the narrator sits down to record a particular experience in a particular place, only to coordinate that experience with the moment of writing and the moment of reading: "I remember the address (you can drag the 'pegman' icon onto the Google map and walk around the neighbourhood on Street View, floating above yourself like a ghost; I'm doing that in a separate window now)" (163). Perception, remembrance, and verbalization operate on the same plane, as do experience, writing, and reading. What matters is less the ontological distinctions between reality and fiction than the novel possibilities of feeling and relation. In moments like these, the novel cancels the emotive processes through which readers normally relate to the fictional world and invites them to expose themselves to the possibility of different and unregimented forms of connectedness.

Withdrawing from predictable emotive patterns in order to prefigure a transpersonal future: this is the movement that *10:04* is interested in, and the one it reflects on through the art project of the narrator's girlfriend Alena, who creates an "Institute for Totaled Art" (the project is based on artist Elka Krajewska's "Salvage Art Institute"). The idea is simple: Alena collects and displays works of art that have been damaged and that insurance companies have declared to have "zero value." Objects are "formally demoted from art to mere objecthood" (129–30). The remarkable thing is that this changed status is often invisible. Contemplating a seemingly unharmed Cartier-Bresson print, the narrator reflects how "[i]t had transitioned from being a repository of immense financial value to being declared of zero value without undergoing what was to me any perceptible material transformation—it was the same, only totally different" (133). The totaling of art liberates the object from the cash nexus: totaled art works are officially withdrawn from circulation, and can never again acquire monetary value. If the late capitalist artwork—or indeed, work of literature—is normally a mere placeholder for future financial gain, totaled art exorcizes "the fetishism of the market," and is, for the narrator, "a utopian readymade—an object for or from a future where there was some other regime of value than the tyranny of price" (134). Withdrawing literary works, emotional investments, and indeed open cities from customary forms of circulation, this suggests, is one way of opening them up to transpersonal connections. It is only when affects are affirmed as radically impersonal, as belonging to no one (like a worthless work of art), that such transpersonal connections become available at all.

The novel ends by imagining a blacked-out New York—an open city, and now also a totaled city. Threatened by Hurricane Sandy, it is the backdrop to Ben's friendship with the woman who is, at the end of the novel, carrying his baby. New York is called a "totaled city"—a city that, because it has been liberated from customary economic dictates and emotional expectations, prefigures a transpersonal future. On the last two pages, the novel, as it has done a couple of times before, directly addresses its readers in order to enlist them for the transpersonal connections it forges—for what it calls "the fantasy of coeval readership" (93). It also suddenly shifts to the future tense, as if to signal that this totaled city presents a future that is no longer the threat or the source of anxiety for the narrator it was at the beginning. The two last paragraphs continue to describe the walk in the future tense, and the remarkable thing is that, apart from this shift in grammatical tense, nothing else really changes: events are still described in great, seemingly trivial detail; indeed, the events are so mundane that, the narrator notes, they "would sound improbable in fiction" (239). Yet this is a novel that has totaled the conventions of fictions, and that, even if it still looks and feels like a conventional novel, has made a wealth of as yet unnamed and untamed affect available. The point, it seems, is that the translocal city, or what the novel's very last lines call "the totaled city in the second person plural" is already a fact, and that the unsettling affective work of literature is one way to make us see that (240).

Works Cited

American Psychiatric Association. *Diagnostic and Statistical Manual of Mental Disorders*, 4th. Edition. Washington: American Psychiatric Association, 2000.

Brickell, Katherine, and Ayona Datta. "Introduction: Translocal Geographies." *Translocal Geographies: Spaces, Places, Connections*. Ed. Katherine Brickell and Ayona Datta. Abingdon: Routledge, 2011.

Buck-Morss, Susan. "The Flaneur, the Sandwichman, and the Whore: The Politics of Loitering." *New German Critique* 39 (1986): 99–140.

Cole, Teju. *Open City*. London: Faber & Faber, 2011.

Cooppan, Vilashini. "Memory's Future: Affect, History, and New Narrative in South Africa." *Concentric: Literary and Cultural Studies* 35.1 (2009): 51–75.

Foden, Giles. Review of *Open City*, by Teju Cole. *The Guardian* 17 Aug. 2011. Online.

Freitag, Ulrike, and Achim von Oppen. " 'Translocality': An Approach to Connection and Transfer in Area Studies." *Translocality: The Study of Globalising Processes from a Southern Perspective*. Ed. Ulrike Freitag and Achim von Oppen. Leiden: Brill, 2010, 1–22.

Gallagher, Catherine. "The Rise of Fictionality." *The Novel, Volume 1*. Ed. Franco Moretti. Princeton: Princeton UP, 2006, 336–63.

Greenwald Smith, Rachel. *Affect and American Literature in the Age of Neoliberalism*. Cambridge: Cambridge UP, 2015.

Greenwald Smith, Rachel. "Postmodernism and the Affective Turn." *Twentieth Century Literature* 57.3-4 (2011): 423–46.

Greiner, Clemens, and Patrick Sakdapolrak. "Translocality: Concepts, Applications and Emerging Research Perspectives." *Geography Compass* 7.5 (2013): 373–84.

Hacking, Ian. *Mad Travelers: Reflections on the Reality of Transient Mental Illnesses.* Charlottesville: U of Virginia P, 1999.

Massumi, Brian. *Parables for the Virtual: Movement, Affect, Sensation.* Durham: Duke UP, 2002.

Messud, Claire. "The Secret Sharer." Review of *Open City*, by Teju Cole. *New York Review of Books* 14 July 2011. Online.

Ngai, Sianne. *Ugly Feelings.* Cambridge: Harvard UP, 2005.

Rabinovitz, Lauren. *For the Love of Pleasure: Women, Movies, and Culture in Turn-of-the-Century Chicago.* New Brunswick: Rutgers UP, 1998.

Ramazani, Jahan. *A Transnational Poetics.* Chicago: U of Chicago P, 2009.

Smith, Michael Peter. "Translocality: A Critical Reflection." *Translocal Geographies: Spaces, Places, Connections.* Ed. Katherine Brickell and Ayona Datta. Abingdon: Routledge, 2011. 181–98.

Terada, Rei. *Feeling in Theory: Emotion after the Death of the Subject.* Cambridge: Harvard UP, 2001.

Vermeulen, Pieter. *Contemporary Literature and the End of the Novel: Creature, Affect, Form.* Basingstoke: Palgrave Macmillan, 2015.

Vermeulen, Pieter. "Flights of Memory: Teju Cole's *Open City* and the Limits of Aesthetic Cosmopolitanism." *Journal of Modern Literature* 37.1 (2013): 40–57.

Vermeulen, Pieter. "How Should a Person Be (Transpersonal)? Ben Lerner, Roberto Esposito, and the Biopolitics of the Future." *Political Theory* 45.5 (2017): 659–81.

Wilson, Elizabeth. "The Invisible Flâneur." *New Left Review* 191 (1992): 90–110.

Wood, James. "The Arrival of Enigmas." Review of *Open City*, by Teju Cole. *New Yorker* 28 Feb. 2011. Online.

CHAPTER 2

Body, Trauma, Theatricality – Rereading Testimony in the Stage Performance of *Sea Lavender, or the Euphoria of Being*

Miklós Takács

Abstract

In October 2015, at the age of 90, Holocaust-survivor Éva Fahidi became a permanent actor in The Symptoms' (Tünet Együttes) *Sea Lavender, or the Euphoria of Being* performance, along with Emese Cuhorka, dancer, 60 years her junior. There is no other such account of Holocaust survivors participating in theatre performances. The lack of similarities points out the uniqueness of *Sea Lavender*, but the true magnificence of it lies in the fact that it creates a perfect blend of various elements (theatre, dance, psychodrama) and hence provides an entirely novel and well-functioning framework for testimony. Here the witness appears actively precisely through her body, in opposition with the former perpetrators, who reduced the victims to their bodies. Thus, Éva not only testifies to trauma, but also her victory over it. As a result, intense positive emotions such as joy and euphoria are released and staged, which is very uncommon in the case of trauma.

This chapter explores testimony as a performative act and the ways theatrical space affects these acts. Capitalizing on Peter Brook's definition of theatre, one might say that the empty space in which two people, an actor and a spectator, meet, is by no means neutral, but is interwoven with emotions. The person who offers testimony by turning her trauma into a narrative, first of all, must defy the sense of shame, which is a burden for every victim of violence – without this, no testimony may occur. This is especially difficult in a public space such as a theatre, even though its spatial structure simulates intimacy. Stage appearance, however, places a lot more emphasis on bodily presence than testimonies in general; these performances feel intimate. One might as well listen to them with one's eyes closed. In this case, however, the listener is turned into a viewer, making the impact of the testimony much more intense: it is not only empathy, but also admiration that a spectator may feel towards the person performing the testimony. Therefore, testimonies not only transform the witness, but also the spectator, performatively creating a community based on affect.

All this can be explained by the distinctive features of theatre as opposed to other art media: since the act of performance, by definition, always takes place in the present moment, it moves both players and spectators out of their daily routine. Besides, theatre provides a fixed locality–due to which the Hungarian context must be taken into consideration–where everyday dichotomies can be temporarily suspended.

In the following analysis, the contrast of fictitious versus real and young versus old, will play a major role. The first opposition loses its affectiveness due to the genre of testimony. The co-author of *Testimony* (the common origin of trauma and testimony studies), psychoanalyst Dori Laub argues that *a testimony is never merely a reproduction of facts,* it is much more than that: it is a "genuine advent" due to the fact that the witness unavoidably uncovers the secrets to survival and to resist violence (62). Another important assumption of Laub's is that *testimonies are not monologues,* they have a continuous need for the presence of the "Other" (Laub 70). The performance analyzed in this paper is entitled *Sea Lavender.* Its protagonist is a Holocaust-survivor, who often enters into dialogue with her younger partner and with the audience as well, which creates the framework for questioning the opposition between the old and the young.Their gestures (for example, sticking out their tongues) permanently suspend our expectations concerning old age. Their behaviour is not childish; they appear in front of the audience in a relaxed manner, exempt from any prescribed roles.

Thus, performance is not an ordinary testimony, as in that case Éva Fahidi would be no more than a "talking head." I argue that the generalizability of uniqueness is only valid for oral or written testimonies, but it does not work for theatre performances that emphasize bodily presence. Theatre performances can function as media to stage traumas for a twofold reason. First, trauma can be defined as a kind of memory written into the body (Assmann 94), and second, trauma, just like the space itself, is of an extratemporal nature. However, trauma suppresses emotions and leads to the symptom of emotional numbing. The theatre performance is very much reminiscent of therapy, especially of the method of *body mapping*, where the first step of therapy is the therapist outlining the patient's body, which lying on a large sheet of paper or textile – hence aiding the individual to focus on the "here and now" instead of the traumatic past (Crawford 710). Additionally, emotions gain a larger significance both for the audience and the actors, and these include positive emotions as well, not only those connected to trauma. The dominant presence of the dance intensifies this effect: dance becomes a medium of expressing these emotions in a non-verbal form and of constituting emotional ties between dancers and between actors and audience.

Due to this constellation, the theoretical link between space and affect can be explored in a theatrical milieu. In the case of the performance of *Sea Lavender, or the Euphoria of Being*, there is a unique reason for this connection: the fact that the four concepts of the title of this essay–and an additional fifth and sixth one, *therapy* and *dance*–can be linked, is due to the person, life and courage of Éva Fahidi.

1   Introducing Éva Fahidi

In October 2015, at the age of 90, Fahidi became a permanent actor in The Symptoms Company's (Tünet Együttes) theatre production, along with Emese Cuhorka, a dancer, sixty years her junior. This was by no means a single production; the performance is still on the programme in Vígszínház Theatre three years later, along with regular performances at festivals, elsewhere in Hungary and in Germany.[1] This achievement would be admirable in itself, but the fact that Éva Fahidi has gone through serious traumas makes it even more unique. In 1944, she and her family were deported to Auschwitz from Debrecen. She lost almost all of her relatives; she herself, along with a thousand Hungarian women, was recruited for forced labor in a military factory hidden in a forest near Allendorf. The government of the town, which grew into a city after the war – hence the name change: Stadtallendorf – contacted the former prisoners, including her, and invited them to the so-called "week of encounters" in 1989, where they were publicly offered an apology (Fahidi 19–20). The leader of the documentation centre at the time asked Fahidi to write a memoir, but she was only able to do so a decade later (Fahidi 21). Her autobiography first appeared in German in 2004 (republished in 2011), followed by the Hungarian version in 2005 titled *Anima Rerum – The Soul of Things*. It is no exaggeration to say that she has held hundreds of readings and lectures, participating in discussions in Hungary and abroad to raise awareness of the Holocaust. Her appreciation and acknowledgement are well illustrated by the fact that she delivered a speech in front of Angela Merkel on 27 January 2015, for the 70th anniversary of Auschwitz's liberation (Fried).

Éva Fahidi's activity up to the present day and the Stadtallendorf initiative around the fall of communism is well suited to the memory culture that emerged in Western Europe by the end of the 1970s, and which is based on the

---

1   This is due to the fact that I had the opportunity to watch the performance twice, in Vígszínház Theatre on 8 October 2016 for the first time, and in the Csokonai Theatre's Chamber Theatre in Debrecen, on 6 March 2017.

testimonies of survivors (Kékesi 2). In Fahidi's case, the role of the witness is self-reflexive and conscious, which is also underlined by her announcement at the beginning of the *Sea Lavender* performance: she declares that she would like to write another book, this time about communism/socialism in Hungary, as she feels that giving her explicitly subjective account is also her responsibility. In this way she would be able to comply with the "social imperative" of memory culture (Kékesi 3) regarding another segment of Hungary's recent past which, like the Holocaust, has not yet been overcome. The same social responsibility can explain why Éva Fahidi, along with fourteen of her companions, testified in the trial of the Auschwitz guard Oskar Gröning at the Lüneburg Province Court on 21 April 2015 (Thüringer). However, following the current theories of testimony, we must draw attention to the fact that the role of a (judicial) witness in the world of law is entirely different from the testimony of a Holocaust-survivor. Following Avishai Margalit, Aleida Assmann calls the latter type a "moral witness," distinguishing the term not only from legal witnesses, but also from religious martyrs and the witnesses of oral history (Assmann and Hartman 22–29). A moral witness is similar to a martyr inasmuch as the term combines the roles of witness and victim, but the differences are even more striking. On the one hand, it is not the death but the survival that creates the witness. On the other hand, it is impossible for a witness to transmit a positive message; they cannot claim that there is someone/something (God) worth dying for (Assmann and Hartman 30).

2 The Relationship between the Memoir and the Performance

Éva Fahidi is a moral witness, who became a judicial witness on a single occasion only. The question, however, remains: why did she choose another medium for testimony? Why not be content with the traditional forms of written and oral narratives (*Anima Rerum*) and orality (talks, lectures and discussions)? Naturally a text-focused theatrical performance can be related to both of these basic forms, but if one examines the relationship between the text of the memoir and the performances, it becomes clear that due to the dramaturgical alterations, the performance relies on a rather abridged version of the book. What remains is some orientation regarding the title of the performance. *Anima Rerum* makes it clear, for instance, that it is Éva's favorite flower:

> But I have seen this very same field at the end of July, when the Sea Lavender–Limonium gmelini – blossoms with its tiny, purple, branching

arms, craning itself in all directions and up to the sky, while the whole field was as if it was covered with a huge, soft, purple duvet.

> FAHIDI 158

The episode is, apparently, a mise-en-abyme: not useful, but beautiful, just like the playful movement of the body, which is accentuated in the performance, be it dancing or a simple warm-up. Two longer excerpts from the text relating parts of the family history are included in the performance. One is the tale of the father. The other is the recollection of the Holocaust itself. Surprisingly, both of them gain dramaturgical emphasis: the father's tale is interrupted and finished only at the end of the performance, while the narration of the Holocaust is the climax of the performance.

This event is certainly a significant factor in the performance, as all the viewers are aware of the fact thatÉva is a Holocaust-survivor. Besides, right at the beginning, after warming up, when they both recall three memories from their "life tableaus," Éva's second image is the trauma of returning to Debrecen, which, in a slightly different version, can be found in *Anima Rerum*:

> A stranger came to open the gate. I told him that this house is mine, I'm home. He said he didn't care. Now it is theirs, it's more than ten of them living there, various families, I have no place here, I should go wherever I wish to. Now all my hopes have dissolved. Now reality hit me: I'm all alone in this world. I have no one.
>
> FAHIDI 236–237

Along with the two text fragments, the personification that is emphasized in the title *Anima Rerum,* which becomes a strategy of survival and remembering, is also uttered at a certain point in the performance, although not precisely the way it appears in the memoires:

> The frenzied research that I am conducting to get back our remaining objects is not for the sake of the objects only. It's for my mother and my father, the education that says that objects must be appreciated because of the work that was put into them. Their spirit and beauty give the framework of the bourgeois existence, in which our family and our likes used to live, which defined my childhood–now faded into the fog of dream–, the first decades of the 20th century.
>
> FAHIDI 80–81

Therefore, the focus of the performance is different from the portrayal of the scene in the memoir: *Emese's and Éva's bodies are foregrounded* (during the Debrecen performance, I witnessed that the audience of university students were audibly fascinated by Éva's movements).

3   The Uniqueness and Interchangeability of the Witness

If we look at the general situation of testimonies, following Aleida Assmann and Geoffrey Hartman, we may say that the empathic listener is a secondary witness, who stands by the "moral witness," gives account to her story and acknowledges her sufferings (Assmann and Hartman 39). The secondary witness occupies an empty position, which can and should always be taken. It is, however, unique to *Sea Lavender* that, due to a significant directorial/dramaturgical decision, the presence of the dancer, Emese Cuhorka, also stages the process of becoming a secondary witness. It is, for instance, symbolic that, right before the climax, she puts on one of the dresses Éva brought from Paris in the 1970s. After a dance divertissement, Emese is even more obviously presented as a secondary witness. They take turns recollecting their eighteen-year-old selves, and the memories they acquired at that time. Highlighting some details, Éva tells how she experienced the Holocaust, starting from the German officer moving into their home, then she speaks of the ghetto, and of Auschwitz. When they get to the cruelest parts, Emese no longer speaks from her own perspective, but she takes over the part of Gilike, Éva's eleven-year-old sister, uttering only a few sentences. Éva is left alone on the stage, recalling three memories from her "Auschwitz-tableau." This is the single occasion when she is alone, and Emese's absence clearly suggests that there are unexplorable dimensions of the traumatic experience. Later on, Emese returns (not in Éva's dress, however), and sits on one of the empty chairs positioned on the stage, listening to Éva, just like all the other spectators. However, as she is also visible to the viewers: she becomes a secondary witness.

Anyone can take the place of the secondary witness; this is the most significant aspect of the term. Emese's memories, fantasies and desires uttered at the performance seem just as haphazard and banal in comparison with Éva's trauma as anyone else's. Therefore, the question lurking behind the understanding of every piece of art, the relationship of uniqueness and generalizability, also needs to be raised. If we only consider Éva's narrative, there is indeed a duality to it; namely that it is unique, but additionally, as Csongor Lőrincz points out, "the reproducibility of witnesshood also assumes the virtual interchangeability of the witness (»anyone else would have testified just like that«)" (Lőrincz 55).

Éva Fahidi herself claims in the preface to her book that "(M)y story is one of many. To some extent typical, that is partly why I decided to write it down" (Fahidi 22). Playing the leading part in a dance performance at the age of ninety, however, cannot be regarded as typical at all. Éva cannot be replaced in this performance; if she decides to quit the show, the production cannot be continued, as there are no Holocaust survivors whose body would allow two hours of such intense work. Maybe it is no exaggeration to compare her presence to the notion of the aura in the Benjaminian sense, as neither the presence of Éva, nor that of the spectator can be reproduced with any technology. In this respect, it does not matter whether contemporary Hungarian theatre tells about the trauma of Holocaust using global or local narratives, as Noémi Herczog argues (Herczog 145). *Sea Lavender* is local in the most literal sense of the word, because it is where Éva Fahidi is. All the other performances will involuntarily blend the global and the local, especially since the globalization of Holocaust memories.

Therefore, one can argue that there is no real contrast between the individual and the collective. The two can seemingly blend into each other if we converge testimony to a similar genre, that of the memoir. Besides, the literature of testimony agrees on the decisive role of another dichotomy, that of activity and passivity. Giorgio Agamben imagines the passive and active parts as two separate subjects within the speech act of testimony. First, there is the survivor, who is able to speak, but "has nothing to tell," and there is the subject, who "glanced at the Gorgon" and "had hit rock bottom," and hence has a lot to say, but cannot speak (Agamben 104). These two do not exclude each other, and what is more, the survivor and the so-called "Muselmann" are inseparable, it is exclusively their unity/difference that constructs the testimony (Agamben 131).

The "Muselmann," the term for the living dead and the dying of the concentration camps, defined by Agamben as the threshold between human and non-human (47), is also a symbolic marker (first with Primo Levi) for the paradox of testimony. In order to illuminate this claim, Agamben quotes from a collection at the end of his book that contains testimonies from people who survived the "Muselmann"state. Levi considers the title of the collection paradoxical ("I was a Muselmann"), because the speaker utters the following, extreme formula: "I, who is speaking here, was once a Muselmann, I was someone who cannot speak by any means" (qtd. in Agamben 144). Based on her account, Éva Fahidi has also reached this state, not long before her rescue at the end of March 1945, when, escorted by their guards, they were escaping from the Allied forces:

> By now I reached the state of distress. I can't even raise my little finger. When you get to this point, you're not able to do anything spiritually

either. Nothing matters, everything is distant, uncertain, wobbly. You have only one wish: to be left alone so that you don't have to move, don't have to think, you're unable to do so anyway, and everything is barren and indifferent. I don't even know who I am, or who I was.

FAHIDI 222

Knowing all this, we may understand Emese'scurious idea in the first half of the performance, namely, that she wants to become "no one" when they play dress-up. The description of "no one" – a black, faceless figure without personality, an abstract shape – mostly resembles her own shadow. It is only much later, practically before the climax, that they appear in the costumes: Éva with a stork on her back, which can therefore be interpreted as an angel costume, and Emese in black, fitted clothes, which cover even her face.

They do a peculiar dance in their costumes, presumably to one of the compositions of György Ligeti, who was mentioned earlier in the performance, where Emese is more active, writhing around Éva with snake-like movements. Through her dance Emese enacts the one who cannot talk but is present as a witness, in Éva's traumatic present. She is able to do so because the "Muselmann" is reduced to her body, thus it can be recalled in bodily presence–even though this stage is impossible to recreate verbally.

4 Victory over Perpetrators and Shame

Both dance and testimony create a sense of community between witness and listener, dancer and dancer. It is easier to grasp this in the case of dancing: it is a fundamental anthropological experience that every human gathering leads to some kind of movement practiced together (Waldenfels 20). Besides, due to the "synesthesia" (multimediality) and performativity of dancing, people who dance together may not only form social, but also emotional bonds (Wulf 121). What is more, dance could build bridges between generations, as Emese belongs to and represents the third generation after the Holocaust. In the closure of the performance, the two dancers evoke a grandmother-granddaughter relationship: Éva finishes the interrupted tale about her father while Emese listens with her head in Éva's lap. By turning towards the audience, Éva "adopts" them as well, since, after giving a "goodnight kiss" to Emese, she says that we, spectators, are also entitled to this kiss. In addition, this symbolic act takes place in a very significant moment, at the very end of the performance.

Therefore, by the end of the performance it becomes apparent that a moral community has been created between actors and viewers, but strangely, the experience of alienness that was manifested in awe at the beginning of the show is a prerequisite of this. Alienation should not be understood as a generation gap between the old and the young, but rather as the alienation from one's own body. This means not only the experience of exhaustion which can be felt by both young and old when it is not only the body that is alienated, but also all of the movements it performs (Waldenfels 21).

Conversely, it is no exaggeration to say that along with the valorization of youth in consumer societies, the elderly body has become something to be ashamed of. This is by no means as seriously liminal a situation as the shame and guilt that survivors feel, but the structural foundations of the two issues are the same. Therefore, it is not surprising that Agamben devotes a longer chapter to shame, arguing that the double subject of the Holocaust survivor witness can be found in shame too. It occurs when the subject is *witness* to their own collapse, experiencing the loss of their subjectivity; it is this twofold movement, the birth and disappearance of the subject that characterizes shame according to Agamben (91).

The loss of the subject position, the dehumanization during the Holocaust already started with the confiscation of the valuables. Since this was a gradual process, the loss was not apparent at first sight:

> Hungarian authorities were careful not to shock us: they gradually deprived us of our goods and favourite objects. First the plants that ensured our living, then our gardens and houses, then the objects we saved into the ghetto, then we only brought to the brick factory what we thought was indispensable.
> FAHIDI 160

However, in the concentration camp this process cannot be concealed any longer: depriving one of their cultural bodies (hair, clothes) is an obvious sign of dehumanization.

> What you cannot get used to or forget and I don't even want to: the indignity. Häftling is a number. She wears it on her clothes. She has no name, she's coming from nothing, she's going to the gas, she has nothing but her tight fitted present, neither past, nor future. (…) We stayed human no matter what, we raised our heads no matter what, we held the cutlery just like at home, we washed ourselves, brushed our teeth every day, we talked to each other just like at home. We trusted each other, our future,

no matter what, and we appreciated each other. This is why we survived the lager, this is why we came back.
FAHIDI 214–215

Hence a possible strategy for survival is the conscious effort to remind oneself of their humanity. The quote above, besides commenting on the duality of shame in an Agambenian sense, may also illustrate what Ruth Leys calls the positive side of shame. Positive at least in comparison with guilt, because shame promises the possibility of change, as it focuses on one's identity instead of the deeds and their meaning (Leys and Goldman 670, 677).

This attention also includes the body. One can be ashamed of one's body and of what happened to it, and both emotions may paralyze us, but, in fact, shame is paradoxically a possible building block for a new subjectivity. *Sea Lavender* doubly exploits this opportunity, as the traumatized person is obviously held back from testimony by shame (we recall that Éva Fahidi herself only managed to break the forced silence when she was almost eighty years old). Meanwhile, traditional testimonies focus on narrative content, and by directing the attention to her own body and that of the secondary witness, Emese, she not only gets rid of an (indeed useless) burden, but also defies the familiar shame to allude to a victory that was achieved after a much greater struggle.

There could have been no better tools for this purpose than those provided by dance theatre. In traditional, text-focused theatres the spectator is prone to concentrate on the "talking head," but in the case of dance theatre, this is impossible. It is an anthropological tenet that all dance is universally focused on the body, and hence such performances invariably emphasize the body (Brandstetter and Wulf 9, Wulf 123). Consciously or not, maybe exactly because of the dance theatre milieu, the reflections about the body are strongly emphasized in the two characters' dialogues too. And it is quite frequent that they do not talk about their own bodies, but they rather declare their expectations, for instance, about the ideal male body (facial hair is not appealing, belly is a "world view"), while discussing old dating habits. In this scene, Emese is wearing Éva's long dress, and Éva pulls it up to Emese's knees, saying that this is the extent to which a woman could publicly show her body at that time. They do not deconstruct the discourses that define their (and our) bodies, but they very much present themselves in submission to these discourses from the first minute. For instance, shortly after entering, Éva mentions her former dance teacher, Karola Perczel, who taught her proper posture. Interestingly, gymnastics is an important part of an actor's preparation in the Stanislavski method, but this "well-intentioned manipulation" was aimed to move the artist's bodily characteristics towards the beauty ideal of the age (P. Müller 139). The *Sea*

Lavender performance does not aim to question the discourses that view the body as a culturally coded entity, such as gymnastics. The physical exercises that Éva Fahidi performs every day free the body from its object status; instead of an animalistic, vegetating organism, the body becomes an artistic artefact. Violence, therefore, reduces the victim to her physical body, but we can deliberately choose to do the same, if we find joy in it. Jan Philipp Reemtsma gives the example of sexual intercourse (128), but dancing or sports are also such activities. The transformation of both body and mind, which a traumatized person goes through, can have a positive impact. The shocking fact that someone over the age of ninety is able to hold up in a two-hour performance (with no break) is in itself the triumph of life (*trauma to triumph*) over death, but here, in addition, the person in question is a Holocaust survivor: a moral witness.

5 Transgressions: Dance and Imagination

This process can be considered as a kind of therapy too. Therapy and testimony are similar inasmuch as both seek to narrativize trauma. What is less emphasized in psychotherapy, though, is the body, whereas the body has a story to tell, just like the soul. In her father's tale, Éva appears as a fairy, which is a curious coincidence if we take into consideration that the therapist Leslie E. Korn tends to ask her patients (as it usually turns out to be very beneficial) to name their favourite myth or fairy tale and explain what it means to them. More importantly, she asks them to rewrite their stories as myths or heroic journeys (Korn 146). Another therapeutic solution places much more emphasis on the body. According to Allison Crawford, the method of *body mapping* is a bridge for the patient to narrativize bodily experiences, because it is easier to share the visual; defying secretiveness, shame and isolation, unspeakable experiences become communicable (Crawford 715–716). This body-centered therapy obviously positions itself against Freud's strictly talking therapy, which does not focus on the body (Crawford 703) and forbids physical contact (i.e., touching) between patient and therapist (Korn 78).

The act of writing could be therapeutic as well. As Dominic LaCapra argues, trauma in many artistic media (literature, film and fine arts), especially in testimonial pieces, appears in symbolic undertakings, characterized by unexpectability, transgression and free associative play (LaCapra 105). Only those texts can be included in the canon that contest the limitations of representation and try to re-inscribe the system of conventions for Holocaust representations (Kisantal 58) (the most typical example is Art Spiegelman's *Maus*). *Anima Rerum* is not included in the narrower, Hungarian canon of Holocaust-representations (and was left without reflections somewhat undeservingly), but *Sea Lavender* should undoubtedly have a place in the canon, simply because *Sea Lavender* managed to find that unusual framework which transforms the performance of the testimony into an entirely "new event," as Oren Baruch Stier puts it, even if the story itself has been told earlier (84). Éva Fahidi not only had her story published, but she told it many times in front of large audiences – and yet even those who have read *Anima Rerum* and listened to her talks can be seriously affected by *Sea Lavender*. A major element of the novelty and impact of the performance is dancing as a mode of expression that makes tangible what is otherwise unexperienceable (Wulf 129).

The other important element is imagination, because testimony, as we have seen above, cannot be inherently reduced to mere information transmission. It cannot demonstrate openly fictitious elements either, yet these appear in the *Sea Lavender* performance right after three realistic memories taken from the main characters' "life tableaus." From that point on in the performance, the actors announce their ages more and more frequently, but they always introduce themselves as somewhat younger or older than they actually are. It is in this context that they enact one of Éva's unfulfilled dreams (she wanted to be a famous pianist, but the Holocaust prevented her from attaining this goal). Emese takes a sheet of plexiglass and puts it in Éva's lap, who starts to imitate playing the piano, while piano music can be heard, and Emese starts dancing to it. This example can demonstrate that play (as an embodiment of imagination) may also be included in a testimony, because the body remembers those "new ways of moving" (Straus 263), which are similar to dance moves and which were acquired a long time ago during piano classes and can be evoked anytime. One might think that this extent of levity undermines the authority of the witness, but this is not so. Firstly, because the performance is structured from the beginning in a way that it makes such instances acceptable within the testimony, and secondly, because Éva is still playing herself, reminding us that each testimony maker is an actor even if they "play" their parts without pretense (Stier 71).

We cannot find many examples of theatrical representations of testimonies in Western culture. Concerning performances in which a moral witness participates, I have found but one example: In Theatre Groupov's production entitled *Rwanda 94. Une tentative de réparation symbolique envers les morts, àl'usage des vivants* (*Rwanda 94: An Attempt at Symbolic Reparation to the Dead, for Use by the Living*) Yolande Mukagasana enacts and tells about her experiences as a survivor, while an actor accounts for the historiographic explanation of the events (Kalisky 207). However, the Rwanda slaughter took place a little over twenty years ago and there is no such account of Holocaust survivors participating in theatre performances. The lack of similar productions points out the uniqueness of *Sea Lavender*, but the true magnificence of it lies in the fact that *it creates a perfect blend of various elements (theatre, dance, psychodrama) and hence provides an entirely novel and well-functioning framework for testimony.*

6 Play on the Dark Side

Theatre performance and the dance as a new media for testimony have already been discussed, it is only the third one that is left: psychodrama. It could be just as well called sociodrama: even the founder, Jacob L. Moreno argues that the two genres cannot be clearly distinguished; while the one focuses on the individual, the other is centred on inter-group relationships and collective ideologies (Kellermann 15). Presumably the situation here is very similar to that of the testimony, where the boundaries between individual and collective, private and public, are blurred. Both genres can be regarded as therapeutic tools which aim to heal traumatic experiences. They share the same tools: sociodrama uses the practices of psychodrama, such as roleplay, doubling, mirroring or turning into a sculpture, which transform sociodrama into socio-therapy (Kellermann 18). The stake of *Sea Lavender* is not Éva's healing; she appears to be healthy both in body and mind, as far as someone can actually recover from a trauma. The use of therapeutic tools rather refers to the process of healing, exploring how it was possible to defy trauma.

 Although in the first sentence of the performance, the slowly approaching Éva emphasizes the difference between young and old bodies, declaring that "(t)his is the difference of rhythm between us" (*Sea Lavender*), this difference disappears during the warm-up, among other things due to the mirroring game, which recalls psychodrama. They mimic each other as mirrors, naming certain body parts with humorous metaphors, and even sticking out tongues. The viewer must accept that this game allows for both players to act like children – regardless of their age.

 The Hungarian and international reviews, which only have one short headline to catch the attention of the reader, also emphasize the tension between old age and play, as well as between an old body and dancing, is definitely dissolved by *Sea Lavender*. However, none of them mentions therapy. Yet it is apparent that dancing, physical exercise, music and singing all have their therapeutic effects, by means of restoring the internal rhythm of the body that had been broken by trauma (Korn 6, 149, 154, 166). This is why the dance scenes of *Sea Lavender* must be interpreted, but it is also a characteristic feature of dancing that it offers space for free associations and demonstrates the limited nature of our knowledge, or the "limitlessness of our lack of knowledge" (Brandstetter 95).

With that in mind, one cannot write definitive statements, for instance, about the dance choreography of the finale, where both women first wear white clothes (Emese is wearing sporty shorts and a tank top and Éva is in a long-sleeved shirt and leggings, barefooted), adding a sparkling sequined layer. Emese puts Éva into a swivel-chair, moving her, dancing with her. This solution is primarily another manifestation of the childlike attitude, which playfully reconfigures everything. However, this form of movement is two-faced: even though it seems like cradling, one of the most ancient means to ease anxiety, it lacks an even more ancient form of healing, physical contact (Korn 94, 85). Thus, this movement includes a darker tone, evoking the image of a caregiver, moving her inert patient in a wheelchair or a gurney. Emese demonstrates a caring attitude from the beginning: she asks Éva if she wants some water, or if she would like a tissue when she is coughing. These gestures evoke the threat of the body's vulnerability, acknowledging that Éva may partially lose control over her body any time. Depending on the context, this negative side may be found in dancing, singing and music, all of which have a major role in the healing process: although they can create both individual and collective memories (Wulf 127), a piece of music, a song might as well be turned into the signifier of trauma in traumatic mnemotechnics. For example, the still popular song, "Nád a házam teteje" signifies one of Éva's memories, evoked in the "piano scene," recalling the time when the Hungarian "girlies" performed this very song for the Allendorf lager commander's competition (Éva even sings another, also existing variant, beginning with "Zsupp a házam teteje"). Even more absurdly, at the climax of the performance Éva recalls that in Auschwitz, the lager band played Julius Fučik's famous *Entry of the Gladiators* every morning and every night for the prisoners leaving for or arriving back from work. The effect is also underlined by the fact that the march first appears in the performance without any commentary, and it is only afterwards that Éva explains the context.

Previously I have emphasized the two-faced nature of the finale, but there is also a mise-en-abyme here which unites the faces of the two characters in a measure of harmony: the postcard-sized leaflet of the performance (figure 2.1), where the half faces of Éva and Emese form one single image. The manipulated picture claims the very same thing as all the images and moments of the two-hour performance: to step into the other person's world is indeed possible. There is empathy between witness and her audience, and the two of them

FIGURE 2.1   The Symptoms' leaflet of the performance from "Tünet Együttes: Sóvirág"; *Csokonai Színház*; csokonaiszinhaz.hu,https://tinyurl.com/yb2uqfyb (Accessed 26 June 2020)

together are capable of creating something entirely new, without either of them losing their original faces.[2]

7   Conclusion

The complexity of *Sea Lavender* is due to the mixture of six constituents: body, trauma, theatricality, testimony, dancing and therapy, and a radical rereading of all six. Unfortunately, in terms of Holocaust memories, this healing cannot

---

2 Here we must mention that due to the collective authorship of theatre performances, the *Sea Lavender* owes much of its complexity to the creators who did not participate in the production in the flesh: Réka Szabó director, Krisztián Peer and Anna Zsigó dramaturges.

really become exemplary because, as time moves on, the chance of the witnesses' personal participation is growing more and more limited. This is in part the root of the performance's uniqueness and unrepeatability. The other side of this uniqueness can be explained by the fact that the witness appears actively precisely through her body, in opposition with the former perpetrators, who reduced the victims to their bodies. Thus, Éva not only testifies to the trauma, but also to her victory over it. As a result, intensively positive emotions such as joy and euphoria are released and staged, which is very much uncommon in the case of trauma. So far, I have intentionally avoided the interpretation of the subtitle (*"or, the Euphoria of Being"*), as I felt it was exaggerated, focusing too much on the positive aspects of the performance. However, I have to admit that this is the final conclusion of *Sea Lavender*: overcoming the transience of both body and mind over the age of ninety can be nothing else but euphoric.

Works Cited

Agamben, Giorgio. *Was von Auschwitz bleibt – Das Archiv und der Zeuge* (*Homo sacer III*). Suhrkamp, 2003.

Assmann, Aleida. *Der lange Schatten der Vergangenheit: Erinnerungskultur und Geschichtspolitik*. C. H. Beck, 2006.

Assmann, Aleida. "Pathos und Passion. Über Gewalt, Trauma und den Begriff der Zeugenschaft." Geoffrey Hartman and Aleida Assmann. *Die Zukunft der Erinnerung und der Holocaust*, Konstanz UP, 2012. pp. 9–40.

Brandstetter, Gabriele. "Tanz als Szeno-Graphie des Wissens." *Tanz als Antropologie*, edited by Gabriele Brandstetter and Christoph Wulf, Wilhelm Fink, 2007. pp. 84–99.

Brandstetter, Gabriele and Christoph Wulf. "Einleitung: Tanz als Antropologie." *Tanz als Antropologie*, edited by Gabriele Brandstetter and Christoph Wulf, Wilhelm Fink, 2007. pp. 9–13.

Crawford, Allison. "If 'The Body Keeps the Score': Mapping the Dissociated Body in Trauma Narrative, Intervention, and Theory." *University of Toronto Quarterly*, vol. 79, no. 2, 2010: 702–19.

Fahidi, Éva. *Anima Rerum – A Dolgok Lelke* (*Anima Rerum – The Soul of Things*). Tudomány, 2005.

Fried, Nico. "Kanzlerin Merkel: Auschwitz fordert uns täglich heraus." *Süddeutsche Zeitung*, www.sueddeutsche.de/politik/bundeskanzlerin-zum-holocaust-gedenken-auschwitz-fordert uns-taeglich-heraus-1.2321245. Accessed 24 July 2017.

Herczog, Noémi. "A metaforikus zsidó a kortárs színházban." ("The Metaphorical Jew in the Contemporary Theatre") *Holokauszt, újutak, újgenerációk* (*Holocaust, New*

Ways, New Generations), edited by Nikolett Antal and Márton Mészáros, Fiatal Írók Szövetsége, 2016. pp. 131–46.

Kalisky, Aurélia. "Jenseits der Typologien: die Vielschichtigkeit der Zeugenschaft." *Zeugenschaft. Perspektiven auf einkulturelles Phänomen*, edited by Claudia Nickel and Alexandra Ortiz Wallner, Universitätsverlag Winter, 2014. pp. 193–211.

Kékesi, Zoltán. *Agents of Liberation. Holocaust Memory in Contemporary Art and Documentary Film*. Central European UP and Helena History Press, 2015.

Kellermann, Peter Felix. *Sociodrama and Collective Trauma*, Jessica Kingsley Publishers, 2007.

Kisantal, Tamás. *Túlélő történetek – Ábrázolásmód és történetiség a holokausztművészetében* (*Surviving Stories. Representational Method and Historicity in Holocaust Art*), Kijárat, 2009.

Korn, Leslie E. *Rhythms of Recovery – Trauma, Nature, and the Body*. Routledge, 2013.

LaCapra, Dominick. "Holocaust Testimonies – Attending to Victim's Voice." LaCapra, Dominick. *Writing History, Writing Trauma*. Johns Hopkins UP, 2nd ed., 2014. pp. 86–113.

Laub, Dori. "Bearing Witness or the Vicissitudes of Listening." Shoshana Felman and Dori Laub. *Testimony – Crises of Witnessing in Literature, Psychoanalysis, and History*, Routledge, 1992. pp. 57–74.

Leys, Ruth and Marlene Goldman. "Navigating the Genealogies of Trauma, Guilt, and Affect: An Interview with Ruth Leys," *University of Toronto Quarterly*, vol. 79, no. 2, 2010: 656–79.

Lőrincz, Csongor. "A tanúság tétel esemény és differenciaelméleti megközelítése." ("Event- and Difference Theoretical Approach to Testimony") *Az irodalom tanúságtételei* (*The Testimonies of Literature*). Ráció, 2015. pp. 11–59.

Müller, Péter. *Test és teatralitás* (*Body and Theatricality*). Balassi, 2009.

Reemtsma, Jan Philipp. *Vertrauen und Gewalt. Versuch über eine besondere Konstellation der Moderne*. Pantheon, 2009. Quoted by: Pabis, Eszter. "Az interdiszciplináris erőszakkutatás eredményeiről és problematikájáról." *Az erőszak reprezentációi* (*Representations of Violence*), edited by Eszter Pabis, Debreceni Egyetemi Kiadó, 2015. pp. 7–22, 17.

Sea Lavender or the Euphoria of Being (*Sóvirág – avagy a létezés eufóriája*). Directed by Réka Szabó, performances by Éva Fahidi and Emese Cuhorka. Tünet Együttes, 8 Oct. 2016, Vígszínház Theatre, Budapest and 6 Mar. 2017, Csokonai Chamber Theatre, Debrecen.

Stier, Oren Baruch. "Framing Memory – Videotestimonies and the Transmission of Holocaust Remembrance." *Committed to Memory – Cultural Mediations of the Holocaust*. U of Massachusetts P, 2003. pp. 67–109.

Straus, Erwin. *Vom Sinn der Sinne*. Springer, 1978. Quoted by: Waldenfels, Bernhard. "Sichbewegen." *Tanz als Antropologie*, edited by Gabriele Brandstetter and Christoph Wulf, Wilhelm Fink, 2007. pp. 14–30, 23.

Thüringer, Barbara. "Magyar holokauszttúlélők tanúskodnak az auschwitzi lágerőr ellen" ("Hungarian Holocaust Survivors Bear Witness in the Trial of Auschwitz Guard"), *Index*, index.hu/kulfold/2015/04/21/magyar_holokauszt-tulelok_tanuskodnak_az_auschwitzi_lageror_ellen/. Accessed 24 July 2017.

Waldenfels, Bernhard. "Sichbewegen." *Tanz als Antropologie*, edited by Gabriele Brandstetter and Christoph Wulf, Wilhelm Fink, 2007. pp. 14–30.

Wulf, Christoph. "Antropologische Dimensionen des Tanzes." *Tanz als Antropologie*, edited by Gabriele Brandstetter and Christoph Wulf, Wilhelm Fink, 2007. pp. 121–31.

Translated by Zsófia O. Réti

CHAPTER 3

The City as a Lyric Archive of Affects in Lisa Robertson's *Occasional Work and Seven Walks*

Katalin Pálinkás

Abstract

Lisa Robertson's *Occasional Work and Seven Walks from the Office for Soft Architecture* (2003) describes the city of Vancouver and urban space as resonating with an array of affects that are not owned and are often historical, yet call for change. This chapter argues that historicity and collectivity are key to Robertson's project: she compiles an archive of information and affective states about urban life, where the past is mobilized into present action through a radical urgency, and experiments with various forms of plural agency, such as a virtual office for urban architecture and a couple of urban walkers, to render a collectively constructed urban experience. Moreover, in an important revision, Robertson aligns the lyric with affect: the singular lyric subject is replaced with the potential communities and shared intimacies created by affective urban experience.

Lisa Robertson is renowned for her experimentation with generic and discursive expectations: she revisits the pastoral in *XEclogue* (1993), combines the lyric with meteorological discourse in *The Weather* (2001), flouts gender expectations in *The Men: A Lyric Book* (2006), and interrogates autobiographical writing and the centrality of a subjective "I" in *R's Boat* (2010). A frequent exploration of formal aspects, such as rhythm, sentence structure and lineation, along with the impressive breadth of theoretical reading often traceable in the texts, add to the complexity of her writing. In *Occasional Work and Seven Walks from the Office for Soft Architecture* (first published in 2003 and re-issued in 2006) she brings all these concerns together: mixing prose and poetry, actual local history and extravagant descriptions of urban experience, while engaging with a vast amount of literary and theoretical writing. She creates a dense description of both the changing urban texture of Vancouver and the translocal urban experience.

As Robertson explains, she originally wanted to document the rapid change of the city between two commercial transactions: that of the sale of the Expo

'86 site and the purchase of land for the 2010 Winter Olympics. She was driven by her nostalgia for what was disappearing, as she put it in the Acknowledgements section: "for the minor, the local, the ruinous; for decay" (n. pag.). In the book, this personal nostalgia is countered by research on urban space and a creation of "alternative spaces and contexts for the visual culture of this city, sites that could also provide a vigorously idiosyncratic history of surfaces as they fluctuate" (n. pag.). Robertson chooses description as a method: "The *Soft Architecture* texts started with a simple problem—how can I construct a description, a document, that maintains an indexical relationship to this city I experience in my quotidian life? How can I develop a description that moves?" ("Andy Fitch with Lisa Robertson"). Description as a capacious form allows her to "compile the synthesis of bodily intuitions, historical research, friendship, and chance" (*Occasional Work* 59).

With its attention to neglected material forms and practices of the city, and with the compilation of an archive about them, *Occasional Work and Seven Walks* can be read as Robertson's Benjaminian project. The book creates its version of Benjamin's dialectic image: through the archival and theoretical research presented, Robertson uncovers ideologies and economies, aesthetic and social practices, and suggests that the present, in this case the present affect, is never entirely independent of its histories. As I wish to argue in this chapter, the book directs its reader to glimpse the present through the accretions of history.

On the other hand, Baudelaire is also a haunting presence for Robertson's strongly lyric book. The figure of the poet appears in "The Value Village Lyric": the speakers, browsing through the discarded yet extravagant garments of the North American mega thrift store, think of "the casual bravado of Baudelaire's tied black cravat against the scrim of white collar in the photograph by Nadar" (218). They imagine how it would feel to try on Baudelaire's coat, slip their arms into its sleeves, and feel how its "worn cuff would brush [their] books" (218). Such fantasies, with their alignment of economy and rhetoric, memory and present affect, are abundant in Robertson's book. Through performing a belated *flânerie* in the city of Vancouver and documenting it in the prose poems of the *Seven Walks*, Robertson acts like Baudelaire, and, prior to that, by marshalling an archival density of information in *Occasional Work*, she acts like Benjamin. Yet, as I wish to show, she significantly remodels both the lyric poet's and the social historian's view of urban experience.

Critics have explored Robertson's book from the perspectives of feminism, global capitalism, urban and spatial studies. Characteristically, it has been read as a critique of globalism, which intends to unmask the ideologies underlying global tendencies and assert the power of the local and the personal as they vitally shape urban experience. Michael Davidson and Christopher Schmidt also point out that Robertson mixes styles and histories to counter globalizing tendencies: she re-imagines Vancouver as a "phantasmagoric site for neo-situationist projects" (M. Davidson 43) and creates a hybrid style by combining aestheticism and "experimentalist difficulty" (Schmidt 156). Ryan Fitzpatrick and Susan Rudy consider how, for Robertson, urban space is inevitably defined by multiple trajectories, ranging from the global to the local, from the political and historical to the poetical. Maia Joseph focuses on how Robertson, a socially conscious urban poet, revisits the poetic practice of *flânerie*, while engaging with important ethical and political questions of contemporary urbanity. Robertson's style has also proved provocative: Jennifer Scapettone looks at how historicism, globalizing economies, and the excess of social and personal affect create a surfeit for an originally localized poetics and how that excess explodes the boundaries of site-specific description. In a similarly Deleuzian reading, Geoffrey Hlibchuk argues that Robertson's text creates a new kind of postmodern poetics that transgresses both the spatial localization of its object and the rhetorical limitations of description: in the text "the separate elements of urban living meld into a morphological delirium," which is maintained by the extensive use of the tropes of fabric, translucency, and delirium (par. 23).

In this chapter, besides tracing the influence of Benjamin (and that of Benjamin's Baudelaire), I will explore how Robertson's *Occasional Work and Seven Walks* creates an urban discourse, simultaneously reflective and lyrical. Considering in turn central and closely intertwined concerns of the book—collaboration and other forms of collective writing together with Robertson's concept of soft architecture that attends to affective surfaces; the urgency of rhetoric that mobilizes both archival information and affective states; *flânerie* as a lyrical urban practice that creates community and intimacy all at the same time—I will argue that urban space, as a result of its defining collectivity and historicity, resonates for Robertson with an infinite array of affects, emphatically not owned, dispersed, always ready to emerge, and potentially historical, but with an urgency for present change. In response, a revised concept of lyric, which de-centres the lyric subject and replaces it with a vital plurality, the agent of a virtual office and the intimacy of a couple of urban walkers, becomes central to Robertson's project: the alignment of lyric with affect enables the description of affective urban space.

1 Collective Writing and Soft Architecture

Occasional Work and Seven Walks crosses the line between poetry and prose in several ways. The manifesto and the twelve essays, which constitute the first half of the book, are occasional in the strict sense, since they were originally commissioned for various art exhibits and special thematic issues of magazines. In each case, the specific occasion prompts Robertson to expand the topic (e.g., public fountains, the arts and crafts movement, interior design, scaffolding, shacks, etc.), do extensive research, and present what she finds in an experimental catalogue essay, which does not lack lyrical qualities. Here, as elsewhere, she exploits the essay as a highly flexible form that allows for "a series of forays that don't necessarily relate to each other by typical causal, temporal or cognitive chains" and that provides ample opportunity for "[e]quivocation, humour and paradox" ("An Interview with Lisa Robertson"). In Robertson's hands the form guarantees that the exploration remains situated and preserves the complexity of the phenomenon described. On the other hand, as Fitzpatrick and Rudy note, the catalogue essays border on and reconsider the perspectives of such traditional prose forms as the manifesto, the historical narrative, or the research paper (176).

The catalogue essays are followed by the prose poems of *Seven Walks*, taking the speaker and her guide to various, most often not identifiable sites in the city—the book cover of the second edition aptly calls them "poetic dioramas." The prose poems, describing what gets exposed in the "radical aesthetic practice" of the walk through the city, combine lyric with narrative and reflective elements, and thus reinforce the double, lyrical and critical, attention that defines both parts of Robertson's book ("An Interview with Lisa Robertson").

Occasional Work and Seven Walks is allegedly authored by the "Office for Soft Architecture," a fictional office of architecture and urban planning, which is rooted in a collaborative writerly project among Robertson and fellow writers and artists. As Robertson explains, the project grew out of the ideas exchanged with friends living in various cities, and from a workshop on "Walking" at the Kootenay School of Writing, an influential writers' collective in Vancouver. Nevertheless, Robertson did not wish to repress a community and be rigorously collective; rather, she relied on a constant awareness of others' ideas and on being in informal dialogue with them.

Having an "office" as a collective author entails that the first person authorial voice is consistently avoided; instead, a collective "we" is used throughout the book. In the essays this indicates not only an exchange of ideas and shared concerns—Robertson's works are often distinctively situated and collective—, but also a variety of voices and subject positions (e.g., the city dweller, the walker, the architect, the researcher, the historian, etc.) that can be engaged in the exploration of urban experience.

In the prose poems the use of "we" and the avoidance of a singular lyric subjectivity further implies that the authenticity and intimacy of self-expression is replaced by an emphasis on collectively constructed experience and potentially shared intimacy. The prose poems locate the source of urban experience in that shared intimacy and in freely circulating affective states. Such a deconstruction of the lyric "I" is characteristic of Robertson's writing: she persistently avoids a centred subjectivity, a singular and expressive inner voice as the organizing principle and the source of self-representation in her poems. Instead, she experiments with writing strategies that disperse the self and emphasize that "[s]ubjectivity is radically pliable and open to collective practices" ("An Interview with Lisa Robertson"). In *Occasional Work and Seven Walks* the decentered authorial position enables the exposure of collective and profoundly affective urban experience.

The "Office for Soft Architecture" (OSA)—the name itself a pun on Rem Koolhaas's Office for Metropolitan Architecture—, offers an alternative vision of urban space. Robertson refers to the Dutch architect's 1994 essay on "new urbanism": "If there is to be a 'new urbanism' it will not be based on the twin fantasies of order and omnipotence; it will be the staging of uncertainty; it will no longer be concerned with the arrangement of more or less permanent objects but with the irrigation of territories with potential" (qtd. in *Occasional Work* 31). Robertson's version of "new urbanism" investigates not solid built structures, concrete and cement, but the uncertainty, transience, and plurality of "soft architectural" forms, in other words, surfaces: paint and pigmentation, draperies and clothing, interior design and furniture; and temporary structures: scaffolding and shacks. Soft architecture provides a description and intends a metaphysics of urban space by being attentive to "shreds of fibre, pigment flakes, the bleaching of light, proofs of lint, ink, spore, liquid and pixilation, the strange, frail, leaky cloths and sketchings and gestures which we are" (17), as well as to the gestures that originally created such surfaces: "the surface is comprised of bodily traces and fixations—rubbing, flecking, scrubbing, weaving, stroking are tactile instrumentations in time" (149).

Surfaces represent the fluidity characteristic of urban space and, importantly, they preserve not identities but various affects and incidents. They are repeatedly described as affective: the "lyrical tone" of surfaces reveal "peopled sentiment," thus it might evoke coolness, reserve, extravagance, grace, coquetry, etc. (*Occasional Work* 16). The alignment of "lyrical" with "peopled sentiment" reinforces the essentially emotional aspect of lyric, while, on the other hand, as Robertson revises the genre, it replaces the subjective expression of emotion with affective states that are detached from particular subjects and situations and become especially well preserved in urban surfaces.

As "soft" and malleable counterparts to "hard" architectural forms, surfaces could be associated with the feminine, yet Robertson resists such a straightforward connection. Instead, she offers a rich array of possibilities that cut across binaries, as it happens with the man-made and the natural in the case of *Rubus armeniacus*: the invasive imported species of blackberries transforms any manmade structure and creates new hybrid architectural forms. For Robertson, the ubiquitous blackberries demonstrate the incredible richness of a morphology that "include[s] decay, blanketing and smothering, shedding, dissolution and penetration, and pendulous swagging and draping, as well as proliferative growth, all in contexts of environmental disturbance and contingency rather than fantasized balance" (*Occasional Work* 130). On the other hand, Robertson reverses but holds in place a binary central to the book: quoting Ruskin, she notes that if solid architectural structures display human intelligence, decoration manifests affective states—soft architecture reverses the subordination of affect to intelligence and investigates how the former "invades the centre" (130).

For OSA, urban spaces are also inescapably social and historical, being constantly erased and recreated by multiple perspectives and trajectories. The essay on New Brighton Park reveals the layers of history that have shaped the place and have made it into an "inverted utopia" (*Occasional Work* 37). Relying on archival research, Robertson explains that originally it had been an Indian clam beach, before the land was purchased in the first real estate transaction of British Columbia. Then industry moved in and prospered, only to be followed by years of recession, when the place was overtaken by a shantytown of squatters. During World War II, the site witnessed one of the first incidents of racial discrimination against Japanese Canadians who, detained in a nearby location, were not allowed to use the public pool facilities. In more recent decades, the site was turned from an industrial wasteland into a popular recreational area, with a pool and abundant open public space with great views. The park now boasts an official plaque which, Robertson comments, reminds the visitors of only a selected section of this history: the glorious colonial past. Yet, Robertson claims, everything is preserved there, as history accrues around the site; she inverts the Situationist slogan: *sous la plage, le pavé* (beneath the beach, the street). The essay ends with the statement: "Soft Architects believe that this site demonstrates the best possible use of an urban origin: Change its name repeatedly. Burn it down. From the rubble confect a prosthetic pleasure ground; with fluent obliviousness, picnic there" (46).

Robertson's approach recalls Doreen Massey's reconceptualization of space as never neutral, singular, and static, but replete and constantly being shaped with multiple threads of social relations, trajectories, and material histories.[1] Robertson's catalogue essays in *Occasional Work* describe urban sites as such inherently social and historical spaces by emphasizing the masked histories, the unrecognized role of people's movements through space, and the shifting purposes attributed to public sites. In the aleatory *Seven Walks*, the fluidity and multiplicity of urban space is emphasized by a radically open, flirtatious, and emphatically historical imagination: the two walkers await impulses that arise from urban space and its inhabitants, as well as from their memories and historical knowledge. They are constantly up to surprises, to unexpected encounters and impressions, to disorienting otherness—Massey argues that space vitally includes a potential for surprise, which lies not in the palimpsest of accrued histories but in a radical synchronicity: the simultaneous presence of open-ended multiple trajectories that constantly re-shape it (113). Robertson subscribes to an urban practice that resists any attempt at fitting loose ends into all-too-coherent and totalizing narratives—the walks, cutting through different times and spaces in their fantasies, reorganize urban experience into a particular, non-repeatable moment again and again.

The collaborative forms Robertson investigates, and the malleable surfaces she attends to, both emphasize the fluidity and multiplicity characteristic of affective urban experience. As the rich array of soft architectural forms demonstrate, the city for Robertson is endowed with and constantly transfigured by multiple practices, uses, and histories, and, therefore, is best served by a collective writerly practice that recreates the impersonality and shared intimacy of urban experience in writing.

2 Urgency and the Archive

In *Occasional Work*, Robertson's intention is to make a descriptive record about the complexity of urban experience; instead of a monumentalized project, she attends to details, to the various perspectives and fragments of stories that are relevant to particular segments of urban space. The city is imagined as an archive: "The city, also, has that density. It's a mess of documents, really. Any neighbourhood or chunk of architecture or park has so many layers of history and human engagement and argument and suppressed history and colonisations. It's all there if you just start to scratch the surface and mess around and

---

1 Fitzpatrick and Ryan also consider Massey as an influential theoretician for Robertson's *Occasional Work and Seven Walks* (184). Ian Davidson reads her "Utopia" from *Rousseau's Boat* in light of Massey's spatial theory.

slow down and perceive and ask questions" ("A Conversation with Lisa Robertson."). In fact, Robertson's methodology relies on unearthing information in the archives: her impressive list of references includes works on the actual history of Vancouver, as well as an abundance of aesthetic, philosophical, and political writings, spanning several centuries and including, among others, Rousseau, Goethe, Carlyle, Thoreau, Ruskin, as well as Benjamin, de Certeau, Lefebvre, Foucault, Derrida, Agamben, etc. Robertson, as much a thinker as a poet, brings her interest in history and theory to bear heavily on the project of the OSA.

Among these influences, Benjamin's ghost looms large: Robertson's interest in the history of architectural forms and the materiality of urban spaces, along with her preferred method of archival research, all align her with Benjamin.[2] Perhaps the most Benjaminian piece in *Occasional Work* is the essay "How to Colour," in which Benjamin's deeply emotional dream about walking the whitewashed corridors of Goethe's house is summoned (*Reflections* 63). Robertson finds the image of the whitewashed walls particularly poignant because in 1806, when Goethe was working on his *Theory of Colours* in occupied Weimar, Napoleon, for the lack of indigo, changed the colour of uniforms to white. In Robertson's imagination the marching soldiers form a white corridor moving through the city, with the mirage of the impeccable whiteness only ineffectively hiding the bloodstain of battlefields. Considering the affective power of associations of white with innocence and purity, as well as its most frequent natural appearance in bones, Robertson adds: "We think of Goethe's whitewashed hallway, running through Benjamin's dream like a spine. But affect can't be controlled" (141). The essay further details the various ways the rhetoric of colours is relevant and could yield historical insight: how our use of pigment for colour lends mobility to plants and minerals; how colour comes to define economies as it happens in the case of the indigo trade; how the archaeological interest in painted facades of antiquity gives rise to the decorative arts, etc. She repeatedly points out the often masked economic and political interests behind the use of colours—such agendas allow no colour, not even the clearest white, to be innocent. Most importantly, however, Robertson as a poet finds colours disturbingly unstable and deeply affective: they can definitely refresh or seduce, embarrass or repel us, but their affective excess can also erupt

---

2   Critics have interpreted Robertson's indebtedness to Benjamin differently: Skoulding finds the interest in materiality and the attention to neglected practices characteristically Benjaminian (154–55); Michael Davidson emphasizes that Robertson, similarly to Benjamin, investigates the corporate and political intentions behind urban phenomena (44); Joseph claims that Robertson's poetic practice relies on Benjamin's concept of the *flâneur*.

and provoke us in other unexpected ways. As the essay aptly illustrates, Robertson tends to read history with an eye to the potential of affect: she would identify phenomena and experiences that burst apart from their particular historical moment and, through their affective energies, engage the present.

The idea of the archive as it has been established by Benjamin is not based on any conventional form of order. The editors of *Walter Benjamin's Archive* note in their introduction that his work reveals the "passions of the collector" and illuminates "points at which topicality flashes up, places that preserve the idiosyncratic registrations of an author, subjective, full of gaps, unofficial" (2). Benjamin's archive in the unfinished research project on the Parisian Arcades invites a reading which is not linear but immersive: it should attend to the fragmentariness, to the very different character of the quotations and the commentaries, and should establish correspondences between them. The collection of fragments creates a constellation through which the quickly receding past, the present, and the forthcoming future can be perceived—for Benjamin reading becomes an essentially dialectic process.

In *Occasional Work* we do not find a similar collage of materials. Instead, Robertson writes up the various fragments of stories and perspectives in continuous essays, which, however, do not cease to analyze complexities and offer no comfortable closures. In the case of *Occasional Work*, what counters this structure, besides the repeated appeal to the disruptive potential of affective states, is that Robertson frequently lends a sense of urgency to her writing: in the case of New Brighton Park, for instance, the readers are urged to have a picnic there, now aware of the troubled history of the place.

This urgency, and an underlying direct address to us, readers, pervades the whole project: we are invited to take our own strolls through the city, to try on the most outlandish outfits at a Value Village store and thus find a strange mix of poverty and extravagance; to move for the summer to a shack and experience a frugal if sustainable economy; or to taste those delicious blackberries climbing up broken fences (with the natural history of the invasive alien species *Rubus armeniacus*, the eminent migrants of fauna, in mind). The call for such "experimental behaviour" recalls the Situationist movement, the concept of *dérive* and the instructions for creating situations; this influence runs deep in Robertson's work ("Definitions"). However, urgency, as Gregory J. Seigworth and Melissa Gregg emphasize, is also a crucial component of the potential of affect: being affected occasions a spur into action (2–3).

There is, moreover, another important tendency to consider. Charles Altieri draws attention to a significant change in contemporary American poetry: a shift from the poem as an aesthetic object to the rhetorical acts involved in poetry. This entails a revision of rhetoric: "Successful rhetoric does not necessarily persuade but it makes it possible to see what identification might consist in, and thereby allows or even encourages cultivating differences in what might arise by means of the participation" (10). Altieri argues that this new rhetoric could explain the urgency with which contemporary poems emphasize social responsibility: they often describe a compelling emotional situation and solicit response from the readers, urging them to consider the attitudes and paths of action that can be taken. Thus, Altieri claims, contemporary lyric is not that much about the reflective consciousness of the speaker but about creating "affective urgencies" that directly address the readers (11).

Although Altieri reads Juliana Spahr's and Jennifer Moxley's poetries in this light and does not mention the Canadian Robertson, I think her poetry also strongly builds on this revised rhetoric and, in the case of the OSA project, couples it with a call for affective response. In the essays of *Occasional Work* (and implicitly in the prose poems), she repeatedly asks the readers to consider their responses and potential participation in particular situations. Robertson mobilizes the archival information she compiles through this urgency: she invites us to consider historical knowledge, the social, economic, and political forces, as well as our personal memories and reactions, that can all come together to shape our urban experience, and then take action. Thus the book can be read as a reconceptualization of Benjamin's project, an investment of the archive with urgency: Robertson provides us with an archival density of information and copious descriptions about urban life only to prompt us to be affected and to affect by taking action in return (cf. Seigworth and Gregg 2–3, 12).

3   *Flânerie* as a Lyrical Practice and Intimate Pluralities

Often directed by impressions and momentary decisions, the walkers in the prose poems of *Seven Walks* take their routes through the city to various sites, such as parks, markets, bridges, restaurants, residential and downtown streets, and abandoned areas; in each case, the description of the urban space is infused with the memories and imaginary fantasies it evokes. The two walkers are referred to as either "we" or "my guide and I"; only once do they become "amorous colleagues" (235), which suggests that we might take them for a couple with unspecified gender, who share an interest in writing and a budding romantic relationship, which culminates in the "Fifth Walk." The erotic overtones make it tempting to see them as an enactment of de Certeau's "lovers": they similarly compose the texture of the city with their walks, but instead of remaining blind to it, they self-consciously mold their experience and document it (cf. de Certeau 93). This is, however, only one among the several possible scenarios: "we" remains a loose enough denomination to refer to any collectivity (including a Dantean figuration of poet and his guide). In addition, De Certeau's interpretation of walking as a rhetorical act, which "affirms, suspects, tries out, transgresses, respects, etc., the trajectories it 'speaks' " is just as relevant to Robertson's writing that seeks to articulate and disarticulate certain aspects of urban space (de Certeau 99).

As they improvise their strolls and attend to what emerges, the two walkers also become "researchers": in the restaurant they study atmospheres, tastes and textures; in the park, in a *flâneuresque* style, they engage in an exchange of gazes with passers-by; elsewhere they uncover economies that lie outside the monetary system, such as temporary housings, decaying streetscapes, and orchards. Through their research, they wish to create a "passional historiography" of the city (239). Their conscious exploration of the city's (psychogeographical) effects recalls the Situationists and their unplanned walk of *dérive*: the experimental and critical urban practice aims to defamiliarize and explore the sensations that urban settings provoke (Debord, "Theory"). Robertson's version of *dérive* results in a highly metaphorical description, which is both a lyricized natural history of urban space and a passionate account of urban experience.

Beyond these theoretical influences, Robertson admits to reading widely on urban walking, including such lesser known 18th and early 19th century walkers as John Thelwall and Sarah Hazlitt (Interview by Ted Byrne). Indeed, a Romantic version of walking, together with the trope of the Aeolian harp, is ironically summoned in the "Sixth Walk," when the unexpectedly solitary speaker, as if in a weird dreamscape, describes crossing a bric-a-brac bridge:

> There was a sensation of cushioning, of safety, which at the same time was not different from chaos—as if unknowable varieties of experience would be held gently, suspended in an elastic breeze. ... Then the rippling of fibres converted themselves again to foliage, as all speech converts itself to foliage in the night, and I felt this rippling simultaneously all over my skin. It was not necessary to differentiate the sensations of particular organs or leaves since this rippling unknit the proprieties and zones of affect—the entire body became an instrument played by weather and chance. (262–3)

In a postmodern dreamlike cityscape the bridge and all the surroundings seem to be responsive forces and the speaker, characteristically, submits to affect, which blurs the boundaries between subject and object, between the "I," the emotion experienced, and the physical space.

With all its subsumed references, *Seven Walks* exhibits a belated postmodern *flânerie* à la Baudelaire and Benjamin, in which desire, idleness, and affect play key roles. Among the walks, all temporally indexed, the "Second Walk" is of special significance: here the time is late afternoon in July and the two walkers imagine that they inhabit a long nineteenth century, even though they are in late modernity. The space around them is suffused with the memories of strolls distant in time and space, and taken by others. The speakers pointedly note that they are "the outmoded remainder of a class," the "lyric class" (232–3): Robertson echoes Benjamin's description of Baudelaire as a belated lyric poet (*The Writer of Modern Life* 170–2). *Flânerie* is associated with the lyric because it requires a similarly suspended state, a privileged idleness. As *flâneurs* and practitioners of the lyric, the speakers await and attend to the surges of attentiveness and the emergence of ideas and moods. At the same time their subject boundaries become "porous" and this allows the pair to release into affect:

> In this landscape the affects took on an independence. It was we who belonged to them. They hovered above the surfaces, disguised as clouds or mists, awaiting the porousness of a passing ego. By aetherial fornications they entered us. We had observed the images and geometries of such intercourses in the great galleries, print rooms and libraries of our travels, but here we ourselves became their medium. And as in those galleries, the affects that usurped or devised us were not all contemporary. The park's real function was archival. Dandering here, a vast melancholy would alight upon us, gently, so as not to frighten, and the pigmented nuance of a renaissance shadow eased its inks and agitations beneath our skin. Or we were seized by a desperate frivolity, plucked up, cherub-style, into marooned pastels and gildings. … I insist that we did not choose to submit to these alienations and languors. It was they who chose us. "No space ever vanishes utterly," said my guide. (236)

Walking the city, the speakers become open to all emergent affects. Urban space indeed appears replete with affects that are not owned or tied to any subject position, but are freely circulating, available, at hand. Importantly, Robertson emphasizes that such affects can be anachronistic and can issue from the past, from personal memories or historical knowledge: the city in *Seven Walks* resonates with historical affects.

Robertson's take on affect and her strategies of registering affective intensities in writing has much in common with Kathleen Stewart's *Ordinary Affects*. In her anthropological investigation Stewart defines "ordinary affects" as things that "happen in impulses, sensations, expectations, daydreams, encounters, and habits of relating, in strategies and their failures, in forms of persuasion, contagion, and compulsion, in modes of attention, attachment, and agency, and in publics and social worlds of all kinds that catch people up in something that feels like *some*thing" (4–5). Ordinary affects can be captured as a form of indeterminate movement, a tangle of connections, or an emerging event; their significance lies not in attributable meanings but in the intensities they build up and in the movement they elicit as a response: they surprise, shock, embarrass or disorient us, or move us in other ways.

For Stewart the most adequate response to affects is an attention to how the particular scene unfolds, winds its way through time, rushes forward or delays, creates stillness or becomes layered, and gives rise to further resonances. Stewart emphasizes that in the case of affect it is important to resist the quick jump to representational thinking: while emotions can be narrativized and related in a story, affects cannot. Therefore, it is critical to devise a form of address that remains attentive to the state of potentiality and resonance. She finds the open-ended description of various everyday scenes as the most effective method because this way "[f]orms of power and meaning become circuits lodged in singularities. ... They can gather themselves into what we think of as stories and selves. But they can also remain, or become again, dispersed, floating, recombining—regardless of what whole or what relay of rushing signs they might find themselves in for a while" (8). Stewart also considers exemplary texts and writing strategies that convey affective intensities. Besides several American novelists, she mentions Barthes's *S/Z* and *A Lover's Discourse* and Benjamin's *Arcades Project*; the latter provides descriptions that stay close to both materiality and emerging dream worlds. Robertson's *Occasional Work* could definitely be added to the list: consciously choosing description as a method, which also inflects the lyric in the prose poems, Robertson attends closely to how impressions and events unfold, how intensities momentarily gather into forms of meaning and power, and how they disperse again.

In Robertson's work the emphasis on writing as a process and the formal experiments with a hybrid style, fragmentation, shifting perspective, and plural agency invite the disruptive energies of affect to register. Her poetry follows the tendency that Laurel Peacock identifies as initiated by Language poetry and the feminist poets of the 80s, and continued by contemporary women poets: lyric as the expression of a subject is critiqued and often renounced, while clear emotions are replaced with much less explicit affective energies (18). These latter are typically not tied to a singular subject but indicate instead a response, an attitude, a "way of being in the world and in language" (Peacock 17). The shift of focus to "restless" and "unattached" affects becomes one of the most important strategies for challenging the lyric in contemporary poetry (Peacock 18).

As Robertson's work demonstrates, this new direction goes hand in hand with an exploration of potential communities. In *Occasional Work* Robertson uses the agency of a virtual office to create the sense of writerly collaboration, while in *Seven Walks* she describes walking as a performative lyrical act, which enables the two walkers to share their affective experiences and be profoundly shaped by the affective states of others and other times. As she comments: "when we are strolling, we wish to abandon salubrious habit to better welcome spontaneous transitions to collective states" (54).

With the sense of a radically dispersed subjectivity that is open to all experience and is vitally plural, Robertson creates a form of "intimate pluralism" that Juliana Spahr, fellow American poet, finds a central concern in contemporary lyric poetry (11). Spahr argues that, in an important shift from individualism to community, the characteristic "lyric space of intimacy" is expanded in innovative contemporary poems: they "move lyric away from individualism to shared, connective spaces ... [and] reveal how our private intimacies have public obligations and ramifications, how intimacy has a social bond with shared meaning" (11). Spahr's claim takes us back to Altieri's argument about the importance of rhetoric: he contends that contemporary poems are in search of a community with the readers—"community comes to depend not so much on empathetic identification as on simple awareness of the degree [at] which momentary subject positions can be shared" (3). Altieri and Spahr emphasize the same tendency that proves fundamental to Robertson's project: in *Occasional Work and Seven Walks*, she creates a resonant textual site which demonstrates that any urban space, not just that of Vancouver, elicits affective intensities that are there to be taken up, to be shared, and to be explored for the potential actions they provoke and the potential communities they create.

Clearly, all the central issues of the book I discussed in the above sections converge on affect. In *Occasional Work and Seven Walks* urban space is an archive of affects: it is charged with a surfeit of intermingling and radically synchronous past and present affects that call for response, for the appreciation and re-animation of history, personal memories, and current concerns. Robertson confirms that to respond to emerging affects is "an ethical, aesthetic, and political task all at once," which also potentially aligns us, as city dwellers, in various forms of community (Seigworth and Gregg 3). The lyric seems surprisingly well adapted to register and perform this task.

Works Cited

Altieri, Charles. "The Place of Rhetoric in Contemporary Poetics: Jennifer Moxley and Juliana Spahr." *Chicago Review*, vol. 56, no. 2–3, 2011: 127–45.

Benjamin, Walter. *The Arcades Project*. Translated by Howard Eiland and Kevin McLaughlin, The Belknap P of Harvard UP, 2002.

Benjamin, Walter. *Reflections: Essays, Aphorisms, Autobiographical Writings*. Edited by Peter Demetz, translated by Edmund Jephcott, Schocken, 1978.

Benjamin, Walter. *Walter Benjamin's Archive*. Edited by Ursula Marx, Gudrun Schwarz, Michael Schwarz and Erdmut Wizisla, translated by Esther Leslie, Verso, 2015.

Benjamin, Walter. *The Writer of Modern Life: Essays on Charles Baudelaire*. Edited by Michael W. Jennings, The Belknap P of Harvard UP, 2006.

Davidson, Ian. "Picture This: Space and Time in Lisa Robertson's 'Utopia/'". *Mosaic: A Journal for the Interdisciplinary Study of Literature*, vol. 40, no. 4, 2007. https://www.jstor.org/stable/44030395?read-now=1&seq=1#page_scan_tab_contents Accessed 25 September 2020.

Davidson, Michael. "On the Outskirts of From: Cosmopoetics in the Shadow of NAFTA." *On the Outskirts of Form: Practicing Cultural Poetics*, by Davidson, Wesleyan UP, 2011. pp. 23–51.

Debord, Guy. "Introduction to a Critique of Urban Geography." *Situationist International Online*, http://www.cddc.vt.edu/sionline/presitu/geography.html. Accessed 1 August 2016.

Debord, Guy. "Theory of the Dérive." *Situationist International Online,* http://www.cddc.vt.edu/sionline/si/theory.html. Accessed 1 August 2016.

De Certeau, Michel. *The Practice of Everyday Life*. Translated by Steven Rendall, U of California P, 1984.

"Definitions." *Situationist International Online,* http://www.cddc.vt.edu/sionline/si/definitions.html. Accessed 1 August 2016.

Fitzpatrick, Ryan, and Susan Rudy. " 'If everything is moving, where is here?': Lisa Robertson's *Occasional Work* on Cities, Space and Impermanence." *British Journal of Canadian Studies*, vol. 26, no. 2, 2013: 173–89.

Hlibchuk, Geoffrey. "Delirious Cities: Lisa Robertson's *Occasional Work and Seven Walks from the Office for Soft Architecture*." *Studies in Canadian Literature*, vol. 36, no.1, 2011:223–42, https://journals.lib.unb.ca/index.php/SCL/article/view/18637. Accessed 1 August 2016.

Joseph, Maia. "The Afterlife of the City: Reconsidering Urban Poetic Practice." *Studies in Canadian Literature*, vol. 34, no. 2, 2009, https://journals.lib.unb.ca/index.php/SCL/article/view/12706. Accessed 25 September 2020.

Massey, Doreen. *For Space*. Sage, 2005.

Marx, Ursula, et al., editors. *Walter Benjamin's Archive: Images, Texts, Signs*. Verso, 2007.

Peacock, Laurel. *The Poetics of Affect in Contemporary Feminist Poetry*. Dissertation, University of California, Santa Cruz, 2013.

Robertson, Lisa. *Occasional Work and Seven Walks from the Office for Soft Architecture*. Clear Cut Press, 2003.

Robertson, Lisa. "Andy Fitch with Lisa Robertson." *The Conversant*, 2012, http://theconversant.org/?p=4100. Accessed 1 August 2016.

Robertson, Lisa. "A Conversation with Lisa Robertson." Interview by Michael Nardone, *Lemon Hound*, 9 Dec., 2010, http://lemonhound.com/2010/12/09/a-conversation-with-lisa-robertson/. Accessed 1 August 2016.

Robertson, Lisa. "An Interview with Lisa Robertson." Interview by Julie Carr. *Evening Will Come: A Monthly Journal of Poetics*, issue 25, January 2013, www.thevolta.org/ewc25-jcarr-p1.html. Accessed 1 August 2016.

Robertson, Lisa. Interview by Ted Byrne. *The Capilano Review*, vol. 3, no. 15, Fall 2011, https://www.thecapilanoreview.ca/interviews/. Accessed 1 August 2016.

Scapettone, Jennifer. "Site Surfeit: Office for Soft Architecture Makes the City Confess." *Chicago Review*, vol. 51/52, no. 4/1, Spring 2006, pp. 70–76.

Schmidt, Christopher. "The Utopian Textures and Civic Commons of Lisa Robertson's Soft Architecture." *Reading the Difficulties: Dialogues with Contemporary American Innovative Poetry*, edited by Thomas Fink and Judith Halden-Sullivan, U of Alabama P, 2014. pp. 146–157.

Seigworth, Gregory J. and Melissa Gregg. "An Inventory of Shimmers." *The Affect Theory Reader*, Duke UP, 2010. pp. 2–25.

Skoulding, Zoë. "Lisa Robertson: Prosody of the Polis." *Contemporary Women's Poetry and Urban Space: Experimental Cities*, Palgrave Macmillan, 2013. pp. 153–174.

Spahr, Juliana. Introduction. *American Women Poets in the 21st Century: Where Lyric Meets Language*, edited by Claudia Rankine and Juliana Spahr, Wesleyan UP, 2002. pp. 1–18.

PART 2

East-Central Europe as a Translocal Space: Gendering the "Periphery"

∴

CHAPTER 4

A Closet of One's Own: Places of Non-Hegemonic Masculinities and Rites of Retreat in Contemporary Hungarian Cinema

György Kalmár

Abstract

This chapter explores some of the recent, characteristically post-economic-crisis displacements in Eastern European identity politics. Through the investigation of the spatial trajectories created by a number of Hungarian films, the chapter introduces the concept of retreat films and the narrative trope of retreat, which it regards as a symptomatic, post-crisis rearrangement of certain Eastern European concepts concerning identity, social progress, and the meaning of the West in the region's cultural imaginary. The protagonists of these films seem to share a disillusionment about their formal dreams about the urban, hyper-modern lifestyle associated with "the West." Their regressive journeys are motivated by the renunciation of their formal dreams and desires, and take them back to their Eastern European homelands, far from the metropolitan cultural centres, to the homes of their fathers or grandfathers, to places where they desperately seek to establish alternative lifestyles and identities on the margins and ruins of (the fantasy of) Europe.

This chapter explores the relationship of masculine identity, place and space in three Hungarian films of the last decade: *Taxidermia* (dir. György Pálfi, 2006), *Delta* (dir. Kornél Mundruczó, 2008), and *Land of Storms* (*Viharsarok*, dir. Ádám Császi 2014). All three films are important representatives of the "new Hungarian cinema" of the 2000s. They have all gained considerable critical attention, have won awards at international film festivals, and are arguably intimately linked with contemporary Hungarian identity politics. Significantly for the purposes of this study, all three films present male protagonists in some kind of crisis, and the drama of these crises are played out in spatial terms. The spatial arrangements and movements found in these films may be analysed as ritualistic retreats, where (usually as a result of some kind of frustration or trauma) the characters turn their backs on mainstream identity-formations and the associated desires, and withdraw into secluded places so as to hide, heal, find their way back to their roots, or simply die.¹

My title deliberately collapses two spatial metaphors signifying contradictory movements: *a room of one's own,* which Virginia Woolf made famous in her feminist essay of the same title, and *coming out of the closet,* a phrase now inextricably linked to gay identity politics. While in 1929 for a woman to move *into* a room of her own was a significant step forward (and not only if she wanted to be a writer), today coming *out* of the closet is a trope for leaving behind a claustrophobic, clandestine, escapist identity for a more authentic and liberated one. Yet, both metaphors express a belief in *forward* movement, in historical development. They share a belief in a better future and one's ability to act in order to reach that. It is a most revealing aspect of Eastern European gender politics (and Eastern European history in general, for that matter) that "return films" constitute an important group of post-1989 Eastern European cinema (see: Gott and Herzog 13). I argue that many male protagonists of post-communist Hungarian cinema tend to withdraw from these open, public (traditionally masculine) spaces of self-liberation, from the possibilities of establishing more authentic, publicly accepted identities, thus creating unusual spatial patterns and peculiar masculinities. As Hajnal Király argues:

> In Hungarian and Romanian films of the last decade, the central dilemma frequently revolves around mobility, that is, whether to stay or move on, whether or not to leave (the country, the family, a traumatic situation, a beloved person, or ultimately life), which frequently escalates to a deep existential crisis and which signals the ultimate impossibility of either staying or moving on/leaving. Places and spaces performed by bodies in distress become sites of a dysfunctional society, often revealed in the narrative of an aborted, circular, interrupted or regressive journey.

---

1 This study is indebted to a number of books and articles in Hungarian, as well as to the work of a group of Hungarian film scholars with whom I have discussed all these issues at various conferences and workshops. Several issues discussed in this chapter were first explored in Hungarian in the special issues of two excellent Hungarian film journals, *Metropolis* and *Apertura*. A great deal of research in the context of Hungarian cinema, space and gender have been presented at the ZOOM conferences in Debrecen, Hungary, and published in the ZOOM books (that I edited with Zsolt Győri), as well as at the events organised by the Contact Zones research group at ELTE University, Budapest. My research was supported by the Bolyai János Research Grant of the Hungarian Academy of Sciences, as well as the Programme of National Excellence of the Hungarian Ministry of Human Resources. Some of the general ideas I put forward here were also formulated in a different cinematic context in my book *Post-Crisis European Cinema: White Men in Off-Modern Landscapes* (Palgrave Macmillan, 2020).

> ... Additionally, many Hungarian and Romanian films feature characters who return from Western Europe, only to realize that home is not an 'authentic' place anymore ... (170)

This chapter investigates a special sub-category of these "return films," one that I will hypothetically call *retreat films*. In these films, returns become ritualistic retreats with masculinities on "regressive journeys." Their spatial trajectories may typically lead from Western cultural centres to Eastern homelands, from cities to the countryside, from the public sphere to the private, sometimes symbolically from the future to the past, and often from the realm of desire to that of Thanatos. The men of these films tend to struggle to find places of their own on the margins of society, *away* from public spaces: what they seem to have in mind is a place to hide, somewhere to retreat, that is, *a closet of their own*.

Clearly, these films and the spatial movements of their male protagonists cannot be fully understood without the "profound disillusionment" (Shaviro 25) experienced in Hungary not long after the fall of communism, without "the problematic and largely unfulfilled fantasies of integration and redemption that have accompanied Hungary's so-called 'return to Europe'" (Jobbit 4). As Steve Jobbit argues apropos of *Kontroll* (dir. Nimród Antal, 2003), another film showing the same symptoms of men in crisis and retreat:

> For some, Hungary's entry into a much-expanded European Union was seen as the culmination of a long and arduous struggle waged by liberal-minded democrats to rescue the nation from nearly seventy years of political intolerance and dictatorial rule, and to reclaim their rightful place amongst Europe's civilized, progressive, and enlightened nations. For many others, however, the post-communist efforts of Hungarian Europhiles to reintegrate and even redeem themselves in the eyes of the West had come at an enormous cultural and even psychological cost. For a number of Hungarians, the interconnected hopes, or more accurately fantasies, of integration and redemption that had guided liberal-democrats in Hungary over the course of nearly two decades proved to be as much of a burden as they had a promise. (1)

Today, thirty years after the fall of communism, it is clear that Eastern Europeans had much distorted, idealized views of the West, that is, of consumerist liberal democracies, as well as of their chances of turning their own countries into such a society overnight. They (or rather, we) were wrong about both issues: transforming a society (and people's attitudes) takes a long time, (totalitarian) history is not so easy to leave behind, and even if we do manage to change, consumerist liberal democracies are not necessarily the "culmination of all human effort and hope" (Shaviro 26). Gáspár Miklós Tamás argues, the regime change in Eastern Europe led to "an inhuman, unjust, unfair, inefficient, anti-egalitarian, fraudulent, and hypocritical system that is in no way at all superior to its predecessor, which was awful enough" (Szeman and Tamás 24). I would argue that this "atmosphere of disillusionment and demoralization" that Shaviro also considers to be a key background to the film *Taxidermia* (26) has shaped Eastern-European masculinities and the spatial journeys they take (see also: Sághy).

Apparently, the history of gender has unpredictable turns in Eastern Europe, leading away from the Western liberal narrative of gradual liberation and self-fulfilment in a consumerist democracy. For men of the third millennium to find themselves in Woolf's 1929 shoes must come as a shocking surprise. Yet, apparently, some room (or place) of one's own was not only important for women in 1929: the films imply that being a woman is not the only form of marginalised subjectivity. In these Hungarian films, men of all description – white and coloured, straight and gay, bastards and orphans, artists and sportsmen, migrants and catatonics – may find themselves homeless in the "new Europe." The dream people had under state-socialism, the dream of freedom, happiness and self-realization is over: these men have seen democracy and consumerist capitalism, many of them have even tried their luck in the West, yet they have all turned back, bitter and disillusioned, to the past, their real or imaginary roots, the local Eastern home(less)land, or plainly death, the ultimate goal of such regressive journeys. Their narratives are typically not victorious stories of liberation and acceptance (coming *out* of the closet), but rather those of retreat, hiding, escape and exile. They are all defeated in some way, usually even before the film's narrative begins. What we see is already plan B (or C or Z), the last resort, the last try to be someone, someplace.

In what follows, I also rely on R. W. Connell's concept of hegemonic masculinity, and argue that these films present non-hegemonic masculinities on the margins of culture and civilized space, masculinities that are constructed in ways characteristically different from the idealized images of mainstream cinema. According to Connell, "hegemonic masculinity can be defined as the configuration of gender practice which embodies the currently accepted answer to the problem of the legitimacy of patriarchy, which guarantees (or is taken to guarantee) the dominant position of men and the subordination of women" (77). Though forms of hegemonic masculinity may vary depending on geographical place and historical time (and is thus an elusive concept with arguably more functional and relational value than theoretical rigour), the protagonists of the abovementioned films are markedly different from the types contemporary Hungarian society privileges. Their masculinities are reactive and regressive, based on the rejection rather than the legitimization of the dominant patriarchal culture. In the context of the films' narratives the pale, anorexic taxidermist Lajoska of the last episode of *Taxidermia* (which I will analyse below), Mihail, the silent, mysterious hero of *Delta,* who comes home from abroad so as to build a log-house in the Danube Delta with the help of his sister-lover, and the gay failed footballer of *Land of Storms* returning from Germany to conservative rural Hungary, are all cinematic examples of non-hegemonic masculinities. The difference or distance from hegemonic, gender-normative, white male identities often appears in these films through spatial arrangements, as distance from human communities and settlements, where physical separation also expresses emotional, affective distance. These male characters try to establish a room or place of their own, a habitat, a home, where their dishevelled embodied identities can *take place*.

Of course, finding a place to be, a home to live, a room of one's own are deeply symbolic acts closely connected to the key topic of alienation, arguably the most common theme of art house cinema, which new Hungarian cinema often approaches through bodily metaphors (see: Gelencsér 302). In the introduction to *Home / Bodies: Geographies of Self, Place and Space,* Wendy Schissel also calls attention to the multiple meanings these acts may acquire: "home is a fluid concept that needs to be constantly 'negotiated.' Home is also, variously but not exclusively, a homeland – indigenous or adopted – a sexuality, a body prescribed by moral or ableist codes, cyberspace, a community, or a place where caring occurs, sometimes at substantial cost to the caregiver. On the other hand, it may also be what we are prevented from achieving" (1). Indeed, what we see in these films can be read as spatial renegotiations of selfhood, or desperate relocations of embodied identity, where such issues are at stake as national belonging, personal dignity, relating to one's roots, finding spaces in which one's preferred sexuality can be practised, establishing an accepting, caring relationship with others, feeling at home in the world, creating a habitable place where one is accepted and loved, escaping fields of defeat and frustration, or at times simply survival. Thus, the study of places in these films must not ignore the complexity and plurality of place as a social phenomenon: "Places are thereby constructed and experienced as both material ecological artefacts and intricate networks of social relations, being the focus of the imaginary, of beliefs, desires and discursive activity, filled with symbolic and representational meanings" (*Sharp et al.* 25).

My interpretations of these regressive journeys follow a paradigm according to which human identity (including gender) is partly created by spatial arrangements and effects of power. As Lefebvre puts it,

Socio-political contradictions are realised spatially. The contradictions of space thus make the contradictions of social relations operative. In other words, spatial contradictions 'express' conflicts between socio-political interests and forces; it is only in space that such conflicts come effectively into play, and in doing so they become contradictions of space. (365)

Foucault's detailed analyses in *Discipline and Punish, Madness and Civilization* and other works also exemplify the connections between space, power and identity: the position of the prisoners in the prison house of the Panopticon (as analysed in the last part of *Discipline and Punish*), or the ordering and placing of the mentally ill in the institutions left after the disappearance of leprosy from Europe (as described in the introduction of *Madness and Civilization*) set a paradigm for such research. Cultural geography's Lefebvrean-Foucaldian axiom that "geography matters, not for the simplistic and overly used reason that everything happens in space, but because *where* things happen is critical to knowing *how* and *why* they happen" (Warf and Arias 1) goes at least as much for cinema as for ordinary social phenomena. In other words, "the geographies become vital: far from being incidental outcomes of power, they become regarded, in their ever-changing specifics, as absolutely central to the constitution of power relations" (Sharp et al. 25).

However, Eastern European cinema (as well as many Eastern European cultural phenomena, I believe) cannot be convincingly analysed without a theory of resistance, with the all-pervading Foucauldian concept of power in the above-mentioned works. I share the scepticism of such authors as the editors of the volume *Entanglements of Power: Geographies of Domination/Resistance*: "if power is so nebulous, so 'unauthored' [as Foucault suggests in the above mentioned works], can we have any optimism in the potential for individuals or groups to find ways, and we might also say spaces, of resisting the all-encompassing cloak seemingly spun by power in its dominating guise?" (15). As these films stage precisely this drama of finding identities and spaces outside dominant social forms, I turn towards Foucault's later writings for theoretical support, and while analysing the spatial constructions of the films, I will apply his concept of *practices of the self,* which appears in his *History of Sexuality* as well as in the interviews given at this time, and can be broadly understood as embodied practices of self-fashioning and self-discipline. Thus, also in accordance with Connell's approach to masculinity, I will treat identity and subjectivity as things produced through bodily practices, and will read scenes from these films as instances of such *practices of the self,* as bodily, spatial, performative acts, in which distance from hegemonic norms of identity and sexuality can be expressed and lived.

1 The Taxidermist's Den

Taxidermy is the art of mounting, turning once living, now dead bodies into mummies, artworks or bodily memorials. Taxidermy can be an allegory of the film itself: not only *á la* Bazin, who thought that filmmaking in general is driven by the urge to mummify the living and preserve it in dead, celluloid form (Bazin 15), but also because Pálfi's film tells the story of three generations of Hungarian men, all defeated and dead by the time of the act of storytelling.

All three generations are characterised by the spatialized mechanisms of defeat. "Each part juxtaposes the private and the public: a body horror case study in imploding masculinity is joined with a parody of the spectacles of power and privilege" (Shaviro 26). The grandfather Morosgoványi, the halfwit orderly living a debased, subhuman life at an army outpost during World War II, is clearly a loser, who is trained, ordered around and humiliated on a regular basis by the lieutenant he serves. He is also isolated and confined (see: Shaviro 26–27, Strausz 2): not only to the outpost in the middle of nowhere (the whole episode takes place on a few hundred square meters), but also to the little wooden shack next to the pig-sty and the loo, outside the house. The life of the father, Kálmán Balatoni is not much better: he is a fast-eating almost-champion, living and competing (in this imaginary sport) in state-socialist Hungary. His story is another failure narrative: first we see him fail at a competition (his jaw gets locked in the final moments of the competition – a meaningful bodily metaphor in the present context – after which he faints), then we see him being cheated on at his wedding night, not having the money for the operation that helps sportsmen of other nations, and not making it to the West, where he thinks he could be a star. By the time of Lajoska's story, he is confined to a small apartment. He is so grotesquely overweight that he cannot even move: it is Lajoska, who changes the pot under him and brings the enormous amount of food that he and his huge, trained cats consume. Now he is not simply locked up behind the iron curtain, but also in his huge body and in this small apartment that smells of urine and excrement.

Both Morosgoványi and Kálmán have lost the most important battles of their lives, and are forced into exile. As László Strausz argues in the context of embodied memory practices, "Morosgoványi is repressed and he creates a secular bodily mythology and retreats into a private world. Eating for Balatoni is a sport that allows him to escape the repressive bounds of the system, although his body becomes seriously disfigured in the process" (Strausz 3). Moreover, both the little shack and the apartment in Budapest seem small, dirty, and confining, spaces for sub-human existences without dignity or love. Taking Shaviro's and Strausz's arguments one step further, I would argue that these spaces (as well as the forms of subjectivity lived there) can be read as those of withdrawal and retreat; places (and subjectivities) clearly established in the absence of more habitable ones. Both characters' solitude and frustration are expressed through visual and spatial symbols. Morosgoványi's main hobby and passion is to peep at the officer's daughters, two young and beautiful women living in the house. He watches them through the window of the house or through the holes in the wooden planks that separate him from "proper" human beings, often while masturbating (see: Strausz 2). Kálmán's confinement is also emphasised by a poster of a seaside resort behind him on the wall (a common and ironic phenomenon of state-socialist building block apartments). In his case it is the TV that fills the function that the window and the holes in the walls did in the Morosgoványi part: during his son's daily visits (when he brings the food, and empties the pot), Kálmán usually watches a video recording of an American fast-eating competition. While he is boasting to his son how much better he would do than these "losers" and "arseholes," we notice his ex-wife, Gizi in the video, supporting or coaching one of the competitors. The motif of the first episode is clearly repeated: Kálmán watches Gizi and images of sports success similarly to his father, Morosgoványi, watching the unreachable young women through the window and the plank wall. Both are separated from their dreams, and both fail when they try to surpass their limitations. One telling, spatially arranged and highly symbolic representation of this situation is the scene when Morosgoványi watches the two young, joyful women's snowball fight outside his shack. He gets aroused at the sight and starts masturbating: he finds a hole in the wall, coats it with lard, pushes his penis through it, "thrusting it frantically in and out" (Shaviro 27). His sexual practice can be seen as an attempt to exceed the limitations of his life, to go past the borders that separate him from his objects of desire. Significantly, the scene ends before he could reach orgasm, when a rooster (a markedly gendered agent of power) notices his penis on the other side and pecks at it.

This pattern changes somewhat when the film gets to the story of Lajoska. The genre of the family novel already ascribes him, as the member of the third generation, a position of degradation: in the novelistic tradition this is a time of the fall of the family with the appearance of artist figures to record the stories of the past generations. *Taxidermia* seems to follow this pattern: Lajoska's story starts with the picture of a pigeon's backside, from which shit falls to the pavement in front of the taxidermist's entrance. The camera moves from the white stain through the door, into the house, through the claustrophobic corridors of the workshop decorated with hundreds of furs and stuffed animals, till it finds him, pale and thin, working on a huge bear. From the beginning, Lajoska is associated with white: the baby's clothes in the hospital before the camera goes through the window to the pigeon, the bird's excrement, the tiles in the workshop, and his almost albino-like skin. However, in *Taxidermia* white is not the colour of purity, but rather that of a bloodless, lifeless body, a meaningless life, a traumatised subjectivity and death. Lajoska lacks the sexual passion of his grandfather (he does not have a partner, he fancies a pretty cashier woman in the supermarket whom he ineffectively courts by shyly handing over a lollipop each time he pays for his father's supplies), but he also lacks the superhuman appetite of his father (he is skinny as an anorexic, and we never see him eat during the film). I would argue that Lajoska's obsession with dead things, as well as his lack of sexual desire and appetite can be read as physical forms of resistance to the paternal order, a practice of the self in defiance of the qualities, ideologies and identity-formations of his fathers.

Of the three generations of men, Lajoska is the most emblematic figure of retreat, confinement and escape, as there is no external power forcing him into exile. No visible external factor destines Lajoska to live his life surrounded by dead things in his cold, literally lifeless labyrinthine den. The film suggests that his miserable existence is only due to opaque psychological reasons, or the weight of the family's history on his shoulders.

The spaces of his life and his bodily practices are most informative: each day he goes through the same routine: he works in his taxidermist workshop (apparently he also lives there, though we never see any furniture hinting at that), he buys food for his father (always the same quantities of margarine and chocolate), hands over the lollipop to the cashier girl, has a coffee alone in the hall outside the supermarket, and visits his father to clean and feed him and his cats. All these spaces appear empty, cold and lifeless, and all these activities seem joyless repetitions. His life is without passion; his body is pale as that of dead people. He never laughs, eats or has sex, his work is the art of death and mummification, so when the spectator glimpses at his suicidal self-mounting machine, one is not very surprised. His regressive journey through his den of death towards self-mounting is foreshadowed by his last work, the tiny human embryo he mounts for the narrator. I would argue that this small object may be interpreted as a visual metaphor standing for his regressive subjectivity. This figuration could entail seeing his place of retreat, the partly subterranean den of death as a womb, as the non-place of the pre-Oedipal mother, where Oedipal subjectivity is dissolved in something greater and more primordial.

As we have seen, none of the three men in *Taxidermia* manages to overcome the confining difficulties of their lives; all of them escape into meaningless bodily activities (Strausz 3), such as sex without a partner or reproduction, eating for the sake of eating, stuffing and collecting dead animals only to eventually become one of them. Marosgoványi and Kálmán had a view of what they wished for, only, they could never reach it. Lajoska, on the other hand, lacks any prospect of happiness. He has been lost all along and does not even seriously try to escape these spaces of retreat and exile.

2   The House on the River

The regressive movement towards death may be less apparent in Kornél Mundruczó's *Delta* (2008) than in Lajoska's story in *Taxidermia*, but it is just as essential for the coherence of the plot and the motivation of the main character. The film tells the story of the homecoming of a prodigal son, Mihail (Félix Lajkó). He does not collect dead animals as Lajoska does, nor is he pale and anorexic: he would simply like to build a log-house on the river in the astonishingly beautiful and untamed wetlands of the Danube Delta (where his father used to have a fishing hut), so as to hide away from the world. "Mihail looks fragile, shy and stylish in his cord velvet jacket, a trademark of the Western bohemian. Significantly, his character is played by Félix Lajkó, an ethnic Hungarian violin virtuoso from Serbia" (Király 179). Mihail has been to the West, as his banknotes also reveal, he has travelled the world and is back now. Yet, in this Eastern European version of the prodigal son, there is no loving father to welcome him. The remains of his family, his mother, sister and his mother's tyrannical, bad-tempered lover live in a nearby village, in physical and emotional deprivation. They run the local pub, a run-down place for weary "faces" well-known from Tarr's films. When his mother asks him how long he wants to stay, he does not answer. Apparently, he has come back for good.

We do not learn the reasons for his departure or his return: these details (as many others) are left in mystery. What matters in Mundruczó's poetic and almost mythical piece is beyond or beneath such practical or rational details. Mihail's return is simply inevitable, just as his leaving was. His slightly disturbed, traumatised look and silences, his need for solitude and pálinka (home-made, strong brandy) all suggest that he had a troubled past, but that is taken for granted in this tradition of Eastern European art-house cinema reminiscent of Béla Tarr's works. Return and repetition – as Freud so famously theorised apropos of war neurosis (what we call PTSD today) in *Beyond the Pleasure Principle* – are intimately connected to trauma and death. The revisiting of the traumatic site, as well as the symbolic gesture of abandoning the search for a better future so as to turn back towards the past, may very easily lead outside the realm of what Freud called the pleasure principle, the world of desire and satisfaction, towards the inorganic. In that sense, the time of the film is as important as the place: as in Lajoska's story, it is set after the time of desire, action, adventure and conquest, when all these have been tried and all have failed. Time as a measurable, calculated forward movement (towards objects of desire) has stopped. So, it is time to return.

In the Hungarian context, however, the inevitability of return to the (ambiguous) roots and homeland is a long-established poetic tope. Let me only refer to one of the most well-known poems by Endre Ady, arguably the greatest Hungarian poet of the first half of the 20th century, "A föl-földobott kő" ("The Tossed Stone" 1909), which is a key work of the Hungarian literary canon, a poem still many students have to learn by heart in secondary schools. By comparing himself to a stone thrown up again and again only to fall back to the ground, the poem addresses precisely the desire to go away and the inevitability of coming home. Significantly in the context of *Delta*, it also speaks about a certain sadness (that Ady saw as a national characteristic), which cannot be left behind wherever one goes; moreover, it also formulates the intimate connection between returning and death. Ady rephrases a 19th-century figuration of the motherland in ways that prefigure the connection between incest, the homeland and death in Mundruczó's film: whereas in the 19th century paradigm the motherland is usually holy and pure, something deserving sacrifice, in Ady it appears simultaneously as a mother-figure and a lover in a passionate love-hate relationship. Perhaps this cultural background is one of the reasons why the (Hungarian) spectator is not surprised at all when Mihail and his newly found sister, Fauna, who follows him to live in the Delta, fall in love and become a strange, incestuous couple on the frontier between nature and culture, life and death, soil and water. Incest is yet another marker of this *outside* of culture and desire: their "return" to each other is inevitable, without words, outside language, concepts and culture, also lacking the usual dynamism and (cinematic) clichés of desire.

As often in contemporary Hungarian films of return, the characters' motivations are mostly told by evocative, sensuous images of highly metaphorical spaces (see: Király 179). The most important spaces in *Delta*, in this respect, are the village and the river. The village is mostly represented by the pub, a place of cruel, worn-out faces, human degradation, alcoholism, and the industrial wastelands of the river bank next to the village (where the escaping Fauna is raped by her foster-father). These are the spaces of a cruel, patriarchal order, where – in a twisted folk-tale-like fashion – the "good father" has been killed and replaced by the "evil step-father." Human order has gone to usurpers, criminals and rapists – the film seems to suggest. The other place, however, is not a harmonious, bucolic Eden, and not even a place of self-fulfilment: the river in *Delta* is the place of the sublime, beyond human comprehension, beyond good and evil, a heterotopic non-place (so as to use Marc Augé's concept, see Király 176), where life and death flow together inextricably and inexorably.

Mihail's most important embodied practice in *Delta* is building the house on the water. This can be read as an attempt at creating a new life, close to his roots (the dead father's hut), outside the corrupted human world. Building a new house means finding a new place, and thus a new connection to the world in a new spatial-physical arrangement. However, this new (non-)place is on the water, a symbolic element that stands at least as much for death as for new life since Ulysses decided to head back to Ithaca. The ambiguity of the project and the place of retreat (as a figure of both life and death) is emphasised by several details. First, Mihail cannot swim, thus choosing the water as a place to escape from the world already signifies the connection between withdrawal and death. Second, the house on the river becomes a place outside, or rather, *before*, the patriarchal order; a sort of incestuous paradise for traumatised subjects in retreat. This motif of regression is not only indicated by the brother-sister relationship, but also by their "totem" animal, the small turtle, the object of his sister's love that was thrown out by their foster-father and lives here. The turtle, in my interpretation, signifies the child-like innocence of their relationship, as well as the regressive trajectory of their journeys. After all these metaphorical foreshadowing elements, when the drunk villagers finally come to the log-house and kill the couple, the event seems as inevitable to the spectator as Lajoska's self-mounting or Ady's returns from Paris to the Hungarian wasteland. Horror, trauma and death are "natural" destinations on these regressive itineraries. A non-place, after all, is no place to live.

3 The Grandfather's House

Szabolcs's story in *Land of Storms* is deeply linked with post-regime-change Hungarian dreams of success in the West. He is a footballer in Germany, living in an urban setting together with other sportsmen of international background, in a seemingly tolerant and liberal community, equipped with the usual toys of contemporary consumer culture, such as smartphones and fancy clothes. The boys train and play football together, drink beer and smoke marijuana together, watch porn and masturbate together, thus more or less fulfilling one of the dominant images of happiness in contemporary Western teen culture. However, Szabolcs does not seem to fit in. He has "attitude problems," has conflicts with the coach as well as the other boys, and finally decides to leave.

Though his motivations are only hinted at, from the three films discussed, it is here in *Land of Storms* that the spectator gets closest to grasping the working of some kind of ideological failure in these films of retreat. The German scenes at the beginning of the film lack music, and there is often some kind of tension in Szabolcs and the spectator that never lets either him or us enjoy these scenes as those of liberation or joyful self-fulfilment. There seems to be a lack of faith, dissatisfaction or disappointment in the kind of life offered by the West, in cultural connectivity, in the Eastern European subject's satisfactory integration into the great projects of Western culture. Szabolcs's alienation from western dreams is already reflected in the very first scene of the film: while the football coach is reciting a prayer- or mantra-like speech about the feel and love of football to the young players, Szabolcs is lying on his side, playing with the grass, instead of lying on his back and looking high into the sky, at high hopes of success, as are the others.

One must note that by the time these films were made, the progress-oriented mythology of modernity had become tainted, corrupted and broken. Ironically, from the perspective of the Eastern European citizen, the West that we "got" is no longer *the West* that we wanted to get to during state-socialism. Not only because it is a "real West" (rather than the "fantasy West" people imagined in state-socialism), but also because the "real West" of the 2000s is also a place of economic and demographic crises, shrinking welfare functions, spreading Islamism and terrorism, less and less credible political elites, and a quickly growing New Right. Progress and development have given way to crisis, decline, struggle and disillusionment both east and west of the former Iron Curtain. A liberal, philanthropist slogan expressing progress and emancipation for all, "building better worlds" (at least in cinema) has turned into the symbol of the hypocrisy of global capitalism and the ruthless exploitation of human beings for the sake of profit and the System.

In the context of characters who give up the mass-produced dreams of contemporary western culture in order to seek a place of retreat, it is quite significant that space, when conceptualised in terms of the dominant mythology of modernism, usually entails forward movement, becoming, leaving behind one's roots and physical constraints, while place is something located, fixed, an object of nostalgia, a home. In other words, the concept of place often had a reactionary edge in theory even before returns and retreats became such common themes in Eastern European cinema (see: Massey 141).

For Szabolcs, this reactionary place, the closet to hide in, is his grandfather's half-ruined house in rural Hungary, in "the land of storms" (*Viharsarok*), traditionally one of the poorest and most conservative regions in the country. His retreat is often emphasised in spatial terms, in a manner similar to that of *Delta*, with long shots of the landscape and the house, standing isolated from any human settlement. Significantly, the first time music is added to the visual images is when Szabolcs gets off the train and we can face the huge green landscapes of his homeland. These images, in both films, evoke the beauty of nature, the promise of a more authentic subjectivity, but also the loneliness, deprivation and trauma of the protagonists. The concept of wounding (trauma) is literally evoked here: when he gets home, because of a previous fight with other lads after a lost match, Szabolcs is bruised and wounded. Restoring the house with his own hands, mending the roof, installing doors and windows (as the old ones were stolen while the house stood deserted) become the basis of a new practice of the self, a symbolic activity of healing, in which the cracks of an injured self can be patched over.

In the context of the collapse of the ideology of progress it is quite significant that during their retreats, hidden in these deserted, marginal places, all three protagonists engage in manual activities of great sensuous value. Lajoska's work on the animals' bodies, Mihail's construction of the log-house, and Szabolcs's restoration of the house (as well as his work with bees) can be seen as retreats from the shiny digital theme-park of contemporary urban consumer societies to an "analogue" world based on bodily presence and physical activities that engage of all the senses of human perception. Szabolcs has a smartphone, but we never see him surfing on the net or playing games on it, as many teenagers do in their spare time.

Issues of fatherhood are also present in *The Land of Storms*, following a pattern similar to the ones seen in the previous films. Father-son relationships are problematic in all three examples. There is practically no understanding between the different generations. In *Land of Storms*, it is Szabolcs's father who keeps pushing his son to be a footballer, as a compensation for his own misfortunes as a sportsman. There seems to be very little in common between them. Apparently Szabolcs cannot discuss the conflicts he faces in his career, or his homosexuality with his father, either. However, his relationship with his substitute- or symbolic father, the German coach – is no better: most of their interactions consist of verbal abuse and physical violence. His interactions with these two father-figures are conspicuously similar: the age and looks of the two elder men, their insistence on Szabolcs's pursuing his football career, and even the configuration of bodies while training with them (we see Szabolcs trying to take the ball away from them, without success). These similarities become most telling when it comes to Szabolcs's reaction to ideological indoctrination: in his father's house after a "typical" father-son conversation, at night when they are already in bed, he turns on his side and assumes an embryo position similar to the one we saw him in in the first scene. In both scenes an overhead camera records the events, registering Szabolcs's difference from the standard, desiring or forward-looking attitude by this regressive body posture (which is the same position that he dies in at the end of the film).

In these three films fathers tend to represent the dominant patriarchal order, and this is why their sons turn towards other, deeper roots when their lives reach a crisis. Szabolcs moves into his grandfather's old house, away from his father's (and from mainstream teenager culture's) dreams of stardom. As Mihail in *Delta* also did, he moves back to the East (something that most people there probably find very stupid and suspicious). In *Delta* it is the dead father and the mean step-father who play the same roles as the grandfather and the father in Szabolcs's case. Mihail's father is long since dead, and the stepfather, his mother's lover, embodies the worst kind of tyrannical, patriarchal masculinity. The first time we see him he is killing a pig behind the house. He is openly hostile towards Mihail, and also rapes his sister, Fauna. In the case of *Taxidermia*, as I have noted above, Lajoska is exactly the opposite of everything his father and grandfather were: he neither has the sexual vigour of his grandfather, nor the obscenely huge appetite of his father, for which his father reviles him.

Szabolcs's difference is coded mostly in terms of gender, though what problems he faces in Germany is unclear. This connects his story with those of Lajoska and Mihail, whose alienation and ritual retreats are never really explained psychologically. Thus their misery can easily acquire overtones of a more general, philosophical, existential or cultural nature. Having left the West, as a young gay man in rural Hungary, Szabolcs quickly becomes an outcast. The house (the most important symbol of his identity in crisis) never gets completely repaired, though he finds help in Áron, a teenager from the nearby village, who becomes his friend and then lover. Their story is as much about the failure of connectivity as that of Lajoska or Mihail. None of them can make real contact with their home communities or fathers. Though they perform a ritual "attempt of recapturing the deserted, the lost" (Dánél 117), they cannot succeed, "home is always elsewhere for them" (Király 178).

4 Conclusions

All three retreats have ritualistic aspects. Not only do the three men retreat from modern lifestyles into closets of their own, but the films themselves also acquire a ritualistic dimension. All three seem to avoid detailed psychological motivations and explanations, instead they show rituals of death and sacrifice. Lajoska turns his father and himself into memorials of a traumatic family history; Mihail, after inviting the villagers to dinner to share the abundant fish they catch (together with plenty of bread and pálinka) in the newly built house, is murdered together with his sister-lover by the villagers in a scene rich in Christian allusions; and when Szabolcs is knifed to death by his tormented lover Áron, we hear the musical motif of Agnus Dei (God's Lamb). These deaths follow the age-old logic of ritualistic scapegoating and (self-)sacrifice, and stem logically from the narratives of the films. These Hungarian stories of retreat seem to be exceedingly brutal with their protagonists; they make it clear that one cannot simply turn one's back on the dominant ideologies and masculinities of contemporary societies, one cannot turn back to a lost past or a lost childhood, ignoring the imperatives of one's biological and/or symbolic fathers.

This brutality is not necessarily there in retreat films of other former Eastern-Bloc countries. In the Slovak film *The Garden* (*Zahrada,* dir. Martin Sulik, 1995), a beautifully photographed, self-reflexive and often amusing take on the theme of retreat, the protagonist Jakub gets fed up with urban life, and moves to his grandfather's garden house. He repairs it somewhat, finds a female companion, makes peace with his father, and seems to find a more authentic and more spiritual life in the countryside. In another example from the region, the Czech-Slovak co-production *The Country Teacher* (*Venkovsky Ucitel,* Bohdan Sláma, 2008), Petr, a gay schoolteacher leaves his prestigious job in Prague and takes up a job in the countryside. As opposed to the Hungarian films discussed above, he is finally accepted by the local community (even though he openly admits his homosexuality in front of his new colleagues). In the Bulgarian film *The World is Big and Salvation Lurks Around the Corner* (*Svetat e golyam i spasenie debne otvskade,* Stephan Komandarev, 2008) the protagonist suffers serious trauma in Germany when he has a car accident with his parents, in which both parents die and he loses his memory. He is visited by his grandfather, who decides to take him back to their old house in Bulgaria on a tandem bicycle, reactivating his memory through the sensory experiences of the journey to his long-left homeland. All these films avoid tragic endings, show the beauty and richness of one's rural homeland, and present stories in which reconnecting to one's roots and (spiritual, emotional) homeland is possible.

Works Cited

Bazin, André. *What Is Cinema? Essays Selected and Edited by Hugh Gray.* Berkeley, Los Angeles, London: U of California P, 1967. Vol. 1.

Connel, R. W. *Masculinities.* Berkeley, Los Angeles: U of California P, 1995.

Dánél, Mónika. "Surrogate Nature, Culture, Women – Inner Colonies. Postcolonial Readings of Contemporary Hungarian Films." *Acta Univ. Sapientiae, Film and Media Studies,* 5 (2012):107–128.

Delta. Dir. Kornél Mundruczó. Budapest Film, 2008.

Ferge, Zsuzsa. "A rendszerváltozás nyertesei és vesztesei. (Winners and Losers of the Regime Change)" Andorka Rudolf, Kolosi Tamás, Vukovich György (szerk.) *Társadalmi Riport 1996*. Budapest: TÁRKI, Századvég. pp. 414–443.

Foucault, Michel. *Discipline and Punish. The Birth of the Prison*. New York: Vintage Books, 1995.

Gelencsér, Gábor. *Az eredendő máshol: Magyar filmes szólamok*. Budapest: Gondolat, 2014.

Kalmár, György. *Post-Crisis European Cinema: White Men in Off-Modern Landscapes*. Cham: Palgrave Macmillan, 2020.

Király, Hajnal. "Leave to Live? Placeless People in Contemporary Hungarian and Romanian Films of Return." *Studies in Eastern European Cinema*, 2015. Vol. 6, No. 2:169–183.

Kontroll. Dir. Nimród Antal. Budapest Film, 2003.

Gott, Michael and Todd Herzog. *East, West and Centre. Reframing Post-1989 European Cinema*. Edinburgh: Edinburgh UP, 2015.

Jobbit, Steve. "Subterranean Dreaming: Hungarian Fantasies of Integration and Redemption." *Kinokultura*, 2008. http://www.kinokultura.com/specials/7/kontroll.shtml.

Lefebvre, Henry. *The Production of Space*. Oxford: Blackwell, 1991.

Massey, Doreen. *Space, Place and Gender*. Minneapolis: U of Minnesota P, 1994.

Sághy, Miklós. "Irány a nyugat! – filmes utazások keletről nyugatra a magyar rendszerváltás után. (Go West! Filmic Journeys from East to West after the Hungarian Regime Change)" Győri Zsolt és Kalmár György (ed.) *Tér, hatalom és identitás viszonyai a magyar filmben*. Debrecen: Debreceni Egyetemi Kiadó, ZOOM könyvek, 2016. pp. 233–243.

Schissel, Wendy (ed.). *Home / Bodies. Geographies of Self, Place and Space*. Calgary: U of Calgary P, 2006.

Sharp, Joanne P., Paul Routledge, Chris Philo and Ronan Paddison (eds.). *Entanglements of Power: Geographies of domination/resistance*. London and New York: Routledge, 2000.

Shaviro, Steven. "Body Horror and Post-Socialist Cinema: György Pálfi's *Taxidermia*." Anikó Imre (ed.) *A Companion to Eastern European Cinemas*. Oxford: Wiley and Blackwell, 2012. pp. 24–40.

Strausz, Laszló. "Archaeology of Flesh. History and Body-Memory in Taxidermia." *JumpCut*, 2011, 53. Accessed 10 February 2015. http://www.ejumpcut.org/archive/jc53.2011/strauszTaxidermia/.

Szeman, Imre and Tamás, Gáspár Miklós. "The Left and Marxism in Eastern Europe: An Interview with Gáspár Miklós Tamás." *Mediations*, (24) 2 2007, 12–35. http://www.mediationsjournal.org/articles/the-left-and-marxism-in-eastern-europe.

Taxidermia. Dir. György Pálfi. Katapult Film, 2006.

The Country Teacher. Dir. Bohdan Slama. ASFK, 2008.
The Garden. Dir. Martin Sulik. Action Gitanes, 1995.
The World is Big and Salvation Lurks Around the Corner. Dir. Stephan Comandarev. Art Fest, 2008.
Viharsarok (Land of Storms). Dir. Ádám Császi. Cirko Film, 2014.
Warf, Barney and Santa Arias (eds). *The Spatial Turn: Interdisciplinary Perspectives*. London: Routledge, 2009.

CHAPTER 5

Young Mothers, Concrete Cages: Representations of Maternity in Hungarian Housing Films from the 1970s and 1980s

Zsolt Győri

Abstract

The chapter examines state socialist spaces of communal living from a gender perspective using relevant Hungarian films. Informed by Judit Ember's *Fagyöngyök* (*Mistletoes*, 1978), Béla Tarr's *Családi tűzfészek* (*Family Nest*, 1979) and *Panelkapcsolat* (*The Prefab People*, 1982), and György Szomjas' *Falfúró* (*Wall Driller*, 1985) I argue that highrise blocks of flats might have eased the housing shortage brought about by socialist industrialization, they hardly achieved social or gender equality. Emphasizing the resistance of the selected films to play along the official ideological-utopian discourse surrounding housing policies, I point out the collaboration between the paternalistic and the patriarchal regimes, most evident in the subordination of welfare policies to national economic considerations that privilege male control and ensure female subordination in the home. Cinema is a useful tool to study "architectural patriarchy" as it both captures the gendered affective imaginations females and males invest in space and portrays marital relationships as a site of inequality, identity crisis, and (female) entrapment. The second part of the chapter distinguishes between three psychodynamically invested social environments – that of the neighbourhood, the extended family, and the nuclear family (mainly the relationship between spouses) – and offers a close reading of how cinema renders legible the character's affective investments in space through describing their varied associations with patriarchy.

1 Introduction and the Scope of the Research

This chapter explores Hungarian cinematic narratives of family and community life set in housing complexes consisting of concrete tower blocks[1] in the late

---

1 For definitions, I rely on concepts as defined by Tamás Egedy, based on relevant explications of the Hungarian Central Statistical Office. Egedy defines housing complexes of concrete tower buildings as "separate communes within the administrative region of the

socialist period. A general trait and joint motif of the chosen films is their focus on young mothers reliant on their spouses both for income and emotional support to counter the negative psychological effects of postpartum depression, child-raising (for example, exhaustion, anxiety, frustration, low self-esteem), social withdrawal and alienation, monotonous chores, and the financial pressure to make ends meet.

While mapping the physical and affective space of the home in state-socialist Hungary, the films share a common ground with what Edward W. Soja called spatial imagination, a critical perspective no longer "subordinated to the dominant dialectic of historicality-sociality, the interplay between what might more collectively be called the making of histories and the constitution of societies" (262). My examples of housing films – Béla Tarr's *Családi tűzfészek* (*Family Nest*, 1979) and *Panelkapcsolat* (*The Prefab People*, 1982), and György Szomjas' *Falfúró* (*Wall Driller*, 1985) – use the spatial representations of cinema to contest official and dominant perceptions of communal living as a great historical and social achievement to resolve the housing shortage brought about by socialist industrialization. Although the urban housing developments during the 1970s resulted in the construction of the highest number of apartment units per decade in 20th-century Hungary, the contradiction between quantity and quality, as Henri Lefebvre also noted in regard to the social production of space, surfaced: "the dominant tendency, therefore is towards the disappearance of the qualitative" (352). The first sociological accounts of the process of ghettoization, revolving around – as Sándor Horváth notes – the metaphors of chaos and the labyrinth (88–90), stood in stark contrast with official narratives that celebrated the new districts as a decisive victory against destitution, crime, and vulnerability, while advertising this type of communal living as a privilege.[2] Cinema stood opposed to such lofty and self-aggrandizing descriptions and, taking sides with sociological investigations as epitomized by the semi-sociographic films of the so-called Budapest School, rendered

---

settlement – usually surrounded by roadways – which hold a coherent whole of residential flats, buildings and civil engineering facilities ... Housing estates are situated common land, consist of multi-level residential buildings that were constructed according to central planning directives using model designs and organized labor force ... a group of medium high or high residential buildings and rows of apartment blocks constructed using the precast large-panel system." (translation mine) (Egedy Tamás "Kiskedvencből mostohagyerek? A lakótelepek helyzete." http://beszelo.c3.hu/05/0304/10egedy.htm).

2 Almost every chapter in the volume entitled *Lakótelepek, a modernitás laboratóriumai* (High-Rise Districts, the Laboratories of Modernism) (Budapest: Kijárat Kiadó, 2008) makes reference to this narrative and points to the then-prevalent discourse which presented socialist urban modernization as an eminent area of tackling social problems.

domestic space visible without either acknowledging its role in the liberation of the masses from the historical evils of rural poverty and bourgeois alienation, or recognizing socialist welfare reforms as a revolutionary step towards the eradication of social inequality. In fact, films offer symptomatic readings of the affective topography characterizing the estates and the identity crises of its tenants.

The films analyzed in this chapter were not the first to portray urban socialist spaces which challenge the ideologically framed official discourse. My previous research concentrated on how Hungarian cinema followed – from initial enthusiasm to gradual disillusionment – the transitions in public perceptions about this type of communal living.[3] As I argued there, the key stage of this transformation occurred in the 1970s, most notably in Péter Bacsó's trilogy (*The Agony of Mr. Boróka*, 1972; *Let Go of My Beard*, 1975; *A Piano in Mid Air*, 1976), a cycle of satirical stories set in high rise housing estates, which capture the mind-frame of the "homo politicus sovieticus," the socialist version of the regime's dedicated devotee who echoed its empty phrases and stereotypes without self-reflection. Bacsó's films draw close parallels between the grey block-buildings of the estates and thinking through clichés; the spatial regulation of ideal living (confined to uniformly built, small apartments with low maintenance costs) and the psychology of the ideal communist. My choice of films favors realist representations over satirical ones which, furthermore, extend and refine the predominantly masculine experiences of identity crisis by foregrounding female anxieties and entrapment. Their engagement with spatiality, I argue, foregrounds a critical agency focusing on housing policies, which, alongside free education, healthcare, long maternity leave, childcare benefit, full-employment and a dual-breadwinner family model, was a key area of family and welfare reforms. As András Murai and Eszter Zsófia Tóth claim, the films in question "present the dependency of the individual on the system as a social problem" (10). In her exploration of the social policy, Katherine Verdery calls attention to the fact that the state socialist welfare state was another form of socialist paternalism which "presumed [subjects] to be grateful recipients – like small children in a family – of benefits their rulers decided upon for them. The subject disposition this produced was dependency, rather than the agency cultivated by citizenship or the solidarity of ethnonationalism" (Verdery 63) This was the case with pronatalist policies that, in theory, allowed for female emancipation and the

---

3 See "Concrete Utopias: Discourses of Domestic Space in Central Eastern European Cinema." In *Spaces, Bodies, Memories*, edited by Andrea Virginás. Newcastle upon Tyne: Cambridge Scholars Publishing, 2016. 28–49.

equality of the two sexes, but in fact, narratives of lived space and "protagonists with limited room for maneuver and without perspective" (Murai-Tóth 10) often testify the failure of housing schemes to achieve either social or gender equality.

My focus on the affective dimension of young mothers' domestic entrapment extends but is also indebted to previous research that almost exclusively adopted sociological research methods and investigated the relationship between social status, education and income levels (Szelényi–Konrád; Egedy "A társadalmi kirekesztés"; Csizmady "Lakótelep és társadalmi szegregáció" and *A lakótelep*), poverty and social segregation (Egedy "A társadalmi kirekesztés" and "Kiskedvencből mostohagyerek?"; Csizmady "Lakótelep és társadalmi szegregáció" and *A lakótelep*), demography of tenants (Egedy "Kiskedvencből mostohagyerek?"; Csizmady *A lakótelep*), ethnic composition of tenants (Csizmady "Lakótelep és társadalmi szegregáció"; Egedy "Kiskedvencből mostohagyerek?") and the urban ecological effects of housing complexes (Bakay) The scope and nature of sociological inquiry leaves those aspects of lived space unexplored that are best made visible in long interviews or by the analysis of the then-contemporary discourse of young mothers' emotional frailty. David Crowley also relies on different sources, but with a similar message in his interpretation of the ordinary homes of state-socialist Warsaw housing schemes, arguing that "[a]rticles published in this medium represented not only the State's interest in disciplining the home, but also ... attempts to speak for the private – a particular form of the 'publicity of the private' " (189). In Hungary, Eszter Zsófia Tóth's research into the gender politics of the Kádár-era takes this route, and reconstructs a series of debates between readers of the popular women's magazine, *Nők Lapja* (*Women's Magazine*) about the simultaneous presence of comfort and isolation, welfare and emotional impoverishment, boredom and tight schedules, saintliness and martyrdom in the lives of mothers with young children (154–163). Such debates, much the same as life story interviews, made visible contradictions that fade away or remain totally invisible within the framework of the standardized questions in qualitative research interviews. I contend that cinematic representations can be attributed a similar agency, especially since they explore the plight of women in housing complexes with emphasis on the affective layers of spatiality, including conflicts with neighbours, the lack of intimacy and the superior position of the breadwinner patriarch over inactive wives. In its spatial construction of domestic environment, cinema both captures the gendered affective imaginations females and males invest in space and stages marital relationships as a site of inequality, identity crisis, and entrapment.

2   Between Architecture and Patriarchy

The most salient affective quality of housing complexes of pre-fabricated buildings is their vast proportions. Manufactured in factories and assembled on-site, they lend cityscapes an industrial touch: their coarse surfaces, uniform facades and dull colours evoke authority and anxiety in the onlooker.[4] The Brutalist architectural features of these buildings emphasized but also celebrated the stark and self-assertive masculine labor required for their construction. Underlying the material-architectural appearance of these buildings, there is a gendered spatial logic described by Flanagan, Valiulis, and Gialanella:

> every city is a gender regime that ideologically and concretely manifests a distinctive relationship among its political, economic, and familial systems. This gender regime is *patriarchal*: it reflects the social relations of power in any given society in which the values and behaviours of men are presumed normative and thus embedded in urban institutions and structures to privilege male control and insure female subordination.
> FLANAGAN-VALIULIS-GIALANELLA xiii

In the present case, this subordination translates into women being made invisible and hidden in concrete cages which keep their bodies and emotional anxieties under male control. Taking into consideration the paternalistic logic of pro-natalist policies which, according to Verdery, "treated women's bodies as no more than instruments of the state's reproductive requirements" (65) these monochrome buildings could be likened to an incubator.

Although I perceive these homogenous-looking high-rise buildings as architectural symbols of young mothers' entrapment, other constraints need to be considered, including the uneven responsibilities towards domestic chores and the distortive stereotypes that overvalue the (male) breadwinner's role and undervalue that of the (female) homemaker's in supporting family life. Not only was society governed by "a paternalist regime that made the most important decisions in "the whole family's" interests" (Verdery 66) and forced maternal bodies into invisibility, but it also worked invisibly, enforcing normative notions of man/woman, father/mother in subtle ways, weaving gender

---

4   Developing Lefebvre' arguments, David Crowley points to similar tendencies in Warsaw housing projects: "in the Soviet-styled city, space was subordinate to images and effects, and, by the same system, interiors were inferior to the exterior forms that produced them. Space was impoverished by the political imperative to create a particular form of 'representational architecture'" (185).

antagonisms and hierarchies into the texture of (banal) everyday rituals. A vivid illustration is the closing scene of Judit Ember's *Fagyöngyök* (*Mistletoes*, 1978), a semi-documentary portrayal of the quotidian domestic life of a young pregnant mother with two children and her spouse. Although the film points to the limits of patriarchy by presenting self-conscious female characters with remarkable willpower, stamina and playful ways to manipulate men, the concluding scene of the film demonstrates that the social visibility of new life is granted not in its intimate links to the corporeal space of the mother, but through a patriarchal discursive space which attributes meanings to it and symbolically calls it into being. The family gathering organized to welcome/celebrate the newborn becomes an initiation ritual into the realm of visibility and meaningful subjecthood granted by patriarchy. This is also the space, then, where the intimate silence of the maternal body is broken by egotistic voices celebrating adult male virtues, which do not really toast the newborn, only themselves.

The head of the city council, a man of authority (speaking in private) lays the foundation of the discursive space, to which all subsequent addresses will accommodate: he wishes the baby "to grow into an immaculately honest, strong adult male." The godfather speaks next – "You don't know who I am. Let me tell you, I am a policeman and I will look after you and make sure you are very good" – followed by the grandfather – "be strong, blessed and happy. Live as your father and grandfather did" – and the great-grandfather: "be as strong and as honest as your grandfathers and fathers were." Later the father's friends and fellow workers speak. One wishes the baby to grow into an adult as honest as his dear father, to which someone adds: "I ask the Lord to make you into a person like me and your father." An elder colleague concludes: "I wish you a joyful, happy, and prosperous life. I also ask you to be a good lathe operator because we have a shortage of those. I hope by the time you grow up it will be paid better." Not only do male voices dominate this blessed moment of greeting a new life but they speak the language of the patriarchy that recognizes only what is made in its own image. This discourse allows only a male (the strong, happy and honest human) to be an equal member of the community. Symptomatically, the women do not question the legitimacy of this initiation ritual; in fact, one great-grandmother raises it to absurd dimensions: "I wish you a life that takes you to heights, may you become Gagarin. Fly high."

The masculine affective space of familial gathering is a social ritual for itself, as far as it remains blind to the very thing it hopes to honor. This logic of "denial by appropriation" seems to have prevailed not only in the micro-politics of patriarchy but in the practices of bureaucratic empowerment. Tímea N. Kovács's insightful observation about the kitchens of apartment buildings – small enough to not even seat members of the nuclear family – is an architectural example of how planners (bureaucrats of space) failed to disrupt deep-rooted notions about familial co-existence and gender-specific role patterns (10). One participant of the debate in *Nők Lapja* (mentioned above) pointed out the controversy at the foundation of these administrative solutions: "by taking away women from the labor market and locking them within the walls of their homes, the maternity leave conserves the very family model deemed outmoded" (quoted in Tóth 158, translation mine).[5] The failure of domestic space to genuinely advance female emancipation was a result of the collaboration between the paternalistic and the patriarchal regimes, most evident in the subordination of welfare policies to national economic considerations. The endless and uniform reproducibility of dwelling spaces to boost statistics of new housing units and to stimulate reproduction rates amongst young couples was hardly accompanied by the design of emancipatory domestic spaces and gender equality. While socialist industrialization brought about demographic requirements satisfied by adopting targeted welfare policies, these measures did not question culturally encoded notions of family: the patriarchy. The next part of my chapter distinguishes between three psychodynamically invested social environments – that of the neighbourhood, the extended family, and the nuclear family (mainly the relationship between spouses) – and proposes that cinema renders legible the character's affective investments in space through describing their confidence in, dependence on, and resistance to, in short, their associations with, patriarchy.

3   Patriarchal Neighbourhoods

Neighbourly relations as a form of cultural-social-spatial network tell us a lot about patriarchal elements of communal living. The summary Tóth offers of interviews she conducted among female tenants of high-rise blocks points beyond the close companionship we might presume to have existed between people literally living a few feet from each other: "[w]oman workers attributed great relevance to the opinion of their neighbours about their own lifestyles. They intruded into each other's private life. Neighbours provided patterns as to what type of clothes to wear. They also sought to satisfy the expectations of the

---

5 This opinion is almost identical to Verdery's conclusion about state-socialist gender policies: "radical socialism may have been in reorganizing family structures and roles at one level, at another its paternalism dovetailed perfectly with patriarchal forms central to national ideas elsewhere in the West" (Verdery 79).

dwelling community through being first-rate wives and by meeting the criteria of female beauty" (151, translation mine). The panoptic gaze invested with normative power, as described here, opened the way for the patriarchal regime to penetrate the female community even in the absence of males and disallowed for the emergence of intimate female spaces. After men left for their workplaces, young mothers on maternity leave attended to house chores and, pressured by strict requirement of having an immaculate household, were relegated to the role of the domestic servant and the housewife, into a subordinate position bearing the weight of the ever-present specter of patriarchal normativity.

Following from Doreen Massey's definition of spatial uniqueness, "the singularity of any individual place is formed in part out of the specificity of the interactions which occur at that location" (168), we could say that uniform spaces and normative lives of the housing complexes disallowed for any singularity as the case of the *Agony of Mr. Boróka* demonstrates. The homogeneity of spaces, lifestyles and human interactions is foregrounded in the story when the protagonist enters, by mistake, a flat in a neighbouring block. With familiar furniture and similar arrangement of the room he sits down in front of the TV and starts a commonplace conversation with his presumed wife – working in the kitchen – about a refrigerator that needs to be repaired, lunch that is being cooked and the son who needs to be disciplined. Soon the real resident arrives home and the two surprised men have the following conversation:

> What are you doing here?
> Me? I could ask the same question.
> Why would you want to know what I am doing in my own apartment?
> I'm awfully sorry, but this apartment is mine. I can recognize what is
>   mine. That picture on the wall, the TV, the sofa, and the woman in the
>   kitchen.
> Hold on. Which block do you live in?
> D.
> Well, this is G, the apartment of Vince Jonyer. ...
> I must have mistaken the apartments. I really am sorry. Everything was
>   so homely in here. Sorry, I meant to say unhomely. (00:15:33–00:16:17)

Patriarchal notions of domesticity for Boróka are defined by the familiarity of interior design which includes the housewife, "the woman in the kitchen," as an integral accessory of the flat. In addition, uniformity is identified in stark contrast with singularity, hence giving rise to the shared spatial experience of an "unhomely domesticity": communal living as the state of permanent identity crisis. Its permanence is underlined by the scene that follows, in which

Boróka returns to his 'real home', behaves the same way and has an almost identical conversation as quoted above. The housing estate in Bacsó's portrayal becomes a space without singularity, a neighbourhood populated by the clichéd words, activities, and affections of 'really existing socialism'. In addition, this scene identifies the kitchen as female, while the living room as male space.

Whenever this binary is violated, like in *Wall Driller*, patriarchy is under threat. In György Szomjas's film a group of bored housewives set up a secret prostitute circuit and offer sexual services for wealthy clients while their husbands are at work. They secretly repossess the living room and the bedroom to avenge patriarchy for having forced them into a barren, aimless, and depressing quotidian existence. Such acts of extramarital sexuality do not simply allow young mothers, as some commentators have suggested, to earn extra money but to regain control over their bodies, free time, and femininity and, at the same time, resist the disempowering label of the housewife. In the eyes of the neighbourhood, however this transgression will be an open act of rebellion against socialist morality, decency and, not least, patriarchal power. The verbal outbursts at the waitress of the café where the transactions took place is less a personal than a generic condemnation of female sovereignty: "As decent men and women we, the majority, are outraged. This woman should be burnt like the witches were in the past, as she brings calamity to domestic values. As a result of her activities alcoholism spreads, men fight with each other and spend their salary on booze instead of their families" (Fekete-Grunwalsky-Szomjas 41). According to the patriarchal logic of binaries, the opposite of the immaculate housewife is the wicked witch, while the alternative of patriarchy is chaos and destitution.

Béla Tarr's *Prefab People* renders legible another aspect of neighbourhood relations' dependence on the gender regime. The most symptomatic scene to depict shared activities of tenants is a dance party attended by the film's protagonists, a young but emotionally estranged couple. Tarr uses the close-up, the type of shot associated with affectivity and emotionality, to highlight the wife's desperate attempts to capture the attention of her husband, who chooses to dance with a housewife from next door. More and more alcohol is consumed during the night. We see the husband in the company of other men singing a romantic folk song while leaning across the table looking captivatingly at someone whom we presume to be his wife. Yet the camera soon reveals that the person opposite him is a fellow singer and his wife seated further away watches them in frustration. Her spatial position on the periphery of the male company is symptomatic of her unfulfilled desire for tenderness and care, to be recognized by the patriarchal regime as an emotional being.

The male bonding ritual of singing together, just like the celebration in Ember's *Mistletoes*, allows women only a withdrawn presence – the position of the spectator and audience – and a form of communal living in which neighbours live alongside and not with each other. Bearing in mind that most Hungarian folk songs talk about deep male devotion for young girls who are beautiful, loyal and obedient, the marginalization of real women and the ritualistic glorification of (stereotypical) imaginary ones is both an escape from the modern-urban realities of marital relations to rural traditions of male superiority and the reconstitution of the latter in the former.

4 Spatial Conflicts between Generations

Women amongst themselves, while at the hairdresser, shopping or walking together, discussed a variety of topics ranging from summer holidays to their children's education. However marital problems are rarely touched upon, and never openly tackled in the films. Such concealment of domestic disharmonies and the self-silencing of the sovereign voice of female non-conformity strengthened the patriarchal ideology. While the psychodynamics of female neighbourly relations were founded on superficial communication, male bonding, in the form of drinking, gambling, and entertainment, was not intellectual either, and often shifted into infantilism and aggression. Such communal activities, even if they served the purpose of repressing anxieties and were not compatible with ideals of self-improvement, self-control, and good conduct (features of the new socialist self), still allowed men to release stress. Whenever women sought to act out their frustrations, as those involved in the prostitute circuit depicted by *Wall Driller*, they were deemed a menace by the neighbourhood.

The ritual of drinking was equally decisive in the interpersonal dynamics among male members of households shared by two or more generations. The turbulent relationship between the father and two sons in Béla Tarr's *Family Nest* finds temporary peace while consuming alcohol. The roots of their antagonism and the psychological terror they inflict on each other arises from the 'unhomely domesticity' already mentioned in connection with *The Agony of Mr. Boróka*. The single bedroom flat hosting seven members and three generations of an extended family is a dense space in more than one sense: it is a flat overcrowded by bodies but also a psychological wrestling arena and a discursive space of various interpretations and imaginations of home. Gábor Gelencsér points to the psychological credibility of Tarr's depictions which "almost completely exclude the social environment and concentrates only on the changes faces undergo" (260, translation mine), and calls it a chamber drama of faces that pose but does not answer "what deeply hidden conflicts, identity crises, miseries haunt these people" (260, translation mine). I fully share this assumption, and would only add that the psychodynamics and conflicts between the desperate and exhausted mother, the alcoholic husband, the spoilt daughter, and the hypocritical father-in-law are embedded in and arise from their different use and notions of space.

The grandparents represent the generation with a stable income, a flat of their own, and a socio-economic security, which they believe entitles them to lecture family members on honest work, the normal conduct of life, and domestic happiness. The petit bourgeoisie instincts of the homeowner are most prevalent in the case of the grandfather, who speaks about his right to privacy in the morning, and tries to flatter a lady with cheap compliments to the point of harassment in the evening. The character's contradictions and his self-ascribed position of the assertive patriarch need to be considered collectively. More than privacy, he needs a space populated by submissive people who willingly idolize him and blindly accept his demands, values, and moral superiority. By the same token, he agrees to share the flat with his son's family not because of his frequently proclaimed deep emotional attachment to his granddaughter, but because he can easily assert his will on the child and continue the emotional blackmail of the rest of the family. In addition, he uses his superior financial position to deprive his son and daughter-in-law the chance to serve as positive role models for their daughter, and almost poses as the biological father to his granddaughter, ascribing to himself direct parental authority. In his patriarchal perception of domesticity, the home should be the space of total obedience, the spatialization of undisputed authority. When this authority is contested by his daughter-in-law (Irén), he will transform into a sneaky manipulator constructing fake narratives of her infidelity and scheming until the emotional estrangement fully consumes his son's marriage.

Irén is the rebel figure of the younger generation, and resists the instructive manners of the patriarchal father-in-law with a strong sense of maternal responsibility. Almost every aspect of her personality stands in stark contrast with her father-in-law's temperament. Her fluid-permissive morals and bohemian attitudes oppose his rigid principles and petit bourgeois mentality, while her prodigal attitude to money could not be more different from that of the penny-wise older generation. The seminal difference, nevertheless, lies between the maternal-feminine affections, Irén's emotional honesty and the manipulative rationality of the paternalistic regime. The gendered nature of these agencies reaches beyond the scope of the extended family demonstrated by the scene set in the city council's housing department. Tarr emphasizes the spatial hierarchy between the crowded corridors where young mothers queue with their applications for council housing[6] and the spacious office occupied by the technocratic male bureaucrat, the functionary of space with the power to decide who is entitled to council homes (that are not even built) and who is not. Both the administrator – who measures, evaluates, categorizes clients' eligibility for flats – and the father-in-law – who regulates who can stay out and for how long, when one can bring friends, cook and sleep – exercise on the local level the power of patriarchy to penetrate and supervise private lives. The housing official, for instance, urges Irén to bear more children and hence increase her chances for a council flat. This twisted logic which objectifies human life and treats it like a manageable resource is instinctively rejected by Irén who, at one point, bursts out:

> We exist because our parents wanted us to exist. One is so happy with a child! When we are sad, a child makes us happy. They are so gentle. All this social policy nonsense they talk about all the time! One doesn't bear children just to increase the population but because one wants to. It is so good to have a child one loves. (01:27:22-01:27:55)

Despite their contrasting lifestyles and mind-frames, both Irén's and her father-in-law's notions of domestic space are shaped by personal pathologies. The male character's incorporation of patriarchal logic is a strategy to offset the psychological damage of his inferiority complex: the wish for a home with full power and authority probably compensates for his failure to prove his professional aptitude at the workplace. Thus, patriarchy serves him well to keep frustrations at bay and to repress his identity crisis. As for Irén, her yearning for her own home to repair her marriage and create a loving family atmosphere seems to be the constitutive factor. Her imaginations about domestic space are formed within the pathology of escapism and rely on ideals that are self-deceptive to the degree that they disallow her to assess the situation realistically and examine her own responsibility in failures. I regard this as a utopian notion of domesticity, the shortcomings of which I will explore next with reference to the psychodynamics between spouses.

---

6 The scene in question is an accurate illustration of the gendered division of labour, prescribing women the inferior role to queue at social benefit offices (or stand in food lines), while men did work considered as superior.

5   There Is No Place Like Home

Family Nest is about domestic space which despite being absent still stands in between people. The characters of *The Prefab People* seem to have resolved the central problem of Tarr's previous film. Although they live in their own flat located on a new housing estate made of panel high-rise buildings, this domestic space is burdened by regular quarrels and bitter from the emotional isolation of the married couple. The two films form a whole and, whereas the first features people dreaming about home as the epitome of an independent, balanced, and affectionate family life, the second recognizes this promise as unfulfillable. The patriarchal regime in *The Prefab People* takes the shape of spatialized affect that is maternal claustrophobia, which the character of the wife/mother describes as follows:

> You come home, and I try to be humorous and in a good mood. Dinner and the kids are both ready, you don't have to do anything. You don't have to take them to school, check their homework. When you take the kid to see a football match, go for a walk or to the sweet-shop, you both have a good time. I always have to do the hard stuff, I'm always jumpy with him, always quarrelling and I can't, I can't control myself … All the time I have to control myself and be patient. In front of you, in the shops, greet everyone with a smile. I can't take it anymore. I can't stand being either with one of them or with both. You're with him when you feel like it. If you don't, you just lie down, read the paper, watch TV, listen to the radio, or go out. You can go out whenever you feel like and wherever you want to. (00:13:50–00:15:01)

The home becomes a trap after realizing she is left on her own with the house chores and anxieties, when she loses the strength to cling on to the imaginary and utopian promises she used to embrace, and can no longer overlook the actual and real limits of her existence: the fact that the domestic space is a place that lacks emotional attachment. When the husband replies to the above accusations, he makes reference to the grueling monotony of the workplace and tries to calm his wife's frustrations by promises of higher income and more money to spend: "we'd have a car within a year" (*The Prefab People* 00:52:58-00:53:00), "in the second year we might save up enough money to buy a house with a garden" (00:53:10-00:53:17). Patriarchy's answer to maternal claustrophobia is yet another (utopian) promise, a commitment to consumerism as the presumed solution to distress and the key to eternal happiness. It takes assurance in an unforeseeable future, and fetishizes it through amassing material wealth and status symbols: it keeps talking about where the family is heading, because it is less and less sure where it stands. Robi understands Judit's entrapment and claustrophobia, but he is unable to address it with empathy, and continues to yearn for the future and avoid the present. When this strategy fails and the masculine identity crisis takes concrete shape, he takes the easy escape route (the freedom of movement provided by the patriarchal regime) in an attempt to leave the family behind: "You're fed up? And you just say, I'm going? ... Where do I go, tell me, what's going to happen to me? How do you imagine that, tell me? Where do you imagine I'll go to? When I've had enough where do I go to, tell me? ... You think you can just say you're off?" (01:06:33- 01:06:53) Escaping from loud children and exhausted wives is a recurring motif of the films. Hardly does the character of the husband in *Family Nest* arrive home after being discharged from a two-year army service, when he runs off to the pub with his brother, but only after they sexually assault a lady friend in the corridor of the apartment building whom they had offered to walk home. In *Wall Driller* Géza does not hesitate much to take the first escape route he is offered when his wife burst out one evening:

> I don't know and I don't care either. I'm bored with it, do you understand me? Bored! Leave me alone, Géza! Hell, you spend no time at home. You don't give a shit about the kids. And I spend my days by your bloody telephone which never rings anyway. ... Don't explain anything to me, Géza because you don't have to explain anything to me, because I know very well what the situation is. We only have this bloody weariness and nervousness ... And Géza, go to hell!
> Listen then, I'll leave.
> As you please!
> I'm gone.
> Just slam the door when you are gone! (00:58:37- 00:59:53)

In the end, neither does the husband deserts the family, nor do they reconsider their approach to gender roles or refute their inherent hierarchy. Spouses will continue to have the same fights over and over again, and whenever mothers feel they have been forced into concrete cages, the patriarchal regime will continue to feed them empty promises of material welfare and address both female angst and the emotional vacuum of marital relationships with patronizing cynicism. In *The Prefab People,* Tarr lays bare the correspondence between the idealistic male visions of the future and the similar imaginations of the socialist system as the father tries to explain the Marxist principles of history to his elder son:

Imperialism is the most developed form of capitalism and was followed by socialism. We live in socialism today. A more developed stage will be communism when ... [*confused*] Well, in socialism everyone gets ... [*even more confused*] or rather in socialism your needs ... No, in socialism you get as much as what you work, while in communism, everyone will get everything they need. (00:23:42–00:24:23)

The confusion of the character is most visible when talking about the contemporary social context, when trying to grasp the essence of his most imminent reality in time and space. His inability to do that is reminiscent of his failure to address the roots of the domestic crisis, while his eventual definition of socialism as a space yearning for an illusory elsewhere is again an apt expression of his own experience of lacking meaning and emotions in life. Until the logic of utopian socialism continues to characterize the psychodynamics of domestic space, patriarchal males will carry on making promises and, in the process, justify and conserve mechanisms and strategies of how not to face their partner's or their own identity crisis.

6   Conclusion

Cinema's ability to capture living bodies as much as their experience of how it feels to be alive makes screen products into a vast resource of studying affective configurations and structures of feelings. But since these bodies exist in a shared social context defined by interpersonal relations, material and discursive givens, films also inform us about the historical, social and spatial creation of affects. More bluntly put, cinema apprehends people's capacity to affect and to be affected in specific spaces, historical epochs and under the guidance of particular norms.

This chapter focused on cinematic articulations of how mothers with young children feel in domestic space which, to a large extent, owes its existence to state socialist welfare policies. These policies, as the films testify, are grounded on and foreground a gender regime, valuing industrial and administrative male work over domestic work and parenting, making women dependent on their elders' and spouses living facilities and income, furthermore disallowing female emancipation by setting up standards as to how young mothers should look, behave and feel. I argued that the generational and personal conflicts that arise from this gender regime involve not only a struggle in and over domestic space, but different and often contradictory affective investments into the home and the family. For young mothers, it becomes a site of entrapment after it ceases to provide for emotional union, while husbands perceive it as a site of identity crisis, that can be coped with by making promises of a better future, the very strategy utopian socialism adopted to domesticate people's desire for autonomy and turn it into the willful acceptance of dependency.

Acknowledgements

This research was supported by the János Bolyai Scholarship of the Hungarian Academy of Sciences and the ÚNKP-19-4 New National Excellence Program of the Ministry of Human Capacities.

Works Cited

Bacsó, Péter. *Forró vizet a kopaszra!* (*The Agony of Mr. Boróka*). Budapest Filmstúdió–MAFILM/Mokép, 1972.

Bakay, Eszter. "The Role of Housing Estates' Green Surfaces in Forming the City Climate of Budapest." *Applied Ecology and Environmental Research* vol. 10, no. 1 (2012): 1–16.

Crowley, David. "Warsaw Interiors: The Public Life of Private Spaces, 1949–65." In *Socialist Spaces: Sites of Everyday Life in the Eastern Bloc*. Edited by David Crowley and Susan E. Reid. Oxford: Berg, 2002. pp. 181–206.

Csizmady, Adrienne. "Lakótelep és társadalmi szegregáció." ("High-rise Housing Districts and Social Segregation") *Szociológiai Szemle* (1996/3–4): 96–132.

Csizmady, Adrienne. *A lakótelep*. (*The High-rise Housing District*) Budapest: Gondolat Kiadó, 2003.

Egedy, Tamás. "A társadalmi kirekesztés és a lakótelepek." ("Social Marginalization and High-Rise Housing") *Tér és Társadalom* 15 (2001/1): 91–110.

Egedy, Tamás. "Kiskedvencből mostohagyerek? A lakótelepek helyzete" ("From Being Favorites to Being the Odd One Out: High Rise Housing Districts Today") *Beszélő* vol. 10, no. 3–4 (Mar.-Apr. 2005): 77–88.

Ember, Judit. *Fagyöngyök* (*Mistletoes*). Film. Balázs Béla Stúdió–Hunnia Filmstúdió/Mokép, 1978.

Fekete, Ibolya, Grunwalsky Ferenc and Szomjas György. "*Falfúró*: filmnovella." ("Wall Driller: A Film Novelette") *Filmvilág* 28.6 (1985): 40–51.

Flanagan, Maureen, A. Valiulis, and Maryann Gialanella. "Introduction: Gender and the City: The Awful Being of Invisibility." *Frontiers* vol. 32, no.1 (2011): xiii–xx.

Gelencsér, Gábor. *A Titanic zenekara*. (*The Band of the Titanic*) Budapest: Osiris, 2002.

Kovács, N. Tímea. "Lakótelepek – a modernitás laboratóriumai. Bevezető." ("High Rise Housing Districts – Laboratories of Modernity. Introduction") *Lakótelepek – a modernitás laboratóriumai*, edited by Kovács N. Tímea. Budapest: Kijárat Kiadó, 2008. pp. 7–14.

Lefebvre, Henri. *The Production of Space*. Oxford: Blackwell, 1991.

Massey, Doreen. *Space, Place and Gender*. Minneapolis: U of Minnesota P, 1994.

Murai, András, Tóth Eszter Zsófia. "Magánörömök, közállapotok: a szexualitás ábrázolása a nyolcvanas évek magyar filmjeiben." ("Personal Pleasures and Social Conditions: The Representation of Sexuality in 1980s Hungarian Cinema") *Médiakutató* vol. 12, no. 2 (2011): 7–21.

Sándor, Horváth. "A lakótelepek népe és a bűn metaforái: a Mária Valériától a csövesekig." ("The Folks of High-Rise Housing Districts and Metaphors of Crime: from Mária Valéria to the Ragged Youth") *Lakótelepek, a modernitás laboratóriumai*, edited by Tímea N. Kovács. Budapest: Kijárat Kiadó, 2008. pp. 83–100.

Soja, Edward W. "Thirdspace: Expanding the Scope of the Geographical Imagination." *Human Geography Today*. Ed Doreen Massey, John Allen and Phillip Sarre. Malden: Blackwell, 1999. pp. 260–2.

Szelényi, Iván and Konrád György. *Az új lakótelepek szociológiai problémái*. (*The Sociological Problems of New High-Rise Housing Districts*) Budapest: Akadémiai Kiadó, 1969.

Szomjas, György. *Falfúró*. (*Wall Driller*). Hunnia–Mafilm/Mokép, 1985.

Tarr, Béla. *Családi tűzfészek*. (*Family Nest*). Balázs Béla Stúdió/Mokép, 1979.

Tarr, Béla. *Panelkapcsolat*. (*The Prefab People*). Balázs Béla Stúdió–MAFILM-MTVFMS–Társulás Stúdió/Mokép, 1982.

Tóth, Eszter Zsófia. *Kádár leányai*. (*Kádár's Daughters*) Budapest: Nyitott Könyvműhely, 2010.

Verdery, Katherine. *What Was Socialism, and What Comes Next?* Princeton: Princeton UP, 1996.

CHAPTER 6

Queer Sex and the City: Affective Places of Queerness in Contemporary Hungarian Cinema

Fanni Feldmann

Abstract

This chapter analyses the depiction and creation of queer places with a specific focus on how different affective qualities influence the use and production of these places in contemporary Hungarian cinema. The analysis differentiates between mainstream films and queer depictions of queer places on the basis of affects they attach to queer place-making. Mainstream films, while maintaining a functional interpretation of queerness – understanding it exclusively in terms of bodily, sexual practices –, position shame as the central affect in the use, experience, and production of queer places. In contrast, queer historiographic documentaries aim at representing the connection between the creation of safe queer places and the development of a queer subculture and suggest that the sense of belonging makes the creation of queer places possible. Although both mainstream and queer images depict the queer use of the same urban environment – Budapest – as a result of the difference between the affective qualities they attach to place, it is two radically different Budapests they create.

1   Introduction

> Eradication of homophobic violence has been a central goal of lesbian and gay liberation and the creation of *"safe spaces"* has been an ongoing political project.
>
> HODGE 41, emphasis mine

The quotation I chose to begin my analysis with touches on various aspects of queerness from marginalization, through emancipation, to the political aspects of the queer movement. However, I highlighted a seemingly self-explanatory phrase, "safe spaces," as it incorporates two theoretical approaches this analysis builds on: affect and spatiality. From a queer point of view, a safe space not only designates the lack of "prejudice, discrimination and physical and verbal violence" (Myslik 156), but also a space of emotional, communal support, where queer identities can be constructed, lived and performed. Furthermore, safe space itself is produced by carving out a place of one's own, where the intimate practice of homosexuality is in a mutual relation to space. Safe spaces provide home for a (sub)culture by embodying queer desire both on the level of sexuality, and by recognizing and nurturing the communal aspects of queerness. At the same time these spaces are created by these very practices: it is queer desire(s) that bring about a transformation of place. Queer "affective engagement … transforms space in the very instance of creating place" (Duff 886).

In terms of space, affect, and queerness, two attitudes seem to crystallize in Hungarian cinematic representations on queer desire, along the dividing line between mainstream cinema – showing signs of homophobia – and queer self-representations – taking a stance of activism. Although both the mainstream films and the queer historical documentaries analysed in what follows presuppose the city as the central place of queer desire and practices, the concepts of the urban space they create are markedly different. First, the mainstream examples focus only on the "sexual" in homosexuality, and skeletonize queerness to a mere instinctual or functional core: a bodily urge, which has to be satisfied occasionally to be kept at bay. As a result, the urban space is not depicted as a collection of protective shelters or cosy, intimate "homes," but rather as a space offering hiding places for a practice that must be kept secret. Therefore, in these films the relation between queer characters – mostly prostitutes, swindlers and their clients –, queer desire, and space is defined by negative effects, mainly shame. As opposed to that, queer documentaries approach the city as a vibrant place for subcultural development, where a more positive affective relation to place is possible: a sense of belonging to a place and to a distinctive subculture are interconnected.

2 Estranged and Ashamed Hustlers in *This I Wish and Nothing More, Men in the Nude*, and *Chameleon*

Apart from a few examples, representations of homosexual identity development, let alone community formation, are scarce in Hungarian mainstream cinema and television. The queer characters who appear on screen articulate two prominent attitudes. They are superficial, sketchy figures bearing only stereotypical signs of their sexual otherness (as in the case of the 2013 *Coming Out* or the early example of Hungarian gay man on prime-time television, Mr. Oli in

Neighbours),¹ signifiers described by Steve Wharton as "a given set of characteristic behaviour applied to a given group which prevents logical and rational engagement with the issues under discussion" (108). These examples testify how Hungarian cinema discredits nuanced explorations of queerness by sticking to the reductive public discourse. The other type of the cinematic homosexual equally misrepresents queer people and is only perceptive to their sexuality. In this case, the complexity of sexual orientation, non-heterosexual identity formation and coming out is stripped down to a mere bodily function: sex.

Each of the three films (*This I Wish and Nothing More*, *Men in the Nude*, *Chameleon*) depicts homosexuality without linking it to questions of sexual identity, community and subculture, instead, they simplify it to joyless and often dehumanizing sexual acts. The functional aspects of sexuality in the films are emphasised by focusing on queer prostitution with all its negative connotations. As a result, prostitution, which "is regarded by many citizens as a *deviant enterprise*: run by shady people and promoting immoral or perverted behaviour" (Weitzer 2, emphasis in the original) and homosexuality become synonymous. The films fuse public attitudes towards queerness and prostitution and apply to them notions of perversion, deviance and promiscuity.² Furthermore, as Nina Peršak and Gert Vermeulen point out, "a prostitute, in particular, is all body, no face" (13), therefore a homosexual prostitute's sexual identity is skeletonised doubly: on the one hand, their sexuality is reduced to the functional performance of sexual acts, on the other hand, their identity is replaced by an empty, purchasable and "fuckable" body.

What strengthens the functional experience and interpretation of queerness is the film's approach to the city, which – in stark opposition to the countryside –appears as a perverted place allowing "illicit sexualities and nonconformist gender practices" (Johnston and Longhurst 80) – in this case functional homosexuality – to prosper. The positioning of the countryside as the space of traditional (heterosexual) values, such as marriage and family, strengthens the accusation or demonization of urban spaces. For instance, in *This I Wish and Nothing More*, the protagonist, Brúnó, lives with his wife (and her brother) in a secluded, solitary country home, an ideal space for a "normal," that is heterosexual, relationship. The events which corrupt and eventually ruin their lives occur without exception in the city, where Brúnó is gradually caught up in a downward spiral of violence, drugs, deviance, incomprehensible fetishes and

---

1   Orosz, Dénes dir. *Coming out* (*Coming Out*). Megafilm, 2013 and Horváth, Ádám dir. *Szomszédok* (*Neighbours*). Mtv, 1987–1999.
2   For a detailed survey of Hungarian public discourse on homosexuality, see Judit Takács's *Homoszexualitás és társadalom* (*Homosexuality and Society*). Új Mandátum, 2004.

perversions. In *Men in the Nude*, the opposition of rural and urban spaces is similarly present, since the protagonist's wife spends most of her time acting in a small-town theatre and repeatedly asks her husband to join her there. However, he decides to stay in the capital, where his affair with the young hustler leads to the termination of their marriage. In Krisztina Goda's *Chameleon* the countryside appears in a similar manner, since Gábor, the swindler, dreams about earning enough money with his shady, urban business for a family home in a quiet and peaceful rural area.

There is no attempt in any of the three films to depict spaces supporting a positive queer experience either in an urban, or in a rural environment; in fact, the city – usually imagined as a haven for queer culture – is a space characterised by the proliferation of sexual exploitation. At this point it should be noted that apart from a few minor characters, the homosexual prostitutes – or rather prostitutes for homosexuals– do not identify themselves as people with same-sex orientations. The protagonist of *This I Wish and Nothing More*, Brúnó, makes ends meet by occasional hustling in the capital, yet his statement– "I do it for the money" (Mundruczó 14:40) –qualifies the homosexual act as a self-imposed perversion. In *Men in the Nude*, Zsolt, the young hustler, never reveals his sexual orientation and is seen flirting and having sex with a girl. His customer (and lover) repeatedly asserts his interest in women, and justifies his attraction to Zsolt with the hustler's young age and feminine features. Although it could be debated whether these characters provide instances of closeted homosexuality, where prostitution is a secretive and deniable form for experiencing their sexual orientation, the third film, *Chameleon*, leaves less doubt about the heterosexual orientations of the protagonist. He is a swindler by profession whose target group consists of insecure, lonely women who happily share their lives and money with him for the illusion of being loved. However, he falls in love with the victim of a scheme and he is forced to prostitute himself in order to support the young woman and cover up his previous lies.

Instead of depicting the city as a chance for cultural homosexuality to develop, the films stick to a functional interpretation and representation of queerness by drawing attention to the financial inequalities between characters and the contrast between the living conditions of hustler and customer. The customers appear as wealthy men who exploit young hustlers' bodies and financial instability.[3] Considering their homes, similar aspects are revealed in the three films: Brúnó's family home In *This I Wish*, is hardly more than a tin

---

3   This attitude is similar to Czech documentary films by Wiktor Grodeczki *Not Angels but Angels* (1994) and *Body Without Soul* (1996), which concentrate on young hustlers of Prague and depict them as innocent victims of wealthy Western perverts.

shed. It is not by chance that the film starts with his wife reciting the story of "The Little Match Girl" which proves to be an allegory for their situation and living conditions. As opposed to this, Brúnó's customers enjoy financial safety, which is emphasised by his stealing from their apartments. Similarly, in *Men in the Nude*, the customer, a middle-aged, financially stable writer lives with his wife in a downtown bourgeois flat. Their home is supplied with antique furniture, the woman's perfume collection and a populous pile of classic books. The hustler's residence is quite the opposite: instead of the upper-middle class milieu, he lives in a run-down flat of a high-rise block of flats with his parents. The writer's spacious home is in huge contrast with the overcrowded, narrow and suffocating atmosphere of Zsolt's home. *Chameleon* further confirms this image: with his childhood friend and swindling partner, Gábor lives in a run-down office where they co-ordinate their business projects. The space lacks homeliness, furniture is limited to the bare necessities of their shady business: the functionality of their lives is well reflected by this room. Although we get only a glimpse of Dr. Marton, his only male customer's flat, its windows look over one of Budapest's most prestigious places: Heroes' Square. Apart from emphasising the financial and social difference between hustler and customer, the run-down residences are places of retreat and camouflage. As Sara Ahmed reminds us: "[t]he word 'shame' comes from the Indo-European verb for 'to cover', which associates shame with other words such as 'hide', 'custody', 'hut' and house" (104, referring to Schneider). These homes can be interpreted as spaces of shame.

Queer presence and the production and experience of place are influenced by one another in the three films, as "the body's encounters in place involve affective resonances far beyond those experienced between discrete individuals. Just as bodies affect one another in place, bodies are inevitably affected by place" (Duff 885). The central affect in this complex relationship of queer bodies and places is shame. Shame, the compulsion of secrecy and the fear of being found out affect both the hustlers and the (usually closeted) gay customers and also the spaces they inhabit. As Ahmed points out, "[i]n shame, more than my action is at stake: *the badness of an action is transferred to me*, such that I feel myself to be bad" (105). No matter how furiously they deny the effect of their queer acts – functioning as queer – on their heterosexuality, their actions' perceived "badness" (according to the norm) strikes back on their self-image and results in shame, as "the queer subject takes on the 'badness' as its own" (108). No surprise then that in *This I Wish* Brúnó is ashamed of his "denied and disguised homosexual affairs" and tries to protect the image of his heterosexual marriage (Stőhr 269, my translation). He prohibits his business partner (his wife's brother) from touching him or hinting at their city life at home. Likewise, one of Brúnó's regular customers desperately tries to conceal his queer desires in front of his family, and he even assaults Brúnó when he endangers his cover.

In *Men in the Nude* shame is also shared by hustler and homosexual partners, although generational differences prevail, most significantly in the scene when the young hustler and his two older customers are interrogated by the police. The two elderly men try everything to conceal the nature of their relationship with the young man, and when the middle-aged writer finally reveals the queer nature of their connection – in order to provide an alibi for the hustler – he can barely look anywhere but at his own lap. In contrast, Zsolt, who is thirty years younger, seems unaffected by the police officers' spiteful comments. His behaviour, nevertheless, is extremely secretive in front of his family and friends. When Tibor unexpectedly visits him at home, he is visibly tense, introduces Tibor to his parents as his teacher and later confronts him on the corridor. He acts in likely fashion when Tibor appears among his friends: he avoids physical contact with the older man, and ostentatiously flirts with a girl. In other words, it is the opinion of his micro-community (instead of a general public) that motivates his secretive behaviour.

Not only social identity, but also the characters' self-image (and self-loathing) is characterised by shame. The quick glances around, the cautious watchfulness before doing anything queer, indicate how the "badness of an action is transferred" (Ahmed 105) to the queer space produced by means of queer practices. The shamefulness of being and acting queer results in markedly silent spaces that turn into "sites of shame" as they are used in opposition to "what dominant ideas … dictate" (Munt 2). In *This I Wish* the stairs at the Danube embankment, usually imagined as a place for peaceful contemplation, turn into a shamefully open and overly visible spot for a "queer quickie;" a public toilet is depicted as a gathering place for ashamed queers who dare to communicate only through gestures and prices; and when entering a private flat for a quick job we can see the two main hustler characters through the bars of the corridor gate, providing a prison cell-like atmosphere for the flat, where shameful – queer – practices are held at bay.

The culmination of these representational attitudes of queer affectivity and space can be found in *Men in the Nude* condensed into a highly symbolic, rather elusive space, the red room. This room appears several times throughout the film, changing locations, and reaches its climax at the end of the film, when after being found out by his wife, the main character walks in and never leaves it. This space carries at least two layers of symbolic meaning. First, its colour is contradictory: red evokes the notion of love, and also its bodily manifestations, lust, passion and eroticism – sexuality – on the one hand, and aggression, violence and blood on the other.

Furthermore, when being embarrassed or ashamed, the body often reacts by blushing: "shame impresses upon the body" (Ahmed 103), and cheeks turn red. Instead of blushing cheeks which would expose "that which has been covered" (104) and could be interpreted as an announcement of their "deviation," to the world – pointing to at least the hope of coming out and identity development – these queer characters are locked up within the scarlet cheeks and walls of the room of shame, in a confined space, without an exit or windows. However, the lack of a view implies the impossibility of peeping into the room from the outside as well. Therefore, the one safe space for queerness is depicted as a confined room, where the shamed and shameful body – (created by) the bodily, functional notion of homosexuality – is the only carrier of queer desire. The room turns into the prison of the body. It confines, hides and locks up the "malfunctioning" queer body, but it is also the queer body tied by self-loathing, repression and shame, this "intense and painful sensation ..., a self-feeling that is felt by and on the body" (103). The film abides by the functional interpretation of queerness, and represents the body with same-sex desires as a prison for the self, where queer desire is no more than a bodily urge which for a moment escaped the necessary control and has to be hustled back into the scarlet room of shame.

3   "Tile bars,"[4] Gay Bars and Pride Marches – Queer Images about Queering Space

The following section explores two queer historiographic documentaries that revolve around the very same place as the three mainstream films, yet approach it with noticeably different attitudes. Instead of placing shame as the central affect of queer spaces within Budapest, the documentaries focus on the possibilities to experience and create space with positive affective qualities, most significantly with a sense of belonging (to a group, a subculture, a community, etc.). As the two documentaries revisit and recreate earlier sites of queer experience in search of a queer past in the pre- and post-regime change Hungary, they create a radically different queer affectivity of "another" Budapest. The films represent how seemingly functional queer practices, such as cruising or meeting in public toilets can be interpreted and experienced differently from the representational modes of mainstream cinema focusing on a sense of

---

4   *Hot Men, Cold Dictatorships* (M. Takács 26:14). The English lines from the film are quoted from the DVD English subtitles.

belonging instead of shame; and depict how the very same affective quality of gay bars was essential in the queer subcultural development of Hungary.

Mária Takács's 2015 documentary, *Hot Men, Cold Dictatorships* explores the theme of finding a partner, a community and establishing a subculture. The film openly approaches this issue as the trajectory leading from isolated gay identities, through small, isolated groups, to a political, activist and empowered body of peers. The documentary starts with contemporary images of a Budapest Gay Pride March,[5] which is presented as the result of previous gay generations' political and activist struggle. The narrator of the documentary explicitly raises the question of Hungarian queer history during the decades of state socialism as a necessary antecedent for the present visibility of queer Hungarians. His question, "how they could find a partner, a community" (Takács M., *Hot Men* 05:26) links the issue of communal identity formation with the emergence of queer activism. To trace their predecessors' steps the young filmmakers – accompanied by gay men above 50– revisit the places which used to serve as sites for the development of queer connections.

The first sites they evoke are public spaces which were originally not intended as gathering opportunities for gay people. As the filmmakers belong to a generation for whom the Internet provides endless possibilities of meeting other LGBTQ people, they are astonished by the strategies of queering public spaces during state socialism. As Judit Takács asserts in her comprehensive essay on the queer history of Budapest, "gay men had been inventing and applying various partner-seeking strategies, involving bathhouses, public toilets, cinemas, and personal tricks, to name but a few" (198). Although we can listen to the older generation's stories of baths, and how they gathered pieces of information about their queer aspects, these places are only shown in the film from a distance or with archive footage. They are not revisited, and the queer experience only exists as a narrative, illustrated with images, but without the actual presence of the interviewees or the filmmakers. According to Judit Takács, bathhouses could provide "a hassle-free environment in which they could meet and physically interact with one another without raising suspicion" (192), and as the interviewees recall: "sun terraces for example, it was

---

5   Although these images of the Pride March represent the outcome of decades of queer activism, they also serve as a criticism of contemporary Hungarian politics. The scenes are from the infamous 2008 March, when groups representing the strengthening right-wing ideologies organised a counter-demonstration parallel to the Pride which ended up in violent physical collision.

quite clear, [were] an almost exclusively gay community" (Takács M., *Hot Men* 20:49).

The two queering strategies that are actually recreated in *Hot Men* are cruising – or queering the streets – and the use of public toilets as meeting sites for queer people. Both served the purpose of finding occasional sex partners, which might bear a resemblance to the mainstream films' functional interpretation of queerness. As one of the participants, Ádám Nádasdy puts it in connection with toilets: "I had no appetite for this. I wanted a person"(Takács M., *Hot Men* 27:00), making clear the functionality of the toilets and the lack of a personal experience provided an experience that was not personal enough. Still, when they visit a public toilet,[6] an earlier meeting site, the elderly gay men point to the places where benches used to stand near the entrance, where visitors could sit and talk. So, some degree of socialising was inevitably part of the experience.

The ambiguity of the functionality and connection-seeking of public toilets defines both the narratives of the participants and the representational attitude of the documentary. As one of the elderly men summarizes: "it [public toilet] both attracted and repulsed me" (Takács M., *Hot Men* 25:47). On the one hand "[t]oilets/bathrooms were largely understood as functional spaces rather than spaces in which [to] relax and linger" (Longhurst 76). Furthermore, as Ruth Barcan points out, public toilets possess "a number of distinctive spatial qualities: they are multiple, contested, ambiguous spaces of heightened affect and sensory charge" (28). First, public toilets are inevitably perceived as non-hygienic places, loaded with unpleasant sights, smells, and bacteria. The inserted archival images of ugly, run-down, dirty public toilets reflect on these ideas as they represent a repulsive place for lingering, relaxation and socialising, and only quick sexual release is imaginable. Katerina Nedbálková argues that toilets are spaces "for anonymous sex without further commitment" (69) where homosexuality is reduced "to the performance of sexual encounters" (72).

On the other hand, when describing the process of meeting people in/around public toilets, the participants talk about experiences of feeling sheltered and connected. While sitting on the benches near the entrance of the toilet "you could see from a sheltered place who was walking in the sun" (Takács M., *Hot Men* 25:57), and recognize even familiar faces. Nedbálková's other argument that public toilets "represent a kind of subcultural scene within the gay

---

6 Judit Takács's statement that "all public toilets were potential meeting places for gay men" (198) stresses the importance of public toilets as meeting sites.

community" (71) is well exemplified by this statement. Furthermore, sexual encounters in public toilets were based on a mutual yearning and consent that did not involve prescriptive power relations as in the case of hustling depicted in mainstream films. Even if control, fear, and shame were present, these were common and shared emotions counterbalanced by the experience of being in a company of equals. Based on this assertion public toilets can be perceived as predecessors of gay bars, sites of an emerging cultural homosexuality, where mutual trust and the desire to embrace sexual otherness transforms this functional, abject, and heteronormative public space into a shelter of oppressed homosexuality. It is this desire of sharing experiences, moments, and spaces which gives birth to the gay bar as the space of community, belonging and empowerment.

As these public meetings were necessarily risky acts during a regime which might have decriminalised same-sex intercourse in 1961, but continued with the surveillance and intimidation of LGBTQ people, the presence of mutual trust also points to a more subcultural view on these public sites. As a participant reveals, public toilets used by gay men were called "tile bars" (26:14), which supports the connection between queered public places and gay bars. It is exactly this semi-subversive atmosphere that transforms homosexuality from a functional satisfaction of bodily needs into a subcultural experience underpinned by the desire for communal spaces. What is subverted by the developing gay community is exactly the original privacy which is, more or less, provided by toilets for the necessary "maintenance" of the body. Toilets provided gay men with a space for opening up, for sharing the experience of their sexuality and meeting other gay men, however, could not provide a space that was safe enough in the period of a rigidly heteronormative and patriarchal authority and society in which, "after many decades of spatially deprived public existence, there was a tremendous need to have places where … 'men can meet' and women can meet" (Takács J. 198). The affective milieu of these public places – although shares the sense of belonging with gay bars – was not adequate for an exuberant, transgressive and liberating performance of queer identity. These places were too strongly bound and saturated by the heteronormatising strategies which produced them.[7] Occasional acts of queering space were possible, but the queer subculture – in order to be able to transgress

---

7   The lack of social connection was not exclusive to the queer community, it affected the whole society, since "[i]ntimacy issues were practically silenced in state socialist Budapest," furthermore, "the urban environment of state socialist cities did not encourage people to submerge in the world of strangers by meeting and interacting with each other" (Takács J. 195–6).

compulsory heterosexuality – first had to retreat into marginal and invisible spaces – such as house parties and gay bars – to gather its members into a community.

As follows, it is only the spatial and not the affective quality that differentiates gay bars from public toilets. Both allowed for a space outside "compulsory heterosexuality," not only in order to avoid its regulating power, but also to transgress its boundaries and limitations, which define "how one can enter different kinds of social spaces" (Ahmed 145). In the case of public toilets, the scattered LGBTQ community used an existing space in a transgressive way, subverting the socially accepted rules of the space reserved for the most intimate and private bodily functions by using it for socialising, and sharing experiences and ideas that heteronormative paternalism regarded as subversive and dangerous. However, the bars signified the queer community's ability to create its own space. In order to create a chance for solidarity to develop among the homosexual group, who permanently felt the controlling power of the norm, the atmosphere of gay bars was essential. Bars could create "an emotional and psychological safety that comes from being in an area in which one has some sense of belonging or social control" (Myslik 167). In other words, bars provided a protected space for excess, self-liberation and empowerment – everything that the controlling and controlled functional spaces lack.

In a Hungarian cinematic context, the most spectacular scene to display the transgressive experience in bars comes not from the two documentaries analysed here, but from the 1992 Hungarian drama, *Kisses and Scratches*. A cross-dressed duo – featuring the lesbian protagonist dressed as a man doing masculine dance-moves and a gay man wearing feminine clothes and pulling off a submissive, feminine dance choreography – perform on stage the reversal of prescribed gender and sexual norms and playfully embrace the fluidity of sexual and gender categories. The playfulness of their performance reflects the emancipating spatial environment provided in bars and condenses the enjoyment and exuberance of transgression and empowerment. As Nedbálková argues, gay bars could sustain an affective environment that provided the possibility of fully embracing, experiencing and performing queer identities, since "individuals feel relaxed and ... they can shed their masks" (73–74). Liberated from "[t]he perception of vulnerability" going hand in hand with the publicity of toilets, and which "can be related to fear, anxiety and stress" (Myslik 162), different encounters and bonding forces become possible for the emerging queer community. Instead of socialising on a "need-to-know" basis, deeper, more personal connections could develop between members of the group who were not compelled to repress parts of their identity or the way they experience that identity.

Besides the sense of being liberated, it is exactly the realisation of belonging to a community that played a crucial role not only in individual identity formation, but also in the empowerment of the LGBT movement. In Mária Takács's earlier documentary, *Secret Years*, middle-aged lesbian women share how they found self-reconciliation and empowerment through the communities of bars.[8] As one of the participants puts it: "[w]hen you joined a bar, you met not one or two or three people, and you no longer believed that you were the one and only failed genetic trash on a planet with a population of six billion" (29:31, my translation). According to another interviewee, "[i]t was a liberating experience that you were not alone, what is more, that there were many of us, only you hadn't known where to find them" (36:11). Others share memories of long-term relationships that began in the safe, personal, and affectionate milieu of bars. The documentary enhances this sense of belonging by its visual strategies as well. *Secret Years* is mostly structured as a series of talking heads interviews; however, when remembering the first bar-experiences, the viewer is presented with images of various old photographs taken by and belonging to the story-tellers. In other words, the film provides visual information in a personalised manner besides the verbal evocation of memories, which results in a more personal experience. I regard these photographs as ways of connecting the sense of trust and belonging to the space of bars, since their presence is emphatic in these parts of the documentary.

As Vivienne Cass's model of personal identity formation asserts, trust and belonging are necessary components of moving forward in developing a stable and empowered queer identity. However, *Secret Years* also attests that – apart from the importance of the gay bar experience on a personal level – these safe spaces provided shelter and fertile soil for the developing activist community as well. As the personal narratives unfold, we realise the connections between the different interviewees who are friends, (ex-)lovers, colleagues and spokespeople of the community. As such, their personal coming out and the development of the homosexual subculture and political activism are intertwined. For instance, the majority of the founding members of the first Hungarian

---

8 The German feature film, *Coming Out* (dir. Heiner Carow, 1989) presents a good example of individual development, of the formation of homosexual identity on a personal level. The main character, a schoolteacher, at first considers his homosexuality as a defect of character, something to be ashamed of and to be suppressed. Initially he seeks occasional sex partners in shady parks and half-lit toilets, but after a few visits to a gay bar, his secret leaks out, and he is subjected to serious inspection at his workplace. However, instead of breaking under the pressure, he carries out a quiet but powerful protest by keeping silent during a class visited by school inspectors.

lesbian organisation, Labrisz, became acquainted at the most famous location for LGBTQ people, Egyetem Presszó (University Café), described by one interviewee as "The Place" (Takács M. 27:58). Another activist emphasizes that she met several of her co-workers in LGBTQ organizations at her first lesbian party organised at the very same bar. Although their original dream (to buy a whole village and establish a lesbian community) has never been realised, they managed to bring about something similar: a strong, proud and loving community, which has its own legitimate spaces and sense of belonging.

Similar notions are outlined by the participants of *Hot Men* as well, as they share their memories about house parties and first bar experiences. Although these two places differ in terms of establishment, they sustain a similar affective environment that allows for queer subculture to develop. These "unofficial" parties were held at "well-known houses, where 100, 150, 200 or 300 people were invited" (Takács M., *Hot Men* 35:04), while the only place which functioned during state socialism (especially in the 1980s) as a gay bar – even though that was not its original purpose – was the University Café, mentioned in *Secret Years*.[9] Both the house parties and the Café were protected from the heteronormative society and publicity, evoking safety; furthermore, these places were frequented by a numerous queer group, strengthening the sense of belonging. As one of the elderly men recalls: "once you were inside, it was your environment, you were *safe*. It was another world." (47:49, my emphasis). Since "[a]ffective atmospheres capture the emotional feel of place, as well as the store of action-potential, the dispositions and agencies, potentially enactable in that place" (Duff 881–2), the connection between the space of gay bars, individual and subcultural empowerment – the parties were a hotbed for Hungarian drag art – is emphatic. The sense of belonging brought about cultural manifestations of queerness and played a significant role in the formation of the LGBTQ subculture.

Hot Men chooses a different attitude to recreate the atmosphere of bars than *Secret Years*. Although when sharing memories of house parties, archive photographs and video recordings are incorporated into the film, the representation of the University Café differs. Instead of the double mediatisation of archive footage, the filmmakers and participants visit the actual location of the Café, which has been transformed into a bank. As they enter the building, they start identifying the earlier functions of rooms and corners, which inscribes a

---

9 Lacking public places of relaxation and entertainment was a widespread issue of state socialist Budapest: "[l]ess urban diversity was derived from the limited capacity of urban services: for example, there were only a few places to go out and socialize, and existing cafés, terraces or restaurants were shut early at night." (Takács J. 195–6).

queer history on the present-day walls of the bank. Furthermore, the evocation of the previous modes of using the spaces of the café in the narration is parallel to their on-screen movements and actions. For instance, when entering the bank, voice-over informs the viewer that "[i]f you rang the bell – the door was locked – Misike appeared in the doorway to see who it was" (Takács M., *Hot Men* 46:14). Moreover, as the interviewees chat about their memories, and point out the previous locations of certain rooms, archive photographs are incorporated among the present-day images. As a result of these modes of representation, it is not just a queer history, a separated, isolated story of the building that is evoked, but the place itself becomes saturated with queerness.

What is more, they mention a back room which – as it was invisible from the outside[10] – was the centre of events. The scene of queering the bank is transformed with a sudden cut and we can see the participants in a room with black curtains as walls. It is clear that this space is the recreation of the previously mentioned back room; however, it is not certain whether this is the same place or just a staged version. Either way, the filmmakers and participants not only recreate the room itself, but its atmosphere as well, by staging a drag piano performance and the bar also comes to life – with two of the filmmakers dressed up as waitresses. There is a shift from the physical surroundings as attested by the comments: "[t]hose who were lucky enough to get in could feel the magic of the place" (47:14) or "the whole thing had an atmosphere" (47:49).

What is recreated here is not the physical space of that particular back room, but its affective milieu. Here, it is the sense of belonging and togetherness that creates the place itself and not the space that allows for certain affects. This scene, with its spatial ambiguity, represents how the queer community managed to reach a level of empowerment, where the direction of the affect-space relationship and interaction is reversed. It is not the space any more that defines the possible affects, but the sense of belonging creates space. This is a thick space in Edward Casey's term, which is "made in and of affect and practice." Furthermore, "thick places enhance one's sense of meaning and belonging, forging a series of affective and experiential connections in place. ... Thick places, in this sense, are made as much as they are discovered; and they are made in and of affect and practice." (Duff 882, referring to Casey) This room with its black curtains could be anywhere, if the gay community entered it, it would be transformed immediately into a queer space. It is this changed affect-space relationship which makes it possible for the LGBTQ community to

---

10 As the participants give an account of the architectural characteristics of the University Café, it turns out that its walls towards the streets consisted mostly of windows, therefore did not mean protection from outsider gazes.

reclaim the public places as its own. Not by chance, the first gay Pride March in Budapest – as recalled in the film – started its walk through the streets of Budapest from a gay bar: "[t]he venue was the Capella Bar. We set out from there" (Takács M., *Hot Men* 1:23:10). The ability to create a queer space regardless of its location, environment or spatial characteristics is the level of empowerment where the sense of togetherness and trust in the community is strong enough to be taken out proudly onto the streets.

4   Conclusion

As Judit Takács states, referring to Michael Warner, *"what queers want is not just sex –* but a lot more, including a critical reorganization of the use of space" (191, emphasis in the original). As my analysis showed, this critical reorganization is strongly connected to the affective qualities attached to queer spaces. Although both mainstream films and queer documentaries take place in the city of Budapest, it is two different Budapest*s* they create. In mainstream representations, queerness is approached as a bodily, sexual function, which remains locked into the red room of shame. As opposed to that, the two queer documentaries of the state socialist Hungarian queer history depict the creation of places through the positive affective quality of belonging. From the secret queering of existing public (and heteronormatively intended) spaces, such as public toilets, bathhouses, steam houses, the developing queer community step by step creates first its own safe spaces away from the public, which, by providing a cultural experience of queerness, pave the way of empowerment and create an affective milieu of belonging to a community that allows for the open and proud reclaiming of public visibility – Pride Marches. Whereas mainstream cinema cannot supersede a reductionist representation of queer sex in the city, the documentaries depict a queer "sexing" of the city.

Works Cited

Ahmed, Sara. *The Cultural Politics of Emotion*. Edinburgh UP, 2004.
Barcan, Ruth. "Dirty Spaces: Separation, Concealment, and Shame in the Public Toilet." Harvey Molotch and Laura Norén eds. *Toilet: Public Restrooms and the Politics of Sharing*. New York UP, 2010. pp. 25–42.
Cass, Vivienne. "Homosexual Identity Formation: A Theoretical Model." *Journal of Homosexuality*. 4.3 (1979): 219–35.

Duff, Cameron. "On the role of affect and practice in the production of place." *Environment and Planning D: Society and Space*. 28.5 (2010). pp. 881–895.

Esztergályos, Károly. dir. *Férfiakt* (*Men in the Nude*). Centrál, 2006. Film.

Goda, Krisztina. dir. *Kaméleon* (*Chameleon*). Megafilm, 2008.Film.

Hodge, Stephen. "'No Fags Out There': Gay Men, Identity and Suburbia." *Journal of Interdisciplinary Gender Studies*. 1.1 (1995): 41–48.

Johnston, Lynda and Longhurst, Robyn. *Space, Place and Sex: Geographies of Sexualities*. Plymouth: Rowman and Littlefield Publishers, 2010.

Longhurst, Robyn. *Bodies: Exploring Fluid Boundaries*. Routledge, 2001.

Mundruczó, Kornél. dir. *Nincsen nekem vágyam semmi* (*This I Wish and Nothing More*). Coma-Art, 2000.Film.

Munt, Sally R. *Queer Attachments: The Cultural Politics of Shame*. Ashgate, 2007.

Myslik, Wayne D. "Renegotiating the Social/sexual Identities of Places: Gay Communities as Safe Havens or Sites of Resistance?" Nancy Duncan ed. *Body Space: Destabilizing Geographies of Gender and Sexuality*. Routledge, 1996. pp. 155–68.

Nedbálková, Katarina. "The Changing Space of the Gay and Lesbian Community in the Czech Republic." Takács Judit, Roman Kuhar eds. *Beyond the Pink Curtain: Everyday Life of LGBT People in Eastern Europe*. Mirovni Institut, 2007. pp. 67–80.

Peršak, Nina and Vermeulen, Gert. "Faces and Spaces of Prostitution." Nina Peršak and Gert Vermeulen eds. *Reframing Prostitution: From Discourse to Description, from Moralisation to Normalisation?*. Maklu, 2014. pp. 13–24.

Stőhr, Lóránt. *Keserű könnyek: a melodráma a modernitáson túl* (*Bitter Tears: Melodrama After Modernity*). Pompeji, 2013.

Takács, Judit. "Queering Budapest." Jennifer V. Evans and Matt Cook eds. *Queer Cities, Queer Cultures: Europe since 1945*. Bloomsbury Publishing, 2014. pp. 191–210.

Takács, Mária dir. *Eltitkolt évek* (*Secret Years*). Fórum Film Alapítvány: 2009. Film.

Takács, Mária dir. *Meleg férfiak, hideg diktatúrák* (*Hot Men, Cold Dictatorships*). Éclipse Film Kft. 2015.

Weitzer, Ronald. "Sex Work: Paradigms and Policies." Ronald Weitzer ed. *Sex for Sale: Prostitution, Pornography and the Sex Industry*. New York and London: Routledge, 2000. pp. 1–43.

Wharton, Steve. "Bars to Understanding? Depictions of the 'Gay Bar' in Film with Specific Reference to *Coming Out*, *Les Nuits Fauves*, and *Beautiful Thing*." Robin Griffiths ed. *Queer Cinema in Europe*. Bristol: Intellect, 2008. pp. 107–116.

PART 3

Translocality, Border Thinking and Restlessness

∵

CHAPTER 7

"They weren't even there yet and already the City was speaking to them" – The Translocal Experience as Fascination with the City in Toni Morrison's *Jazz*

Imola Bülgözdi

Abstract

This chapter discusses the Southern African American migrant's relationship with the city in Toni Morrison's novel, and demonstrates that the main affect that structures this relationship and the protagonists' response to the change of environment is fascination. Clearly a translocal journey, as the characters' unresolved past is inscribed in their ability to emotionally navigate the city, the novel emphasises their simultaneous situatedness in both locations by their problematic spatial adjustment. Fascination, postulated by Schmid, Sahr and Urry's as a significant element in the construction of new urban subjectivities, is more than aptly highlighted by the affects evoked by various forms of black music, likewise transplanted from a rural environment. The translocal experience and fascination become thus not only building blocks of the new black urban subject, but also that of the black metropolis.

1   Introduction: Fascination

Harlem, 1926: capital of Black America, the nation's largest black city within a city, measuring only 10 km² but home to over 100,000 African Americans, many of whom arrived from the South on the tides of the Great Migration (Fusfeld and Bates 16). The novel's protagonists, Joe and Violet Trace, a country couple from Virginia, arrive in 1906 after a translocal journey from the rural south to Harlem, which, according to Heiko Schmid, Wolf-Dietrich Sahr and John Urry, requires the formation of a new urban sensitivity and cultural emotional competence to cope with the new environment (2). However, it is not only the oft-cited reasons of racism and poverty that motivate Joe and Violet, described by Morrison as nervous, even terrified, to move north. They enter the city dancing to the rhythm of the train: "They weren't even there yet and already the City was speaking to them. They were dancing. And like a million others, chests pounding, tracks controlling their feet, they stared out the windows for first sight of the City that danced with them, proving already how much it *loved* them. Like a million more they could hardly wait to get there and *love it back*" (32, italics mine). Their first experience, while approaching New York, draws attention to the relationship between the individual and the big city, which is to be the main focus of my investigation, since *Jazz* not only describes this nexus but is also organized around an urban experience different from that of the detached, middle-class white flâneur.

Danielle Russell posits the link between individual and place as one of the fundamental elements of identification in Morrison's work, reasoning that place has "both an identity of its own and an impact on the identities of those who experience it. The interaction between person and place can be mutually transforming; a specific site can alter an individual's perspective as effectively as an individual can alter the physical landscape" (Russell 4). Although Russell's discussion of several novels by Morrison leads to the conclusion that "the distortion of identity can accompany a geographic relocation" (42), her analysis of *Jazz* fails to elaborate on the specific nature of how city life affects the newcomers (70–71). The central role of the narrator's comments on the city is hard to miss, yet most critics treat them as subservient to some other major theme in Morrison's writing: the city is "nurturer and agitator as well as *birth-mother* of *Jazz*'s characters" (Chadwick-Joshua 169), a place offering enormous opportunities "for liberal engagement with black individualism and collective group action" (Yeldho and Neelakantan) or "an acting site of reconstruction, of potential and actual articulation of some traumatic traces of the past" (221).

While there is no denying that the urban landscape serves all these purposes and several more, it is my contention that the significance of the very first sentence that mentions the city, positioned right after a brief three-page summary of the novel's events, has been overlooked by the critics cited above. "I'm crazy about this City" (Morrison 7), confesses the narrator, and introduces the concept of fascination with city life as a major affect at work in the novel. What is more, the narrator states that "fascination, permanent and out of control, seizes children, young girls, men of every description, mothers, brides and barfly women, and if they have their way and get to the City, they feel more like themselves, more like the people they always believed they were" (35). It is a type of affect, described by Gregory J. Seigworth and Melissa Gregg as visceral forces other than emotions or conscious knowing, which prompts these people to brave the journey north into the unknown (1), and *Jazz* documents the formation of the protagonists' urban subjectivities as they engage with the city. Seigworth and Gregg succinctly define affect as potential: "a body's *capacity* to affect and to be affected" and the novel explores the full range of possible outcomes from fascination motivating some toward movement, thought and extension to others being left overwhelmed by an uncontrollable world (2).

Morrison's Harlem is definitely not an idealized safe haven, and the characters experience it in far more complex ways than the dichotomous "friend and foe" division formulated by Anne-Marie Paquet-Deyris (222). The novel's narrator is very specific about how the city affects its inhabitants: "the City makes people think they can do what they want and get away with it," and even confirms that the articulation of an urban sensitivity is a necessary survival skill for translocal subjects who need to "figure out how to be welcoming and defensive at the same time. When to love something and when to quit" or they "can end up out of control or controlled by some outside thing" (Morrison 8–9). Morrison here describes affect as potential within the specific context of fascination with the city, which, according to Schmid, Sahr and Urry, is a force that includes not only attraction and the desire for seduction and happiness, but also terror and fear (2–4). The novel very accurately presents both of these aspects of urban fascination: newcomers from the South find themselves in a place "where the sidewalks [...] are wider than the main roads of the towns where they were born" and among people who are in search of "something curious or thrilling" (Morrison 10). Besides jobs, shops, churches and other amenities, the city provides places to "find danger or be it; where you can fight till you drop and smile at the knife when it misses and when it doesn't" (Morrison 11). As sociologist Deborah Stevenson confirms, people are drawn to cities "for work, politics, pleasure, crime and conquest," which provide the contemporary spectacle (108), and indeed, new-comers in *Jazz* stay "to look at their number, hear themselves in an audience" (Morrison 32), construing themselves as part of the urban spectacle, since "it makes you wonderful just to see it" (11). The narrator draws the conclusion that the city affects identity: in this environment, people feel more like themselves, "their stronger, riskier selves" and "they love that part of themselves so much they forget what loving other people was like," becoming infatuated with "the way a person is in the City." Although they are aware of the fact that "the deception was part of it too," country people fall in love with the city the moment they arrive and, according to the novel, this fascination lasts forever (33–34).

The protagonists' Southern past and traumas that are intertwined with the history of the region are, however, indelibly part of their identities, lurking behind the new urban subjectivity they so willingly embraced upon arrival. The novel not only revisits sites of memory, but also elaborates on their effect twenty years after Joe and Violet's first glimpse of New York. This provides the perfect setting for the investigation of translocal geographies, as defined by Katherine Brickell and Ayona Datta, in that Morrison constructs her characters through the experience of "a simultaneous situatedness across different locales" and invites the reader to try and make sense of "the overlapping place-time(s) in migrants' everyday lives" (Brickell and Datta 4). By expanding the concept of translocality, previously almost exclusively subsumed by the notion of transnational migration, to include different scales and locales, such as rural-urban, inter-urban, inter-regional and even local-local journeys, Brickell and Datta provide a framework for the analysis of "the everyday materiality, corporeality and subjectivity of movement" as linked to global forces (5). Harlem, where the black community was established around the turn of the century, became home to over 100,000 migrants from the South, the Caribbean and other areas of New York in the following decades (King 23), whose presence all the more emphasizes that the notion of the local cannot be interpreted in isolation. *Jazz* situates its characters "within a network of spaces, places and scales where identities are negotiated and transformed" (Brickell and Datta 5) as a result of the translocal experience, which, in the novel, very prominently takes the shape of fascination with the city. Therefore, in order to find out more about the affective dimension of translocality, my exploration of the relationship between the individual and the city will be based on the four pivotal dimensions of urban fascination as identified by Schmid, Sahr and Urry: the aesthetic and the emotional dimensions, the context of lived experience, and the networks of power relations.

2   Aesthetics

Schmid, Sahr and Urry, somewhat misleadingly, use this term to denote "the formal construction of a space as social means" and regard fascination as both a stimulus and agitation "for the restructuring of the symbolic dimension of identity, status, and power through the creation of focal points in the urban landscape" (7). This claim is underpinned by research in cultural geography, which posits that the identity and meaning of places are a result of the intersections of culture and geographical context in a specific location, defined by traces, material or non-material, left in place by cultural life. In *Understanding Cultural Geography: Places and Traces*, Jon Anderson argues that "places should be understood as an *ongoing composition of traces*" (6–7), which comprise material objects, traces left by cultural and mundane everyday activities, various ideologies, as well as emotional and psychological traces in people's hearts and minds (12–13). The investigation of traces, which may take the shape of Schmid, Sahr and Urry's focal points in the urban landscape, incorporates inquiry into both cultures and geographies, as well as the identities of both as inextricably linked. Thus, Harlem itself is one such focal point in the 1920s within New York and the United States, since the largest African-American community provides a new basis for identity construction, which is signalled by the appearance of the aforementioned "stronger, riskier selves" in translocal subjects.

3   Emotional Context

In this context, fascination is postulated "as a psychological link that incorporates fetishism, preference, but also dislike, rejection, or fear," establishing a "psychological nexus between the inhabitants of a city and their environment on the edge, between ratio and emotion" (Schmid, Sahr and Urry 7). The narrator provides ample general description of this link, for instance, by detailing the conflicting effect of the City on its inhabitants in spring, when "people notice one another in the road [...]. It's the time of year when the City urges contradiction most, encouraging you to buy street food when you have no appetite at all; giving you a taste for a single room occupied by you alone as well as a craving to share it with someone you passed in the street" (Morrison 118). The novel also implies that most people are not aware of the influence of the city, which makes one do what it wants, while maintaining the illusion of individual freedom and a plethora of choices.

As the affective turn reached the social sciences, the general antipathy to studying emotional connections has abated and the notion of the sense of place has received more attention in the past two decades. According to Anderson, this term refers to "the emotional, experiential, and affective traces that tie humans into particular environments" (35), and is of utmost importance, since "people do not simply locate themselves, they define themselves through a sense of place" (Crang 102). It follows that translocality has a major impact on the geographical context posited as integral to human identity and, what is more, the opposing psychological forces pertaining to fascination further complicate the sense of belonging in translocal subjects, like Violet and Joe Trace, and the other main characters, Dorcas and Alice Manfred.

Violet's experience of Harlem, when she arrives in 1906 as a bold, hardworking and gossipy woman of thirty, is definitely positive: domestic work and hairdressing are a respite from the backbreaking labour she used to do in the fields, and she is quick to seize the opportunities offered by city life, which both Joe and she regard as better than perfect. However, twenty years later she is only a ghost of her former self, she goes practically silent to stop herself from blurting out inappropriate things, and lives in a daze due to the pain caused by her childlessness. Her disorientation, bordering on craziness according to some in the community, also manifests itself in spatial terms: Violet one day sits down in the middle of the street, without stumbling or being pushed, and for about an hour she is unable to understand what people say to her. Her detachment from everyday life is also clear from how she sees her chores and work "in a string of small, well-lit scenes. [...] But she does not see herself doing these things. She sees them being done" (Morrison 22). Where the light fades, however, there is no solid foundation, "in truth, there is no foundation at all, but alleyways, crevices one steps across all the time" and the globe light illuminating the scenes also turns out to be imperfect, with "ill-glued cracks and weak places beyond which is anything" (23). It is these cracks Violet stumbles onto when she is not careful, partly due to the fact that she lost the sense of belonging she had in the South: "I messed up my own life [...]. Before I came North, I made sense and so did the world. We didn't have nothing but we didn't miss it." She confesses she had forgotten she was supposed to live her own life in the city and "ran up and down the streets wishing I was somebody else. [...] White. Light. Young again" (207–8).

Alice Manfred, however, never gave in to the glamour of city life: she brought along from the South the fear planted in her by her parents, which caused the woman of fifty and independent means to feel unsafe in most of New York, confining herself to a shrinking territory in the heart of Harlem, bordered by Eleventh Avenue and Third Avenue, then Park Avenue and nowhere south of 110th Street, with Fifth Avenue being the most fearful place of all, since "that was where white men leaned out of motor cars with folded dollar bills peeping from their palms" and she regularly had to endure the racist behaviour of shopkeepers, passengers on public transport, even white immigrants who did not speak English (Morrison 54). Alice, who resists the glamour of the low-down music that permeates Harlem, regarding it as incompatible with her old-fashioned morality, blames even the race riots on the music that makes one "do unwise disorderly things. Just hearing it was like violating the law" (58).

Much has been said concerning the role of music in the novel in terms of the jazz aesthetic present both in the narrative structure and the language (see Grandt), or the blues persona enacted by Dorcas (see Boutry) but less consideration has been given to music as a representation of affect. Seigworth and Gregg also construe affect as an impersonal force, as

> regimes of expressivity that are tied much more to ... diffusions of feeling/passions – often including atmospheres of sociality, crowd behaviours, contagions of feeling, matters of belonging ... and a range of postcolonial, hybridized, and migrant voices that forcefully question the privilege

and stability of individualized actants possessing self-derived agency and solely private emotions within a scene or environment. (8)

Jazz describes multiple instances of music affecting not only individuals, but also crowds, and general mood surpassing individual emotion. For instance, "the right tune whistled in a doorway or lifting up from the circles and grooves of a record can change the weather. From freezing to hot to cool" (Morrison 51), eliciting reactions very similar to the responses given to the influence exuded by and clearly attributed to the city by the narrator. Music operates through creating the same illusion as the city: dancers are described as believing they know how they are going to dance, but it is the music that tricks them into believing they are in control (65). This confirms, on the one hand, the role of music as an emotional gauge for the city and, on the other hand, also renders more tangible the inhabitants' effect on the overall affective atmosphere, as it is them who provide the all-permeating music, playing "in window frames, or clustered on rooftops, in alleyways, on stoops and in the apartments of relatives" (56).

In *Who Set You Flowin'? The African-American Migration Narrative*, Farah Jasmine Griffin is right to assert that black jazz defines the city and the era, but her claim that it is also a source of constructing black urban subjectivity, as jazz embodies and gives voice to the African-American experience (191), is contested by Peter Brooker based on Morrison's essays "Rootedness: The Ancestor as Foundation" and "City Limits, Village Values." Morrison believes that the art form African-Americans could resort to during conflicts used to be music, but it has lost the power to heal due to the fact that it is no longer exclusively played by black people, having been integrated into contemporary music everywhere. "Black music – jazz – may have misled us into thinking of black people as essentially urban types" (Morrison qtd in Brooker 202), states Morrison, and Brooker concludes that blues, the rural form of black music, has lost its healing, story-telling power. He claims that "black migrants, such as those in *Jazz*, therefore, are thought to have severed a vital connection with the village neighbourhood, especially the wisdom of its elders. They do not belong 'essentially' in the city. And they do not have a music to express their condition" (Brooker 202). It follows that the ever-present jazz music in the novel also highlights the characters' translocal experience and emotional journey, from rural blues to thrilling jazz that also pumps desire like the city to which it is inextricably linked.

The only type of music in the city that Alice Manfred experiences as positive is the sound of drums during the Silent Protest Parade of July 28, 1917, organized in response to the race riots in East St. Louis, where her sister and brother-in-law were killed, leaving their daughter, 9-year-old Dorcas in her keeping. Marcy S. Sacks interprets the events as the black community of Harlem demanding "its rightful place within the American Republic generally and the city specifically" (195) in a very visible location, Fifth Avenue, which Alice regards as the scariest place of all. For Sacks, the disciplined order and patriarchal arrangement of the parade signals the challenging of discrimination and stereotyping African Americans suffered (195), while Alice experiences the sound of drums "like a rope cast for rescue" (Morrison 53), gathering and connecting her with Dorcas, her dead sister, the frozen black faces in the parade and the watchers. The drums are not only capable of expressing what the marchers or the banners cannot, but create "an all-embracing rope of fellowship, discipline and transcendence" (58) that Alice continues to use to anchor herself in a hostile environment. What is more, she discerns that the music affects people just the same way as the city does according to the narrator, underscoring the role of music as a representation of urban fascination:

> Alice Manfred swore she heard a complicated anger in it; something hostile that disguised itself as flourish and roaring seduction. But the part she hated most was its appetite. Its longing for the bash, the slit; a kind of careless hunger for a fight or a red ruby stickpin for a tie – either would do. It faked happiness, faked welcome [...], this juke joint, barrel hooch, tonk house, music.
> MORRISON 59

Jazz is the music of the City and it possesses both the positive and negative aspects of fascination, and as much as she would like to, Alice realizes she cannot dismiss the music she deeply despises, since underneath the glamour she can hear the drums of the Fifth Avenue protest, which speak of all the hardships and injustice African-Americans tried to leave behind in vain when coming north.

Another reason why jazz can be interpreted as mirroring the characters' fascination with the city is the translocal experience at the heart of both, which connection is explored in the novel through Dorcas's relationship to music. She watched the parade, one of her earliest memories after her arrival from East St. Louis, as a kind of funeral parade for her mother and father and remembers the drums as "a start of something she looked to complete," a beginning she imagines as a burning wood chip from her parents' house that entered her throat, while watching her mother burn to death. It "smoked and glowed there" and during the parade "the bright wood chip sank further and further down until it lodged comfortably somewhere below her navel [...] and the drums assured her that the glow would never leave her" (Morrison 60–61). Dorcas's memory of her Southern childhood trauma that she comes to associate with the drums, along with her ensuing boldness and refusal to "shed a tear about anything" (212) is the personal dimension of the collective anger Alice feels boiling under the seduction of what she calls the low-down music. The music, just like the city, is perceived and interpreted through memories of a Southern past, thereby reinforcing the affective dimension of translocality.

4   Lived Experience

This aspect is closely linked to the emotional context of fascination discussed in the previous section and is defined as "a set of cognitive or performative acts that conquer and/or lose, or at least occupy, portions of the urban space as an environment for survival, self-fulfilment and self-expression" (Schmid, Sahr and Urry 7). The narrator of *Jazz* not only emphasizes the need for new cognitive capacities to cope with city life, but also draws the reader's attention to the bodily felt embeddedness in the urban environment, in a city, which "is there to back and frame you no matter what you do" (Morrison 8). The co-ingredience of people and places theorized by cultural geography (Anderson 56) renders physical embeddedness a constitutive element of making place, and, consequently, a prerequisite for the formation of the sense of place of the individual or its opposite, the feeling of being out-of-place. As a poor African American couple arriving from the South with a single suitcase, Joe and Violet had to work hard to carve out their own place in Harlem, slowly saving enough money to move from the Tenderloin, the red-light district, via Little Africa in Manhattan, to Harlem, where by the early 1920s the majority of residences were black, though the area remained commercially and residentially under white control. Violet and Joe witnessed as Harlem "rapidly transformed from a scattering of black residences in a white neighbourhood to a thriving black neighbourhood and eventually the cultural and intellectual epicentre of black America" (King 23), and had to fight light-skinned African-American renters for the apartment on Lenox Avenue, a prime location, as if they were whites.

Despite the fact that the apartment's windows give on the inner courtyard without much access to sunlight, Joe likens the buildings to castles in pictures, and the couple claims the place as their own, not only by filling the rooms with birds and plants, but also by arranging the furnishings in a way that "suits the habits of the body, the way a person walks from one room to another without bumping into anything, and what he wants to do when he sits down" (Morrison 12). The apartment reflects that they manage to shape the urban environment on a microscale, not following the principles of the *Modern Homemaker*, as pointed out by the narrator, but creating a cosy, comfortable place where "everything is put where a person would like to have it, or would use or need it" (12). By the time the narrative begins, however, this apartment has ceased to be a cherished home and has become a dark and haunted place instead, as all life is gone: Joe is depressed and cries all day, Violet, dubbed "Violent" after the funeral, is silent and has put the birds out in the January cold, and the shells and pretty stones on the mantelpiece have been replaced by a ghost: "the picture of Dorcas Manfred [...] in a silver frame waking them up all night long" (13).

Though Dorcas, Joe's young lover, dies at his hands, it is not only her ghost that haunts the apartment: she also comes to embody Joe and Violet's traumatic Southern past. Joe, once a skilled woodsman, tracks Dorcas down in the city the way he had tracked his mother, Wild, in the woods of Virginia in a futile attempt to find out something about his parentage. For Violet, the photo of the hated rival, whom she tried to disfigure at the funeral, turns into the face of one of her miscarried babies, who did not survive "mammymade poisons and mammy's urgent fists" (Morrison 109). The three members of the love triangle share a profound lack, the memories of dead or unmotherly mothers and homes destroyed by racism, which continue to inform their daily existence. The translocal experience of the individual translates into a postmodern use of the uncanny, as argued by Petra Eckhard, who posits the uncanny in *Chronotopes of the Uncanny: Time and Space in Postmodern New York Novels* as "a literary tool that [...] articulates subjective post-traumatic experiences, which, however, can also point to larger, national memory discourses" (20). It is her contention that the main characters of the two novels she analyses – *Jazz* and Paul Auster's *City of Glass* – are unable to read and make sense of the ambiguous signs of the city, which provides a cultural contact-zone that renders otherness apparent in the subject's present social reality due to its contrast with a subjective past (62–64), in this case all the more emphatic due to the translocal journey.

Eckhard, who regards the uncanny as a product of spatial practice in the postmodern city, states that Morrison presents cognitive maps of Harlem, and concludes that these "spatial practices are acted out as a translation of subjective obsessions" in the city, which she believes to be depicted and perceived as a non-place, as theorised by Marc Augé: "a space of ongoing transit and/or transition, lacking myth, history, or identity" (151–52). In my view, Eckhard's postulation of the city as a non-place for the characters of *Jazz* is too radical in the light of Augé's definition:

> If a place can be defined as relational, historical and concerned with identity, then a space which cannot be defined as relational, or historical, or concerned with identity will be a non-place. [...] supermodernity produces non-places, meaning spaces which are not themselves anthropological places and which, unlike Baudelairean modernity, do not integrate the earlier places: instead these are listed, classified, promoted to the status of 'places of memory', and assigned to a circumscribed and specific position.
>
> AUGÉ 77–78

On the other hand, Augé also accentuates that neither place nor non-place exists in pure form, and the two should be conceived as opposed polarities forming palimpsests which provide the base for the ongoing process of identity formation (78–79). Thus, the way the main characters experience and navigate the city is more in accordance with a palimpsestic composition of places and non-places, derived both from the present and their Southern past. They do not live in the City in a void, like travelers in transit, postulated by Augé as the archetype of the non-place (86), and the process of recovery which starts with Violet's visits to Alice and is later facilitated by Felice, Dorcas's friend, clearly shows that identity negotiation is taking place.

5 Power Structures and Forms of Governance

What makes identity construction and re-negotiation problematic for the translocal subject in the city is the fact that fascination, having become a powerful factor structuring daily life experiences, came to condition social relations "through new *power structures and forms of governance*" (Schmid, Sahr and Urry 7). While these characters have some control over private places, like flats, they often lack agency in public, since "power relations are central to the question of public space as an aesthetic and emotional landscape" that translocal subjects need to navigate (7). This fourth aspect of fascination, considered in terms of networks of power relations, also becomes a form of urban structuring and binding, argue Schmid, Sahr and Urry, a statement in agreement with cultural geography's tenet that it is power relations that order and border space differently for different groups and individuals (Anderson 75–80). Violet and Joe's train journey North is very much affected by the spatial ordering required by segregation, and is emphasized in the novel by the disappearance of the physical borders after crossing the Mason-Dixon Line, such as the removal of the curtains dividing the black and white sections of the dining car. However, the psychological and cultural borders that prevent white women from sitting next to black ones on public transport are deeply ingrained in the North, as well. Therefore, it is not surprising that Harlem, despite being the largest African-American community, does not provide safety in numbers, as attested by the severe beating Joe endures as a bystander during a 1917 riot.

Besides racially motivated violence which aims to control City space, *Jazz* also exposes the gendered violence women are subject to in the urban environment. Sixteen-year-old Dorcas's death at the hands of Joe, her ex-lover, makes her aunt, Alice face the ubiquity of the danger she has been dreading all her life. Alice tried to protect her niece by prohibiting makeup, high heels and making her wear childish clothes, as well as by spatial camouflage: she "taught her how to crawl along the walls of buildings, disappear into doorways, cut across corners in choked traffic – how to do anything, move anywhere to avoid a whiteboy over the age of eleven" (Morrison 55). After Dorcas's death, Alice comes to realize that the newspapers are full of reports of violence against black women, perpetrated by men both black and white. Although Alice has surrendered the streets, she has to admit the victims were not defenseless: "black women were armed; black women were dangerous and the less money they had the deadlier the weapon they chose," resorting to razors and packets of lye (77). In the contest for public space, only very religious women or the very wealthy remained unarmed besides the ones who were attached to armed men or found protection in various clubs, societies and sisterhoods. "Any other kind of unarmed black woman in 1926 was silent or crazy or dead" (78), like herself, Violet, and Dorcas, respectively. It was not only black men, but also black women, for the majority of whom working outside the home has always been a necessity, who were asserting their right to the city as public space.

At the same time, *Jazz* also challenges the masculinist reason and feminized emotion dichotomy through the figure of middle-aged Joe, who suffers on silent and distant Violet's side, and tries to reconcile himself as best he can to the fact that "old age would be not remembering what things felt like" (Morrison 29). Besides sexual pleasure, he finds someone he can open up to in Dorcas, not only telling her very personal things he has never talked about before, but things he has not even admitted to himself (123). When she quits him, he kills her in an attempt to preserve this feeling, even though he knows the memories will fade. After the murder, Joe is crippled by his emotions: a grown man crying openly, "a strange sight you hardly ever see" (118) sitting around the flat month after month, whose healing process starts likewise by reconnecting with Violet and his Southern, traumatic past: "a lot of the time ... they stay home figuring things out, telling each other ... little personal stories" (223).

6   Conclusion

It was this new urban environment that African-American translocal subjects had to make their own, inevitably challenging existing power structures on various levels, as "the struggle for place is [...] both the manifestation of cultural struggle and the medium of that struggle, it is in place that power is constituted and played out" (Anderson 76). By operating in all four dimensions of fascination, *Jazz* links collective social structures to individual experience and the new urban self, justifying Schmid, Sahr and Urry's claim that fascination is a prime element in the border zone between urban structures and new subjectivities (12). The simultaneous exploration of both the city and the translocal subject through the lens of fascination reveals that the novel is not only structured around a specifically urban form of affective geography, but also encompasses affects that lead "far beyond ... the conception of the rational subject" (Schmid, Sahr, and Urry 5), which is analogous to the effect jazz has both on individuals and crowds.

By portraying fascination with the city both in terms of succumbing to its glamour, and withdrawing from its temptations and asserting its ubiquitous and inescapable nature, Morrison describes an affective relation that transcends gendered and public/private boundaries and fosters transpersonal connections. The novel presents the affective geography of translocal subjects in the 1920s, an age generally characterized by increased mobility, as a major site of identity construction, which results in new urban subjectivities intertwined with the creation of the black metropolis.

Works Cited

Anderson, Jon. *Understanding Cultural Geography: Places and Traces*. London and New York: Routledge, 2015.

Augé, Marc. *Non-places: Introduction to an Anthropology of Supermodernity*. Transl. John Howe. London and New York: Verso, 1995.

Boutry, Katherine. "Black and Blue: The Female Body of Blues Writing in Jean Toomer, Toni Morrison, and Gayl Jones" in *Black Orpheus: Music in African American Fiction from the Harlem Renaissance to Toni Morrison*, edited by Saadi A. Simawe, pp. 91–118. New York: Garland, 2000.

Brickell, Katherine and Ayona Datta. "Introduction: Translocal Geographies." In *Translocal Geographies: Spaces, Places, Connections*, edited by Katherine Brickell and Ayona Datta, 3–20. Farnham: Ashgate, 2011.

Brooker, Peter. *New York Fictions: Modernity, Postmodernism, The New Modern*. London and New York: Longman, 1996.

Chadwick-Joshua, Jocelyn. "Metonymy and Synecdoche: The Rhetoric of the City in Toni Morrison's *Jazz*." In *The City in African-American Literature*, edited by Yoshinob Hakutani and Robert Butler, 168–180. London and Toronto: Associated U Presses, 1995.

Crang, Mike. *Cultural Geography*. London and New York: Routledge, 1998.

Eckhard, Petra. *Chronotopes of the Uncanny: Time and Space in Postmodern New York Novels, Paul Auster's City of Glass and Toni Morrison's Jazz*. N.p.: Transcript, 2011.

Fusfeld, Daniel R. and Timothy Bates. *The Political Economy of the Urban Ghetto*. Carbondale and Edwardsville: Southern Illinois UP, 1984.

Grandt, Jurgen E. "Kinds of Blue: Toni Morrison, Hans Janowitz, and the Jazz Aesthetic." *African American Review* 38, no. 2 (2004): 303–322.

Griffin, Farah J. *Who Set You Flowin'? The African-American Migration Narrative*. New York: Oxford UP, 1996.

King, Shannon. *Whose Harlem Is This, Anyway? Community Politics and Grassroots Activism during the New Negro Era*. New York: New York UP, 2015.

Morrison, Toni. *Jazz*. London: Vintage, 2001.

Paquet-Deyris, Anne-Marie. "Toni Morrison's *Jazz* and the City." *African American Review* 35, no. 2 (2001): 219–231.

Russell, Danielle. *Between the Angle and the Curve – Mapping Gender, Race, Space, and Identity in Willa Cather and Toni Morrison*. New York and London: Routledge, 2006.

Sacks, Marcy S. *Before Harlem: The Black Experience in New York City before World War I*. Philadelphia: U of Pennsylvania P, 2006.

Schmid, Heiko, Wolf-Dietrich Sahr and John Urry. "Cities and Fascination: Beyond the Surplus of Meaning." In *Cities and Fascination: Beyond the Surplus of Meaning*, edited by Heiko Schmid, Wolf-Dietrich Sahr and John Urry, 1–13. Farnham: Ashgate, 2011.

Seigworth, Gregory J. and Melissa Gregg. "An Inventory of Shimmers." In *The Affect Theory Reader*, edited by Melissa Gregg and Gregory J. Seigworth, 1–25. Durham and London: Duke UP, 2010.

Stevenson, Deborah. *Cities and Urban Cultures*. Philadelphia: Open UP, 2003.

Thien, Deborah. "After or Beyond Feeling? A Consideration of Affect and Emotion in Geography." *Area* 37, no. 4 (2005): 450–456.

Yeldho, Joe V. and G. Neelakantan. "Toni Morrison's Depiction of the City in *Jazz*." *Notes on Contemporary Literature* 36, no. 1 (2006): n.p.

CHAPTER 8

"I again put on my veil" – Autobiographical Narrative, Feminism, and the Emergence of Border Thinking in Marjane Satrapi's *Persepolis* Books

Márta Kőrösi

Abstract

This chapter discusses Marjane Satrapi's *Persepolis* in terms of Walter Mignolo's concept of "border thinking," a kind of "historical thinking" that exposes a "double critique" of multiple geographical-cultural locations. While the actualization of border thinking may be examined in various aspects of Satrapi's text, the focus is laid on how *Persepolis* – both as a product of a specific visual-verbal medium and as an autobiographical story – presents a series of literal and metaphorical/symbolic border-crossings that create, as Joseph Darda puts it, tensions, "fissures," holes and interruptions which may engage the reader in an affective and ethical reconsideration of societal norms. The type of border thinking and identification that emerges in Satrapi's graphic novel, accentuated by the characteristic features of the graphic form, constitutes her work as a site of ideological contestation that provides a contemporary transcultural feminism of dislocation.

1   Introduction

Marjane Satrapi's graphic autobiographies, *Persepolis: The Story of a Childhood* (2000) and *Persepolis 2: The Story of a Return* (2001) are narratives that engage with what Walter Mignolo calls "border thinking," a kind of historically generated thinking that exposes a "double critique" of multiple geographical-cultural locations (66–7). In the *Persepolis* books, border thinking emerges by virtue of a productive interplay between formal and thematic elements, that is, the specificities of the graphic genre and the series of border crossings the narrator experiences in the course of her journeys. Satrapi's autobiographical narrator, Marji, faces political and religious oppression in her native country, Iran, and when she travels to Europe as a teenager, she has to deal with rejection and contempt because of her cultural and ethnic origin. As a result of her sense of dislocation in both places, Satrapi's autobiographical "I" develops a kind of "border subjectivity," which is generated both by Iran and Europe but is tied to neither place. She is in an imaginary borderland where a new, non-territorial epistemology may be born because it cannot be exclusively derived from either of the geographically and nationally "fixed" territories Marjane has resided in. Thus, Satrapi's graphic autobiography is not only a narrative of transnational migrant experience shaped by a sense of spatial and geopolitical difference, dislocation, and transience but also an alternative to hegemonic epistemology described by Mignolo as "a celebration of the possession of true knowledge, an Occidental achievement of universal value" (3).

Marjane's border epistemology develops in the markedly visual, iconic genre of the graphic novel, which becomes a medium for the representation of the dynamics of ideological, political, and affective contradictions the *Persepolis* books operate with, as they narrate Marji's travels between Tehran, Iran and Vienna, Austria (and eventually Strasbourg, France). These contradictions gradually increase not only her sense of alienation in both Tehran and Vienna but also her critical attitude, especially because in both locations she experiences gender-based discrimination as it intersects with political, religious and ethnic oppression. The result of this dynamics of contradictions is a unique epistemology of transcultural feminist dislocation, which can be identified as a specific form of border thinking to the extent that it offers a double critique of patriarchal regimes both in the Islamic state of Iran and Western Europe.

Due to the interdependence between graphic form and critical content in Satrapi's autobiographical narrative, I find it useful to examine her double critique by focusing on places in the two texts where the formal dis-closures of the visual-verbal medium emphasize how a change in Marjane's geographical-cultural situatedness modifies her perception, epistemology, and sense of identity, and how these modifications affect the role and interpretation of such ideologically loaded signifiers as the veil or the mythical land of Persepolis. The narrative of Marjane's experiences featuring these elements explores the intersections of gender, class, ethnicity, and location in terms of the East-West divide, but this binary is gradually overcome to make space for an emergent border subjectivity, or, in Gloria Anzaldúa's terms referring to *mestiza* consciousness, "a third element which is greater than the sum of its severed parts" (101–2). Thus, in what follows I will concentrate on a selection of scenes in which emphasis is placed on some cultural-ideological-geographical divide or where these divides are transgressed by virtue of Marjane's experiences related to her movement across borders. But before dealing with these scenes in detail, some useful aspects relevant to the reading of comic books in general must be discussed, since the medium of the graphic novel has a constitutive role in the development of the narrator's border subjectivity and her imaginary borderland.

2   The Gutter as a Tool of Border Epistemology

What makes the reading of comics unique, in comparison with traditional written texts of prose or poetry, is that comics present a mixture of words and images that must be interpreted simultaneously, with respect to each other, and as such, they constantly emphasize the physicality and spatiality of the text. Thus, a comic book, with its conscious formalism, entails an interpretive journey that constantly switches between two kinds of signification, and the tension between word and image is an integral element of meaning-making. Both Hillary Chute ("Comics as Literature?") and Joseph Darda point out the importance of this tension, emphasizing that comic books do not simply juxtapose the verbal and the visual, or use one to illustrate the other, but are rather "prone to present the two nonsynchronously," since the reader "not only fills in the gaps between panels but also works with the often disjunctive back-and-forth of reading and looking for meaning" (Chute, "The Texture of Retracing" 452). That is why, as Darda asserts, the comic form is "an ideal space for interrogating epistemological assumptions and placing extratextual 'demands' on the reader" (32). Consequently, the recent criticism of comics in general, and graphic memoirs in particular, is concerned with the instabilities, the disjunctures between word and image, which are connected with the conflicts inherent in the present narration of a past self (32), in which autobiographical narratives typically invest.

To understand how these instabilities and disjunctures are formulated in comics, it is worthwhile, as Darda suggests, to look at two important concepts in the analysis of comics: the icon and the gutter. Based on cartoonist and comics theorist Scott McCloud's pioneering work, Darda describes the icon in the context of the graphic novel simply as a representation of an object, the abstraction of which may vary to a great extent depending on the type of graphic work in which it features (33). The gutter, which is the liminal space between panels the readers are expected to close by way of interpretation (33), is the more intriguing of the two concepts, and especially appropriate for the purposes of analyzing Satrapi's *Persepolis* in terms of border thinking. Darda also emphasizes that gutters make the reading of comics fractured and discontinuous and that readers are made to turn this discontinuity into a continuous reading experience. He also adds that one of the most compelling questions in the recent criticism of comics is what happens when the gutter does not close

(33), that is, when this discontinuity is the fundamental experience of reading a comic book.

In the discussion of Satrapi's *Persepolis* books, the critical analysis of the gutter as a formal-textual element that produces a discontinuous reading experience may fruitfully be linked to the formation of border subjectivity and epistemology. Satrapi makes a conscious use of the gutter to generate critical meaning by making juxtapositions between conflicting aspects of life, different geographical locations, ideologies, feelings, and interpretations, and as a result of the medium's visual specificity, these juxtapositions are always spatially contextualized. For example, at the very beginning, she uses the gutter to establish both her autobiographical character as a unique individual (who is nevertheless veiled in the same fashion as the other girls in her class) as well as her situation as an outsider, "sitting on the far left" in the second picture, thus the readers cannot even see her (3, figure 8.1).

The critical importance of these first two panels in terms of establishing and destabilizing the autobiographical "I" in the graphic narrative form of *Persepolis* has been emphasized (Chute, "The Texture of Retracing," Chaney, Darda). By presenting two "copies" of Marji in conceptual interplay, in a "structural threading of absence and presence" (Chute, "The Texture of Retracing" 94), Satrapi exposes and refutes "the historical practice of erasure" (Darda 38). I would like to link this critical gesture to the development of Marjane's border position, the very first step of which is manifest in the literal fragmentation of the ten-year-old "I" right at the beginning of the autobiographical narrative. Being (non-)represented on the border (margin) in the second frame puts Marji into a liminal position, which foreshadows not only her transnational

FIGURE 8.1   Satrapi in a liminal position
SOURCE: SATRAPI, *PERSEPOLIS* 3

journeys but also the development of her border identity. The importance of this initial position is realized only after the reader has perused the story of Marji's border-crossings, which induces the need to "return for meaning" to the beginning after reading the whole story, thereby bridging the gap between the first and the last panels of the graphic autobiography and retrospectively comprehending the significance of the narrator's initial "self-erasure."

The panels of the first page establish Marjane's position in the story as the main character and set the temporal and geographical frame for the narrative. The frames that immediately follow Marji's introduction (figure 8.2) complicate the narratee's initial liminal position by specifying the historical event, which has a range of effects on the everyday life of the people in 1980s Iran. However, the epistemological connections between the political (national and religious) and the personal, that is, the Islamic Revolution of 1979 and the compulsory wearing of the veil, and their effects on the life of Marji and her community, must be made in the reader's imagination, again by way of "suturing the gap" (Chaney 28, Darda 33) created by the gutter in-between the two frames.

Thus, in Satrapi's *petit histoire*, the panels and the gutters together create an alternative historical epistemology in which the autobiographical subject's *Künstlerroman* is to be interpreted. In this "border epistemology," or rather, "gutter epistemology," Iran's national history and Marjane's personal experience of growing up in a city of conflict and terror are juxtaposed in the margin, literally "in the gutter," often creating a surprising comic effect by jumping from the realm of the tragically sublime to the ordinary, funny, or absurd. For example, when later in the first *Persepolis* book, Marji tries to smoke a cigarette

FIGURE 8.2 The effect of the Islamic Revolution
SOURCE: SATRAPI, *PERSEPOLIS* 3

to rebel against her mother's "dictatorship" (117), the terror the Islamic regime has inflicted on its opposers and Marji's development into adolescence are juxtaposed in a self-ironic way (figure 8.3). It can also be seen in these six panels how the gutters function to create interpretive links both between the individual frames within each scene (the executions and the smoking, respectively) and between the two scenes, contextualizing Marji's personal "rebellion" in terms of political opposition.

This technique of embedding "grand" historical events into the narrative of the autobiographical subject's development within the framework of the graphic genre provides a powerful and informative representation of history in general and state oppression in particular. In *Persepolis*, Satrapi shows the effects of the Islamic Republic on the nation, not necessarily by presenting what "the people" in general (may) feel or think but what material, cognitive, and affective effects the political events have on Marji, her family, and friends.

FIGURE 8.3 Adolescence
SOURCE: SATRAPI, *PERSEPOLIS* 117

Marji's life story gains a more general relevance by way of inserting essential elements into the plot that bear import on the narratee's everyday life, while they also serve as key metaphors with ideological and historical significance. In the case of the veil, for example, Satrapi draws in simple pictures of what school was like before the revolution of 1979 and what it was like in 1980, what the kids looked like, how they behaved, what they could and could not learn, and how they were grouped. The methods of juxtaposing panels (of past and present, for instance) or presenting images that contradict the verbal information in the speech bubbles make readers active participants in the process of making meaning by compelling them to search for narrative links between the verbal and visual elements, and also to remain affectively involved in the reading process as they follow Marji's life story.

Making the child (and later adolescent) Marjane the focalizer and the main consciousness of the book, from whose point of view most of the events are narrated, serves to show how pointless and unintelligible "grand history" may be, not only for kids but for adults, as well. Thus, the gutters, which provide cognitive spaces for the readers to make sense of cause-and-effect links between events and consequences both on the historical and the personal level, have a vital role in the interpretation of Marji's character as an "unreliable" narrative persona, while they also provide a tool to understand and critically evaluate the historical context of her story. As Chute explains, this interpretive work is largely the result of how the graphic narrative form works in *Persepolis*: Satrapi repeatedly uses the gutter to stress the gap between the knowledge (and imagination) of the reader and that of Marji, which creates a tension that is "structural to pictorially depicting trauma in a visual idiom shaped by the discursive scaffolding of a child" ("The Texture of Retracing" 100). I also argue that the graphic form largely defines Marjane's border subjectivity and epistemology in *Persepolis*, since the tension between the traumatic and horrifying events and the stylized nature of their presentation, as well as the visual and verbal representation of the gap between the narratee's and the narrator's understanding of the events, are constitutive of Marjane's ideological development and ensuing double critique.

3 Marjane's Feminism

The feminist ideology of the *Persepolis* books naturally unfolds within Marjane's personalized historical context, as well. Her rebellious character, which is gradually channeled into feminism, largely stems from her mother's and grandmother's "matriarchal inheritance." Marji's mother is already presented as a rebel in the first chapter of *Persepolis* by way of a photo taken by a German journalist at one of the demonstrations in Iran and picked up by "all the European newspapers" (5). Marjane's middle-class, intellectual, secular, and liberal family background is thus established quite early in the story, which partly explains how and why she can develop a border subjectivity later on. The mother's role in the revolution, her modern views and feminist readings (Simone de Beauvoir, for instance), combined with the family background, are key elements in the story of *Persepolis* both because they inevitably lead Marjane to feminism and also because they provide her with both motivation and means to leave and return to Iran, and then leave again, whenever her life takes a critical turn. Marjane's and her mother's feminism, however, is not just the outcome of reading Simone de Beauvoir and other critical thinkers: it is also (and perhaps more importantly) a reaction to the fundamentalist regime's oppression of women in the name of Islam, as thematized not only in the *Persepolis* books but also in *Embroideries* (2003), another graphic novel by Satrapi. As such, Marjane's feminism develops not only (or not primarily) out of western ideology derived from her readings but also as a reaction to her specific local historical and social context, which changes several times in the course of the story. As a result, her feminism comes to be defined by a transnational border epistemology that endows her with a critical position from which both eastern and western regimes can be seen.

As a focal point of this double critique, the conflicting views and discourses about the veil[1] – on the one hand, fundamentalist, and on the other, "western

---

1 Haleh Afshar argues in her book *Islam and Feminisms: An Iranian Case-Study* (1998) that "[a]lmost two decades after the Islamic revolution, [...] the only visible sign of Islamification that remains in Iran today is the presence of veiled women (Omid 1996) and substantially lower standards of living (Karshenas 1996)" (197). She goes on to state that women "have become the major emblem of Islamification and their dress code the most significant identifier of revolutionary success" (197). No wonder the veil becomes a central element not only in Satrapi's *Persepolis* but in discourses on Islam all around the world. Thus, for the Islamic government, it becomes crucial to insist on the veil and women's *hijab paziri* (acceptance of the veil), since it shows that democracy is indeed viable on Islamist grounds. At the same time, the nation state wishes to protect itself from "westoxification" (Afshar 209), which is supported by *bad hijabi*, poor veiling, the non-acceptance of Islamist dress codes (206). All of this is justified on religious grounds, when proponents of the veil refer to verses from the Koran to show that the foundation of Islamic law orders women to "cast down their looks and guard their private parts" and "not display their ornaments" (Koran XXIV: 31, quoted in Afshar 198). There are conflicting views about the necessity of the veil: for one thing, it is supposed "to cover lasciviousness, which is attributed to women [...] and protect men and morality" (Afshar 199), for another, it is meant to honor and protect women "by showing their modesty" (199). In this rhetoric of protection, a marked binary is set up between Iranian and western women: "Iranian women are warned that failure to be properly veiled would make them into

and enlightened" – are both criticized in *Persepolis*. Marjane understands early in her childhood the literal and symbolic significance of the veil in the formation of her Iranian identity, as well as its importance as a site of contestation for women in her country. The young Marjane also presents an internal conflict concerning *hijab*: "I really didn't know what to think about the veil. Deep down I was very religious but as a family we were very modern and avantgarde" (6). This personal conflict is effectively represented in the panel below with another self-portrait of Marji, whose torso is divided in the middle, having thus two "sides" to her character, one modern and rational, the other traditional and religious (figure 8.4). This portrait may also be seen as an icon that literally inscribes Marjane's border position onto her body.

Throughout the two books the veil remains a significant ideological marker: for example, in *Persepolis*, when Marjane's mother is assaulted in the street by "two bearded guys," that is, "two fundamentalist bastards," because she is not wearing a veil (74); when Marjane explains how people dress quickly becomes "an ideological sign" (75); and more significantly in *Persepolis 2*, after she returns to Iran to study fine arts and graphic design in Tehran, when she publicly criticizes the sexism that permeates the "protectionist" ideology behind *hijab* (143). Her criticism of this ideology, more exactly, that the veil is supposed "to cover lasciviousness, which is attributed to women […] and protect men and morality" (Afshar 199), is most emphatically presented in an "absurd situation" in *Persepolis 2* when she is running to catch the bus and is stopped by two policemen, who tell her that when she runs, her "behind makes movements that are … how do you say … obscene!" (147). She replies with such a surprisingly big yell that the policemen are too stunned to arrest her. This scene also exemplifies how the narrator's rebellious and critical attitude manifests both on the level of the story and that of political commentary: the easily accessible graphic frames, which depict an everyday episode in Marjane's life, provide political critique by way of recalling and reflecting on the scene in a retrospective autobiographical narrative mode.

---

sex objects" (200) much in the same way as "women in the West" have become the objects (victims) of male desire (201). On "the other side," that is, according to mainstream western beliefs, one of the most visible signs of women's oppression in Islam is the veil; thus, casting it off would certainly mean a large step towards women's liberation in Islamist countries. Therefore, the veil becomes an overburdened symbol of femininity in the context of the Islamic Republic, while veiled women are abstractions standing in for the nation state. In this chain of signification, women's activism, which, as Hamid Dabashi argues in *Iran: A People Interrupted* (2007), was a crucial and spectacular part of the revolution (152), is downplayed and neglected in its aftermath.

FIGURE 8.4 Border position illustrated by Satrapi's self-portrait
SOURCE: SATRAPI, *PERSEPOLIS* 6

As can be seen from the examples above, the veil functions in the story as one of its most important ideologically loaded signifiers by virtue of its physical (omni)presence in Marjane's Iranian life – as a clothing item on women's bodies as well as her own. As such, the veil not only stands as an abstract marker of the oppression of female sexuality in Iran, but in its material capacity as a tool inducing this oppression, it also defines the everyday reality of women's existence in the public spaces of urban Tehran. As the episode of Marjane's shouting at the policemen also shows, women cannot virtually "use" the public spaces of the city without being veiled (protected as well as hidden) in and from it, which also suggests that they are posited *vis-à-vis* the city both as beings in need of protection from the male gaze, for whom the public sphere is dangerous, and as alien bodies that present a threat. In either case, they are not first-class citizens existing in the public sphere by their own right, and thus they are decreed to remain covered.

One of the chapters in *Persepolis 2* to best illustrate the contradictions of women's life under Islamist oppression is called "The Socks," which mainly relates the everyday life of Marjane and her fellow college students "in public" and "in private." A pair of the chapter's panels (figure 8.5) gives a dichotomous representation of the two spheres, with the usual gutter standing in-between as a liminal space of division and connection. Satrapi asserts that the women's behaviour in public and their behaviour in private are "polar opposites," and the disparity makes them schizophrenic (151). As in many scenes in the graphic novel, it is the gutter again that holds a critical space for the interpretation of all the affective and cognitive controversies the students' schizophrenic state entails, since the cause-and-effect relationship between their state of mind and the political regime is not explained in detail in either of the two frames.

Apart from demonstrating how misguided and stereotypical some of the western ideas held of women in Iran may be, namely, that they uniformly accept their oppression with no means of resistance whatsoever, the two frames in figure 8.5 also exemplify the kind of "logic of adjustment" in the ordinariness of trauma Lauren Berlant talks about in *Cruel Optimism* (10). As the narrator of *Persepolis* asserts, "to find a semblance of equilibrium, we partied almost every night" (152). The whole chapter of "The Socks" and several other parts in *Persepolis*, which present stories and images of parties, drinking, police raids, and more parties despite the raids, show everyday acts of resistance and strategies of survival that make life for Iranian people in the Islamic Republic bearable. Since life in a city of one's birth typically constitutes an affective texture of the familiar, traumatic experience (for example, the death of a neighbour, a friend, or a family member in a raid or a bombing) entails the unraveling of this familiar texture of not just one's life but also one's affective ties to a specific location and a set of people. *Persepolis* is thus one of those "stories about navigating what's overwhelming" (Berlant 10) in the face of losing the familiar. A tragic example of such loss in the same chapter of *Persepolis* is the story of a house party raid, which results in the death of one of Marjane's company, who falls off the roof of a block of flats while trying to escape from the police (that is, "guardians" of the Islamic Republic). The black-and-white images of the staircases and rooftops, the running policemen and the partygoers escaping from them, with no verbal explanations to accompany the panels, have a very immediate and dramatic visual effect (153–5). Yet, the end of the chapter shows that most of Marjane's friends are resolute in not succumbing to the threat of the police as they insist on not giving up their parties. Marjane comments in the last panel of the chapter, which depicts her at another party immediately after the tragic raid, that she "never drank so much" in her life (157). The affective repercussions of losing a friend, her grief and desperation at the political

FIGURE 8.5 Women's public and private behaviour
SOURCE: SATRAPI, *PERSEPOLIS 2* 151

situation are all expressed in this single frame as much as her resolution not to give in.

Although Marjane takes part in the "dissident" social life of her college, her liminal position, which is indicated at the beginning of the narrative, still stands out: when it turns out that under her veil she is a modern woman who has sex with her boyfriend and generally has a "liberated" understanding of women's right to their own body, many girls in her college group turn away from her (149). Her feminist ideas expressed at this point in the narrative are the result of having already become familiar with western feminism after her stay in Vienna as a high-school student and having been able to negotiate it with her Tehran reality. Obviously, it is a long way until the autobiographical "I" gets to the point where she can fully recognize the mechanisms of women's oppression in the Islamic state and take a double critical stance concerning gender, ethnicity, and class. In order to be able to speak from a firm standpoint of her own, she has to travel both physically and metaphorically (narratively) to-and-fro between Iran and Europe, which also entails the types of losses I have mentioned earlier. Thus, *Persepolis* is one of those stories that narrate and cope with the trauma of losing people and places not only because of war and dictatorship in the home country but also because of migration. In this respect, Marjane's life story also presents the shifting locations of navigating the overwhelming – most importantly, from Tehran to Vienna. In what follows, I will dwell on some affective, narrative, and ideological aspects of this navigation which are specifically linked to Marjane's travels, while I examine how her attempt to cope with loss and intersecting inequalities eventually leads to the emergence of her border subjectivity.

4   Migration as a Catalyst of Border Thinking

The geographical and spiritual starting point on the road to Marjane's feminist enunciation is her travel to Vienna in *Persepolis 2*. She expects to leave "a religious Iran for an open and secular Europe" (1). However, in Vienna, she is put into a religious boarding house run by nuns, so eventually she leaves behind one "great narrative" (Islam) just to be circumscribed by another (Christianity). In Europe, she is caught in the snare of consumerism, too: "I was so bored that to buy four different products, I would go to the supermarket at least four times" (20). On the upside, she also has the possibility and time to become more familiar with European thought by reading as many books as she can. She starts with Simone de Beauvoir's *The Second Sex*: "To educate myself, I had to understand everything. Starting with myself, me, Marji, the woman.

So I threw myself into reading my mother's favorite book" (21). Trying to apply de Beauvoir's symbolic thinking to her own life (women peeing standing up as a symbol of liberation), Marjane realizes that "as an Iranian woman, before learning to urinate like a man" she needs "to learn to become a liberated and emancipated woman" (21).

This scene is crucial in Marjane's self-realization as an emerging feminist from Iran who has migrated to Europe. As Anastasia Valassopoulos points out, Marjane needs to take up different positions (including de Beauvoir's) before realizing that the metaphor offered by de Beauvoir is inadequate for her (203). Coming from a different geopolitical location, she has to learn how to be a feminist in a different way. The critique of ready-made hegemonic epistemology (in this case, western feminism) and a new border epistemology thus emerge as a result of Marjane's transnational dislocation. As Valassopoulos puts it, Marjane travels "from awe [of western feminist symbolism] to practicality [sitting back down to pee]" (203). The negotiation of everyday life in the face of oppression and overwhelming loss, which characterizes Marji's earlier life in Tehran, thus gives way in Vienna to ideological negotiation between canonized western feminism and personal migrant experience.

Marjane's border feminism, as a vital part of her border thinking, thus develops through "trials and errors" (Valassopoulos 201). As opposed to her mother's self-assured "second-wave" feminism, Marjane does not automatically know what she wants or what she should think about either western feminist ideologies or the situation and treatment of women under the Islamic regime of her own country. She is born into a modern, "enlightened" family; yet, her faith in God, as has been previously pointed out, is very strong at the beginning (later it diminishes due to all the terror she has to experience and the death of her beloved uncle Anoosh). She goes to Vienna because her parents see that she is too outspoken to be safe in Iran, and she believes she may find freedom, a satisfactory sense of identity, and a life goal there, but she ends up going home feeling depressed, ill, and worthless. After breaking up with her boyfriend and leaving her rented room at the racist Frau Doctor Heller's, who, in the meantime, accuses her of stealing her brooch (*Persepolis 2* 79), she endangers her health and life by spending several nights in the street in winter: "I think that I preferred to put myself in serious danger rather than confront my shame. My shame at not having become someone, the shame of not having made my parents proud after all the sacrifices they had made for me. The shame of having become a mediocre nihilist" (90). Weakened and depressed, Marjane decides to go back to Iran after her high-school career in Vienna comes to a dissatisfying end.

Marjane knows that the decision to return to Iran comes with a price of having to say good-bye to her "individual and social liberties" (*Persepolis 2*

91). In this definitive moment, the veil becomes a key symbol re-appropriated to stand both for the acceptance of Marjane's defeat in the battle to become "somebody" in western terms and for home (in terms of national identity as well as Islamic oppression). Figure 8.6 shows in four panels the process of donning the veil "again," with the last and biggest frame representing Marji's sad face and veiled head in the mirror. Michael A. Chaney discusses the significance of mirrors in subjectivity-formation in graphic novel autobiographies, stating that the "duplicitous self-consciousness" created by the graphic narrator representing herself in the mirror helps assuage the anxieties inherent in the construction of the autobiographical subject as being simultaneously narrator and narratee, thereby endeavoring to construct the impossible presence of absence (22). Chaney chooses Satrapi's *Persepolis*, specifically its first two panels, to illustrate how the graphic medium exposes "a narrational strategy well suited to articulate the liminal conditions of transculturality" (26). He states that Satrapi's establishment of the autobiographical subject in the first two panels of *Persepolis* is like a moment of Lacan's mirror stage, in which "the larger chasm of the gutter" accentuates Marji's difference and liminality (26). In line with Chaney's argument, I suggest that the "mirror moment" in figure 8.6 also plays a vital role in the establishment of Marjane's liminal transcultural subject-position from which her border critique emerges. In this instance, the veil, which is literally a means (tool) for her to enter the country, becomes a (reluctantly worn) symbol of Marji's national identity as well as her act of succumbing to codes of conduct dictated by an oppressive regime, in order to regain her affective balance after four years of desperation in Vienna. Thus, the "Lacanian moment" in the panel below, which is induced by Marjane's border-crossing, presents three levels of subject-construction: the subject-formation of the individual by dis/identification (the psychoanalytical level), the representation of the paradoxical autobiographical subject as both narratee and narrator (the narrative level), and the emergence of border subjectivity in the margins, in the liminal critical space of the gutter, in the nowhere land between the body and its image in the mirror (ideological level).

The two cities, Tehran and Vienna, where the majority of Marjane's life story in *Persepolis* takes place, mark the two sides of her mirror of subject-construction, in terms of not only geography but also affect and ideology. While both urban settings are places of loss and alienation, the causes of these existential states are rather different in the case of the two cities. Marjane's sense of dislocation in Tehran is largely generated by political oppression as well as the destruction of the city and the people in it. Her alienation in Vienna is of a different nature: it is the result of her sense of isolation, as well as the racism and loneliness she experiences there as an immigrant. However,

FIGURE 8.6 Donning the veil again
SOURCE: SATRAPI, *PERSEPOLIS 2* 91

after spending four years in Vienna and returning to Iran, she immediately feels "the oppressive air of [her] country" (92) and becomes distanced from her friends and family, too. This distancing is already apparent at the Tehran airport – another liminal or transitional urban space –, where Marjane's parents do not even recognize her at first upon her arrival (92). The affective conflict that Marjane experiences in Vienna as an ethnic outsider gives place to emptiness and a sense of dislocation in Tehran, partly as a result of the city's turning into a "cemetery" (97) and partly because Marjane herself has changed so much in the meantime. Being at home in neither place, she feels that she has lost her sense of identity and purpose: "I was a westerner in Iran, an Iranian in the West. I had no identity. I didn't even know anymore why I was living" (118).

Eventually, Marjane tries to commit suicide, but she miraculously survives, and her survival makes her realize that she is "not made to die" (*Persepolis 2* 119). From this point on, her travel towards self-fulfillment as a feminist seems to be on the right track: apart from training at college as a graphic artist, she meets her future husband. After some ideological struggle with her friends, she can negotiate a balance in this respect, too: "My friends and I had evolved. I had tempered my western vision of life and they, for their part, had moved away from tradition. As a result, many unmarried couples had formed" (158). Yet, it is exactly the issue of marriage where this optimistic train is derailed: in order to be able to appear in public together, Marjane and her boyfriend Riza get married. Marjane's mother is not happy: "I have always wanted for you to become independent, educated, cultured … and here you are getting married at twenty-one. I want you to leave Iran, for you to be free and emancipated …" (163). Again, in this instance, the different feminist views of mother and daughter become clear, as Marjane "jumps into marriage" for political reasons. And indeed, as soon as the couple arrive home and the apartment door closes, Marjane has a bizarre feeling: "I was already sorry! I had suddenly become 'a married woman.' I had conformed to society, while I had always wanted to remain in the margins. In my mind, 'a married woman' wasn't like me. It required too many compromises. I couldn't accept it, but it was too late" (163). In this picture frame (figure 8.7), Marjane is represented behind prison bars, which confirms her sense of being oppressed by the institution of marriage. Inevitably, after one month, husband and wife sleep in separate beds (165), and after three years of "marriage" they finally divorce (184).

Marjane's metaphor in this panel of always wanting to "remain in the margins," which recalls her sitting "on the far left" at the beginning of *Persepolis* (figure 8.1), aptly describes her epistemological position for border thinking,

FIGURE 8.7 Marriage as prison
SOURCE: SATRAPI, *PERSEPOLIS* 2 163

which is impossible behind the "closed doors" of her Tehran life and marriage. Thus, after the divorce, she decides to go back to Europe, as remaining in the margins, a precondition for double critique, also entails being constantly on the move. Her mother's words at the departure reaffirm Marjane's liminal position as an Iranian woman: "This time, you're leaving for good. You are a free woman. The Iran of today is not for you. I forbid you to come back!" (*Persepolis* 2 187). Her mother's words of farewell demonstrate the importance of personal and affective dimensions in Marjane's ideological development: her strong bond with her family and friends, which is activated and tested whenever she leaves and returns to Iran, and also while she is away, provides an affective framework for her transnational migrant experience, while it also plays a vital role in shaping her feminism and political ideology.

Although Marjane's second departure to Europe closes both the narrative of *Persepolis* and the Iranian chapter of her life story, it opens up new possibilities for her to actually create her autobiographical narrative in graphic format. She is admitted to the School of Decorative Arts in Strasbourg, which gives her the chance to publish her graphic novel and get it translated – in Iran, this would not be possible because she would be imprisoned immediately. Thus, for Marjane, departures mean arrivals at the same time: new ways of narrative expression open up for her "in the margins," which require that she move and negotiate between two cultural contexts, experiencing, comparing, and contrasting them in order to be able to scrutinize them in her double critique.

While the political oppression and sexism in Tehran motivate Marjane to leave Iran, the ethnocentrism and racism she encounters in Vienna induces her self-declaration as an Iranian. Although at first she lies that she is from France, her accent gives her away, which she realizes from a conversation she overhears in a café. She justifies her lie stating that "[a]t the time, Iran was the epitome of evil and to be Iranian was a heavy burden to bear. It was easier to lie than to assume that burden" (*Persepolis* 2 41). Denying her ethnic origin, however, is in opposition with her grandmother's teachings: "Always keep your dignity and be true to yourself" (41). When Marjane hears the racist and nasty remarks made by some girls in the café, she is so enraged that she exposes herself and declares her identity: "You are going to shut up or I am going to make you! I am Iranian and proud of it!" (43). From this instance on, her ethnic origin becomes "public" in a sense that it is written into her "European narrative." She realizes that she is indeed proud, "for the first time in a year," and she understands her grandmother's words: If you are not comfortable with yourself, you will never be comfortable (43). This teaching applies not only to Marjane's ethnic identity but also to her gendered position in society: her realization that marriage is an oppressive institution for her, especially in an Iranian context, also contributes to her identity-formation.[2]

The intersecting aspects of discrimination and oppression construct Marjane's subjectivity as an "outsider" in both places: a modern woman in an Islamic state, a middle-class "third-world citizen" in Europe. Her border thinking derives from her "margin sensitivity" to inequalities and puts her in a liminal position from which she can speak. Even though in Iran she is denied, on grounds of Islamic belief, to realize an extraordinary dissertation project of a theme park of Persepolis, in which the complex mythology of Iran would serve as the source of inspiration for the imagery (174–7), she can create an alternative Persepolis in the form of her graphic novels. I consider these novels instances or spaces for border thinking, where a special, "Satrapian" border epistemology is created in the form of a historical narrative that juxtaposes words with pictures as well as presents a double critique of both Islamic ideology and "western" notions of Islamic oppression.

---

2   Satrapi's 2003 book, *Embroideries*, is dedicated to the subject of male-female relationships, examining it through the gossip and discussion of several "relationship-narratives" among some women with differing viewpoints and experiences.

5 Conclusion

Marjane Satrapi's choice of the graphic novel as an intelligible form of narrative was motivated by her endeavor to present an alternative interpretation of Iran and its history to her reading public in a widely accessible and "universal" form. She asserts that "[i]mage is an international language. [...] And when you draw a situation – someone is scared or angry or happy – it means the same thing in all cultures. You cannot draw someone crying, and in one culture they think that he is happy. He would have the same expression. There's something direct about the image" (Weich).

While the directness of the image certainly makes *Persepolis* more accessible, the minimalist black-and-white style of the drawings, as Chute argues, is meant "to present events with a pointed degree of abstraction in order to call attention to the horror of history by representing endemic images, either imagined or reproduced, of violence" ("The Texture of Retracing" 98–9). Thus, by virtue of its popular yet abstract narrative form, which juxtaposes history, autobiography, and fiction, *Persepolis* stands witness to terrible historical trauma outside the realm of official national history, while it addresses and criticizes both "eastern" and "western" practices and notions of inequality from their very locales, be these inequalities of gender, ethnic origin, or class. Satrapi's *Persepolis* presents "a new form of engagement" (Valassopoulos 204), which entails a "sophisticated, and historically cognizant, means of doing the work of seeing" (Chute, "The Texture of Retracing" 99).

While Valassopoulos states that "the question of difference, subjective experience and the various levels at which gender is experienced and understood, do not seem to be part of the feminist agenda at work in the production of popular culture" (206), I argue that Satrapi's *Persepolis* and her later works, such as *Embroideries*, not only give way to the question of difference and subjective experience but present them as constitutive elements in the narrative formation of the autobiographical subject and her border thinking. Expressing difference and subjective experience in a way that moves beyond the personal and internal is achieved by Satrapi through the inclusion of multiple locations, voices, and points of view. First, the "small histories" of the various relatives and acquaintances together form a mosaic of "real lives" and give a more general sense of the fate of people in Iran, as their lives are influenced by larger historical forces in different but related ways and with each character trying to negotiate their way through life by different means and methods. Second, although Marjane is the narrator of the *Persepolis* books, she brings in several other voices that make her work polyphonic, which reassures the belief that even in the most oppressive political circumstances, there are not only silent victims subjugated by totalitarian regimes, but there is space for resistance, and there are always self-styled ways to come to grips with oppression.

In Ella Shohat's words, there is a possibility for a multicultural feminism that "questions the benevolence of 'allowing' other voices to add themselves to the 'mainstream' of feminism" and focuses on "feminism as *itself* a constitutively multi-voiced arena of struggle" (15–6, emphasis in original). The multi-voiced feminism in the *Persepolis* books gives strength to the double critique that emerges in the narrative, thereby also displaying the gendered nature of both Islamic and western hegemony and patriarchy. As Mignolo states, a double critique always "implies to think from both traditions and, at the same time, from neither of them" (67), which, in the case of the *Persepolis* books, equally applies to the critique of geopolitical-cultural regimes and the re-evaluation of feminist traditions. This is how Satrapi's graphic novels manifest a specific form of border thinking that derives from their narrator's transcultural feminist dislocation.

Works Cited

Afshar, Haleh. *Islam and Feminisms: An Iranian Case Study*. St. Martin's Press, 1998.

Anzaldúa, Gloria. *Borderlands/La Frontera: The New Mestiza*. Aunt Lute Books, 1987.

Berlant, Lauren. *Cruel Optimism*. Duke UP, 2011.

Chaney, Michael A. "Terrors of the Mirror and the *Mise en Abyme* of Graphic Novel Autobiography." *College Literature*, vol. 38, no. 3, *Visual Literature*, Summer 2011: 21–44.

Chute, Hillary. "Comics as Literature? Reading Graphic Narrative." *PMLA*, vol. 123, no. 2, March 2008: 452–65.

Chute, Hillary. "The Texture of Retracing in Marjane Satrapi's *Persepolis*." *Women's Studies Quarterly*, vol. 36, no. 1–2, Spring-Summer 2008: 92–110.

Dabashi, Hamid. *Iran: A People Interrupted*. New Press, 2007.

Darda, Joseph. "Graphic Ethics: Theorizing the Face in Marjane Satrapi's *Persepolis*." *College Literature*, vol. 40, no. 2, Spring 2013: 31–51.

Mignolo, Walter. *Local Histories / Global Designs: Coloniality, Subaltern Knowledges, and Border Thinking*. Princeton UP, 2000.

Satrapi, Marjane. *Embroideries*. 2003. Translated by Anjali Singh, Pantheon Books, 2005.

Satrapi, Marjane. *Persepolis: The Story of a Childhood*. 2000. Translated by Mattias Ripa and Blake Ferris, Jonathan Cape, 2003.

Satrapi, Marjane. *Persepolis 2: The Story of a Return*. 2001. Translated by Anjali Singh, Pantheon Books, 2004.

Shohat, Ella. "Introduction." *Talking Visions: Multicultural Feminism in a Transnational Age*. Edited by Ella Shohat, MIT Press, 1998, pp. 1–63.

Valassopoulos, Anastasia. "Also I Wanted So Much to Leave for the West: Postcolonial Feminism Rides the Third Wave." *Third Wave Feminism: A Critical Exploration.* Expanded 2nd edition, edited by Stacy Gillis, Gillian Howie and Rebecca Munford, Palgrave Macmillan, 2007.

Weich, Dave. "Marjane Satrapi Returns." Interview. Powell's Books, 2006, https://www.powells.com/post/interviews/marjane-satrapi-returns. Accessed: 24 September 2020.

PART 4

Translocality and Transgression

CHAPTER 9

"Whichever way you go, you are sure to get somewhere." Dysgeographic Mappings of Playable Loci and the "Compass" of Girlish Curiosity in Lewis Carroll's and China Miéville's Spatial Fantasies

Anna Kérchy

Abstract

The embodied experience of spatial and narrative disorientation is epitomized by Lewis Carroll's Victorian nonsense fairy-tale fantasies mapping adventures in Wonderland and through the looking glass (1865, 1871). This essay explores how Alice's journey driven by a transgressive girlish curiosity invites readers to reinterpret the notion of space in terms of affective psychogeography. Surpassing the category of ontological locatedness, place becomes meaningful as an epistemologically and metaphysically conceived way of seeing, knowing, sensing the world and of empathically relating to its inhabitants. Both in Carroll's classic and its urban fantasy adaptation, China Miéville's *Un Lun Dun* (2007), the penchant for straying off the path to aimlessly wander holds psychoanalytical, language philosophical, ideology-critical and environmentalist implications. The dreamchild's fluid ego boundaries – matching the coming-of-age itinerary of young adult adventure novels – evoke a nomadic wanderlust and a blurring of borders between one's self and others, be they fellow human subjects, built objects or companion species living on the green continuum.

The embodied experience of spatial and narrative disorientation is epitomized by Lewis Carroll's Victorian nonsense fairy-tale fantasies about Alice's adventures (1865, 1871). Falling down the rabbit hole, crossing through the looking-glass, wandering aimlessly in Wonderland, getting lost in the woods where things have no names, or returning to an unhomely home that will never be the same after the incredible journeys are all affectively charged, transgressive moves in and out of enchanted loci, driven by the heroine's relentless, girlish curiosity. The aim of this essay is to explore how Alice's journey (in Carroll's classic and Miéville's contemporary adaptation alike) invites readers to reinterpret the notion of space along the lines of affective psychogeography: much more than just a category of ontological locatedness, place becomes meaningful as an "epistemologically and metaphysically conceived way of seeing, knowing, sensing the world" (Dewsbury 148) and of sensitively relating to other inhabitants of this space and their ideas thereof.

I wish to prove that Alice's aimless movement, her readiness to wander from the path is just as stimulating in a philosophical as in a feminist political sense. The dreamchild's fluid ego boundaries – fitting the coming-of-age subtext of the young adult (YA) adventure novel genre – not only bring about a nomadic wanderlust but also become responsible for empathically opening up the borders of oneself to the needs, cries, and visions of others, both fellow human subjects and all beings living on the green continuum. Eventually, the reluctance to fear getting lost allows for a harmonious cohabitation with nature, even in an urban environment: our surroundings turned into a playground can reinforce communal belonging. My spatially engaged study of emotions represented in and elicited by literary texts, with a focus on interconnections of geographical, corporeal, and psychic transformations adopts an affective psycho-geographical methodology, too, insofar as I "form new linkages or assemblages of (and between) ideas that connect different knowledge systems [literature, geography, feminism] so as to form new connections and possibilities for meaning" (Dewsbury 148).

1 Curious Spaces of Nomadic Meanderings and Empathic Relationality

In the preface to *Alternative Alices* (1997), a collection of rewritings of Carroll's classic, editor Carolyn Sigler summarizes the quintessence of "the Alice type story" along the lines of the significance of spatial mobility. According to her formula, a heroine is involved in a transition from 'real,' waking life to a fantasy dream world; she undergoes rapid shifts in identity, appearance, and location in an episodic structure centering on chance meetings with nonhuman fantasy characters who force her to mentally map unimaginable and unspeakable impossibilities; and after her curious adventures in an alternate universe returns to a domestic consensus reality (xvii).

The interpretive approaches to Carroll's classic Alice tales hold an impressive variety of spatial implications which all deal with the negotiations of emotional landscapes. Instead of mundane spaces devoid of passions, ordered by rational principles, and demarcated according to political, economic or technical logics in which the geographical discipline is traditionally interested (Bondi 1), the random stations of Alice's journey are associated with sentimentally charged terrains which foreground the ambiguous affective elements at play beneath our experience of (real and fantastic) topographies.

Psychoanalytical readings find in the novels symptoms of the introvert author's fear of growing up or the growing pains of the girl (implied reader/muse) troubled by an unstable relation to space fundamentally defined by her misbehaving body and unruly language, dwelling in an ambiguous sphere of in-between, almost thereness, between child and adult. The stories can be alternately criticized for trapping the heroine within a child's body or praised for granting an adventuress' freedom to the female figure historically confined within the drawing room privacy. They can offer a feminist critique of the claustrophobic anxiety of the Victorian "Angel in the House." The infernal site of the Duchess' kitchen is a parody of a domestic feminine space, where a latent maternal violence is brought to surface in a wicked lullaby fuelled by death jokes which permeate the text from the beginning, topographically mapped onto the heroine's downward movement, initiated by the fall down the emblematic rabbit hole.

The paradigmatically metaphorical readings typical of poststructuralist literary analyses follow a similar direction by investing Alice's spatial manoeuvres, such as her legendary fall down the rabbit hole, with affective charge. Gilles Deleuze interprets the Alice tales in terms of a traumatic combat of depths and surfaces. For him, Wonderland narrates the struggle to leave the horrific, suffocating underground where "boxes are too small for their contents," toxic food stretches entrails and bursts bodies, things and words weld together into non-decomposable blocks, until Alice manages to gradually rise and return to the surfaces she creates to survive, making the chimeras of nonsensical depths become cards without thickness, and allowing the frustrating "movements of penetration and burying give way to lighter lateral movements of sliding" (21), which peak in her subsequent passing through the all-transparent looking glass. For French feminist Hélène Cixous, Alice's diving into dreamlands is a blissful experience that results in the blurring of the dividing line between reality and imagination, presence/surplus and absence/loss of sense, and a succeeding free, uncorrupted eroticization of the indeterminacy of meaning that can outline subversive "libidinal" writing/reading strategies motivated by feminine bodily energies. If the fall down the rabbit hole means falling in love while falling deep into the story's transverbal regions, the passage through the looking glass leads to the "sonorous other side of words" "to the outside of the inside of this outside, to this place where language is situated between monologue, soliloquy, and dialogue" (235), a transitional realm where "womanspeak" can flourish beyond phallogocentric discourse. Jacques Derrida's analysis celebrates Alice's treading in the footsteps of the White Rabbit as a revolutionary step towards the post-human recognition of one's own animal alterities. With a Carrollian pun the phrase "l'animal que je suis" (369) – the animal that I am, that I follow, that I am to follow – undoes the hierarchical positioning of humans over non-human entities and calls forth a deconstruction of our anthropocentric worldview and a movement towards the emancipation of othereds within oppressive social and semiotic systems of meaning.

In the light of her episodic adventures, Alice's figure can be regarded as an oddly twisted take on the traditional picaresque novel's protagonist. She is an honest, bourgeois, juvenile, female *picara* who encounters many surprising creatures – each representing different worldviews and apparently illogical ways of thinking – in an indifferent environment that fosters misunderstanding and celebrates the nonsensical nature of being. Despite the innovatively anti-didactic, non-moralizing agenda of this children's classic, Alice communicates a lesson in *empathy* by her willingness to identify with a multitude of unusual perspectives, readily alternating between a variety of viewpoints attributed to Wonderland's locals, animals, things, and in-between hybrids. In this respect, Alice is humane because of her toying with the option of becoming non-human, repeatedly re-considering the odds and implications of her serial dislocations, her transformations into a beast, a thing, or a mythical monster.

Her survival skills in a maddening universe so radically different from her own consensus-reality spring from the fact that she embraces personas of an adventurer longing to be enchanted. She is a child at play reconceiving its surroundings as if it were a playground's semi-public safe terrain where all dangers belong to pretense play. Mimicry, the adaptation to one's environment is part of the game in lands inhabited by humans fused with playing cards and chess figures. Alice performs a rather sophisticated camouflage by taking on properties of her special surroundings. Her numerous shrinkings and growings represent a kind of experimentation with protective coloration, an assimilation into the nonsensical functioning of a wondrous realm where a baby can transform into a pig, a grin can remain without a cat, creatures based on neologisms and portmanteau word coinages – like bandersnatches, bread-and-butterflies, or slithy toves – and anthropomorphic animals prosper, and metamorphosis rules on discursive, corporeal, and societal planes alike (in flexible meanings, shapeshifting bodies, changing, illusory power relations, and roads running into each other like a Moebius strip).

When in Wonderland, Alice does what Wonderlandians do. Respectful of the beliefs and practices of the local culture, no matter how anarchic they seem, she conforms to the strange discursive customs too. Her polite conversations with Wonderland creatures share rhetorical similarities with the Socratic dialogue's attempt to explore others' views of moral, philosophical issues by means of gentle questioning, as Gillian Beer argues. By familiarizing herself with the unfamiliar nonsense discourse, excelling in turning meanings inside out, Alice trains herself in a verbal implementation of *dysgeographia*, a tendency to miss the correct path and lose one's way – that is, in her case, not an inaptitude but the wanderer's joy at recognizing the relativity of the right directions. Just how much carefreeness this self-afflicted directional disability can grant is perfectly illustrated by the dialogue of Alice and the Cheshire Cat in which the pair communally trace a tentative psycho-geographical agenda. Their phrases complement each other's to encapsulate the essence of Guy Debord's notion of the *dérive* (1956), a semi-conscious drifting, an unplanned journey through a landscape where the subtle aesthetic contours of the geographical and built environment imperceptibly direct the traveler's path towards entirely new experiences of being.

> 'Cheshire Puss,' she began, rather timidly, as she did not at all know whether it would like the name: however, it only grinned a little wider. 'Come, it's pleased so far,' thought Alice, and she went on.
> 'Would you tell me, please, which way I ought to go from here?'
> 'That depends a good deal on where you want to get to,' said the Cat.
> 'I don't much care where –' said Alice.
> 'Then it doesn't matter which way you go,' said the Cat.
> '– so long as I get SOMEWHERE,' Alice added as an explanation.
> 'Oh, you're sure to do that,' said the Cat, 'if you only walk long enough.'
> CARROLL 67

Alice's journey has nothing to do with the masculine appropriation of space, it lacks a conquistador's colonizing intent, it never aims to reach a final destination, nor does it give account of a teleological development. More of an "armchair flânerie," it provides a metafictional celebration of wondering about wandering, a speculative strolling towards a multitude of possible becomings in a Deleuzian fashion. It remains rather indecisive just how her interactions with the Wonderland or looking-glass space transform Alice's character. Even her coming of age and mature separation from the dream realms remain highly dubious. It is so, because her attitude to space is not in the least possessive but tentative, re-negotiable, fluid and relational. The adventurer Alice's reaction to Wonderland is an overwhelming enchantment that is primordially a spatial experience implied in the etymology of the word "amazement," a stupefaction by the recognition of maze-like, labyrinthine structure of reality that entails getting lost as an enriching self-exploration, not a traumatizing identity crisis.

More like a nomadic subjectivity in Rosi Braidotti's understanding of the term: a multidifferentiated, non-hierarchical sense of the self is always in the process of becoming and gets perpetually engaged in creative relations via a strategic deterritorialization that unsettles the fixed borders of patriarchal hegemony. Alice neither really strives to get back home, nor aims to stay in Wonderland. Her aimless strolls are driven by this strange realm's major geographical guideline, which she quickly masters: "whichever way you go, you are sure to get somewhere." As a child-woman dwelling in the 'in-between,' she re-embodies her modernist foremother, Virginia Woolf's woman artist who has no country, and wants no country, since her country is the whole world (Woolf 197) – mappable from within the space of a room of one's own, too. Unlike the privileged, bourgeois, male *flâneur*, the participant of the *dérive* playfully suspends class and gender belongings and instead of detached omniscient observing, daringly interacts with her environment and puts herself "out of place" to reach a heightened receptivity of the "psychogeographical relief" (McDonough 257) of the public and private arenas experienced as sites of surprising explorations and connectibility to previously unknown realms of being, thinking, feeling. Paradoxically, Braidotti's nomadism, like Alice's wanderings, is grounded in an insistence on intensive interconnectedness and empathic proximity.

Just how much locatedness, or rather, dislocatedness, holds a phenomenological, existential significance, is reflected in Alice's recurring self-questioning: instead of the obvious enquiry "Where am I?" she keeps asking herself "Who am I?". Projecting spatial destabilization inward, she attempts to find meaning in an irrational universe by embracing existence, freedom, and an endless array of choices, including the choice of not choosing.

2   Urban Fantasy Wonderlands

Because of their numerous anthropomorphic animal and plant characters, and the memorable mock pastoral scenes – the pool of tears, the forest of nameless things, or the garden of live flowers – the Alice tales are associated with a natural environment, albeit the cognitive dissonance provoked by Carroll's nonsense fantasy is enhanced by the fact that instead of awe and love for a natural environment considered inherently worthy of protection and respect, we keep being stupefied by the radically strange surroundings. This surprising defamiliarization is further complicated by contemporary adaptations when the fantastic topoi of Wonderland are redeployed in an unfamiliar context: the urban sphere of the city.

The "urban" descriptor applied to the fairy-tale fantasy increases the spatial fantasy features of the source text, while the collision of the make-believe, magical motifs with the realistic urban milieu of a more or less recognizable city turns the mapping of the fantasy space into a genuinely challenging experience. In (post)millennial YA urban fantasy Wonderlands, "two common figurative and symbolic vocabularies" (Irvine 201) are juxtaposed, those of the fairy-tale adventure and the tale of urban initiation. However, these stories also bear characteristics of Alexander C. Irvine's other category of urban fantasy in which "the city is not just a field on which the naturalist and the fantastic play out a series of thematic collisions" but rather embodies a genius loci that animates all the fantastic elements derived from the history and character of the city. Certainly, these two urban fantasy modes are difficult to separate neatly in terms of binary oppositions and rather constitute two far ends of a literary axis, with "urban" as one terminus and "fantasy" as the other, as Irvine suggests (201).

An almost real city hosts fantastic events in Jeff Noon's *Automated Alice* (1996), a dystopian steampunk fantasy about Alice and her doll, Celia, who pass through a grandfather clock to solve a murder mystery in a futuristic Manchester city ruled by chaos theory, jazz music, puns and puzzles, along with human-machine-animal hybrid Newmonians, and Alice's termite-driven, robot "twin twister," the title character. The landscape, an actual geographical region emerges as a source of fantastification in Bryan Talbot's *Alice in Sunderland: An Entertainment* (2007), a graphic novel fantasy inoculated with history, detective story, biography, literary theory, music-hall turns, jokes and homages mapping how Carroll's Alice tales gained inspiration from the Sunderland area's rich folklore heritage, local legends, like that of the Lambton Worm, the Walrus in Whitburn, and a monkey hanged in Hartlepool. China Miéville's YA urban fantasy girl's adventure story *Un Lun Dun* (2007) does not simply locate magical happenings in a fantastic city, but tells the story of this fantastic city itself, a nonsensical mirror version of London mostly constructed from trash discarded by Londoners, a complex space I will analyze in depth.

These contemporary YA fantasy rewritings of the Alice-theme remain faithful to the original in so far as their heroines' mapping of make-believe spaces allows for an affirmation of women's creative spatial agency in diegetic universes which lend themselves even more easily to being studied in terms of affective psycho-geographical notions, given that they relocate Carroll's originally solitary character into densely inhabited regions of metropolitan setting. The stories recycle and challenge archetypal figures like the "lost little girl" associated in cautionary tales with the vice of curiosity and a resulting debilitating spatial dyslexia; the "nymph" as an eroticized tutelary divinity of a landform, a *genius loci* reduced to a mere symbol of the fertility of nature; or the modernist *haute bourgeois* "flâneuse" whose "spectacular invisibility" participated in the "ocular economy" of the city (Pollock 1988, Wolff 1990, Nead 2000) and was both threatening to and threatened by the white, masculinist urban space. Dysgeographia and curiosity are identified with a multiplicity and mobility of perspectives and sensations, a resulting environmentalist empathy and a female authorial empowerment fueled by the embracement of unpredictability. They are reinterpreted in terms of the feminist psycho-geographer's self-reflective, metafictional gambit, a feminist pedestrian politics and poetics, a capacity to explore "a new way of walking [or meaning formation!] that changes our city [or fictional!] experience, a whole toy box full of playful, inventive strategies for exploring cities [or narratives!] ... just about anything that takes pedestrians [or readers!] off their predictable paths and jolts them into a new awareness of the urban [or literary!] landscape" (Hart in Bucher and Finka).

In Clute and Grant's seminal *Encyclopedia of Fantasy*, the entry "urban fantasy" defines spatial experience in terms of the subjective filter of the city-dweller, who functions as an unreliable narrator because of the emotional investment of her geographical locatedness.

> A City is a *place*; urban fantasy is a *mode*. A city may be an Icon or a geography; the urban fantasy recounts an experience. A city may be seen from afar, and is generally seen clear; the urban fantasy is told from within, and, from the perspective of characters acting out their roles, (hence) it may be difficult to determine the extent and nature of the surrounding reality.

What strikes me in this definition is how it resonates with the notions of the partial perspective and situated knowledges celebrated by contemporary feminist thinkers, such as Donna Haraway, who argues that "having multiple viewpoints that are put into dialogue with one another is what gives our individual knowledge value and worth" (583). She argues in favor of putting feminism's partial, even fallible, and self-admittedly vulnerable objectivity into practice in order to yield productive "knowledges from limited locations potent for constructing worlds less organized by axes of domination" by doing away with illusory transcendence and the splitting of subject and object in favor of collective connectibility (Haraway 583). These ideas remarkably match urban fantasy's notion of the city as a site of social and imaginary interactions, a heterogeneous web of real and fictitious knowledges coming from distinct yet interrelated cities within the city. Moreover, the 'cities within the city' as a labyrinthine spatial structure, augmenting playfulness and uncertainty, conforms to today's urban trends shaped both by local colours of institutionalized city districts and metropolitan hotspots as well as those micro-spatial urban practices – from community gardening to shock tactics of graffiti and flash-mobbing – which perform a certain "do-it-yourself urbanism" to express differing, individual "rights to the city" (Iveson 941).

This fuzziness of our surrounding reality has been remarkably well represented by China Miéville, a figurehead of contemporary urban fantasy, who has earned a reputation for trespassing generic boundaries, combining maps and methods of epic and urban fantasy, social and hard science fiction, crime, and horror into a literary bricolage alternately coined by critics as "new weird," "fantastika," "literary speculation" and "hauntological slipstream." His obsession with the urban milieu shows already in the titles of his bestsellers ranging from *Perdido Street Station* (2000) to *The City & the City* (2009) to *Embassytown* (2011). Several of his novels take place in a more or less fictionalized version of London. *King Rat* set in the '90s suburbia is a modern-day sequel to *The Pied Piper of Hamelin*, *Kraken* presents a dark comedy about a squid-worshipping cult and the end of the world, while *Un Lun Dun* – admittedly inspired by Carroll's *Wonderland* and Neil Gaiman's *Neverwhere* – leads into a parallel universe version of the city, with not one but two Alice type protagonists, Carrollian language games, a living radioactive cloud attacking the city as an ungraspable arch enemy replacing the monstrous Jabberwock, and many strange creatures – grotesque mixtures of humans, animals, plants, objects, and ideas – matching an equally amazing urban landscape and architecture.

3 Parallel Universe in an Organic Junkyard. Saving a Green City Built on Waste

In *Un Lun Dun*'s opening scene set in contemporary London, four girls come across a fox in their school playground. The wild animal, incompatible with the civilized urban environment, is an uncanny embodiment of the invisible, all-knowing underworld lurking beneath the mundane consensus reality that is threatened by an emerging thinning/wrongness conforming to the conventions of the fantastic fictional genre. The stillness of the beast contrasted with the bustling of the metropolis, and the meeting of human and animal eyes invite characters and readers to explore their habitual surroundings from a different perspective. The fox acts as a harbinger to the strange things that have been happening to the protagonists who, as emerging flâneuses-detectives, gradually learn to read the city space, decoding hidden signs – graffiti on walls, smoke boiling out of drains, and an odd version of the London travel card in the name Schwazzy (distorted phonetic transcript of the French word 'choisie' meaning The Chosen One) – all messages from a parallel universe that needs to be saved by them. "Zanna['s gaze meeting] the fox's gentle vulpine stare [that] seemed to get lost in something" (7) signals the initiation of adventures, the opening of an alternate world by virtue of the intimate encounter with the non-human other. However, instead of Alice's White Rabbit, the girls watching the fox are reminded of the Big Bad Wolf, and hence the story of Little Red Riding Hood, a classic cautionary fairy tale about misbehaviour resulting from feminine curiosity, where straying off the parentally prescribed path is punished in the Grimm Brothers' *Kinder und Hausmarchen*. This association is crucial in so far as the novel very consciously plays with overturning normatively gendered cultural scripts and narrative patterns. Besides rejecting the misogynist moralizing of traditional bedtime stories, *Un Lun Dun* plays a trick with the mythical hero figure, the portal quest fantasy genre, writing, and fictitious urban spaces, too.

The two little heroines descend to a cellar, turn a giant wheel on a waste water pipe that turns off all the traffic, all the lamps and lights, and, eventually, all London, to transport them to a parallel universe, the titular *Un Lun Dun* where Zanna is meant to fulfil a prophecy, defeat the Smog, and liberate the land. However, with an unconventional plot twist, Zanna the Schwazzy, the Chosen One falls in the first battle, and returns to London amnesiac, forgetful of her adventures. So, it is her friend Deeba, catalogued in *Un Lun Dun*'s talking and sentient book of prophecies as just a "funny sidekick," who decides to explore the two cities, collect evidence and weapons, and with the help of allies she manages to save both worlds. With a unique skill of adaptation, a daring challenging of narrative conventions, a readiness to "write beyond/against the (set) ending" (see DuPlessis), and a series of clever Carollian puns, she becomes the Unchosen to free Un Lun Dun with the help of the Ungun from Unstible, a prophesier turned smombie (a corpse reanimated by the smog), Brokkenbroll the master of broken umbrellas, and other villains.

Reimagining the protagonist and sidekick relationship beyond a hierarchical arrangement points towards a challenging of the engendered spatial arrangement of the predominant, masculinized foreground vs the lesser, feminized background, a distinction so often criticized by feminist geography. In Marilyn Frye's words, a phallocentric reality of space, figures, motion and adventurous action defines itself against the monotonously repetitive, uneventful activities of women constituting the background scenery. "It is essential to the maintenance of the foreground reality that nothing within it refer in any way to anything in the background, and yet it depends absolutely upon the existence of the background" (Frye in Rose 5). Deeba's story takes over Zanna's plays by unsettling this spatial exclusion/domination.

Questioning the authority of the master narratives is a major theme of leftist juvenile fiction, which strategically aims to avoid the moralizing and manipulation inherent in the genre of children's literature, and instead encourages young readers to think for themselves (a major feat of the Alice tales, according to Jack Zipes (73)), to believe in social justice, to be politically engaged, and become involved in issues which could affect one's environment and community (see Mickenberg and Nel). Deeba's agility and commitment are reflected in the mode of her second entry to Un Lun Dun: instead of an accidental fall down the rabbit hole, or a tentative turning of a wheel, she very self-consciously climbs up on booksteps, on "storyladders" – the portal is next to a book called *Wasp in a Wig*, the title of a chapter omitted from Carroll's *Wonderland*, and a metafictional allusion to the possible continuations of Alicedelic adventures. After she finds out that the weatherwizards Armets are just a mishearing of the Royal Meteorological Society's name, and that klinneract in not a magic weapon but the rather dubious Clean Air Act that seeks to channel back all London's polluting material into Un Lun Dun, Deeba decides to rewrite her own place in the story. She questions the reliability of the prophetic book and urges her allies to communally co-author their own adventures by constantly negotiating and challenging the ambiguous prophecies of the animated book they kidnap ("booknap") to learn and unlearn about their mission, and ways of defeating the Smog. Leftist and urban children's fantasy fuse: reading is never an isolated act of class-privilege, but a collective partaking in social action prompting environmental protection, anti-consumerism, and democratic egalitarianism.

Never a lonely *flâneuse*, Deeba considers the city as a site of social interactions, a heterogeneous web of knowledges accessible via the partial perspectives of inhabitants of different urban regions. Her friends assist her quest with different spatial skills. Hemi, the half-ghost boy from Wraithown can pass through things and knows how memories can infiltrate the built environment haunted by "ghosts of earlier forms." Curdle, the milk carton comes from a deserted alleyway, the Backwall Maze full of discarded detritus, and hence knows about the trashpack's desire to overtake order and cleanliness. Obaday Fing, the pincushion-headed couturier dressed in neatly sawn book pages from a market called Location, knows how to stitch a few wrinkles in space, while bus conductors "Un Lun Dun's champions, protectors of the transit, the sacred warriors" (58) know secret passageways to hardly accessible locations and also know how to conduct electricity in their enemies. With the help of these Un Lun Duners – each coming from distinct cities within the city conforming to today's strange urban political aesthetic – Deeba breaks rules to reclaim the city from Smog. In Gillian Rose's view, the relational mode of identity formation and the contextual epistemology that Deeba excels in constitute specifically feminine ways of mapping the space, while deliberately contradicting masculine hegemonic mapping methods based on the conquest, marginalization, domination, or closure of socio-scientific space (Rose 112).

At another station of her picaresque journey, a feat of her rebelliousness, embodied locatedness, and an example of Miéville's leftist politics and postmodernist metafictional penchant, Deeba teaches animated words that they can rebel against their speaker and deviate from their intended meanings. The utterlings are strange creations sprung from the "despotic logorrhoea" of Mr. Speaker. Whenever the tyrant of Talkland says something, his utterings take the form of mouthless grotesque creatures: "search" is a tiny beakless bird, "cartography" is a bowler hat with several spidery legs and a fox's tail, and Deeba's allies "bling," "brer," and "cauldron" are a silver-furred locust; a bear with a pair of legs too many; a four-armed four-legged several-eyed little man, respectively.

Deeba's argument on words not necessarily meaning what their users want them to is a nod towards Carroll's famed eggman Humpty Dumpty's mock language philosophical rant boasting about the mastery over meanings being a question of willpower. But, as Joe Sutliff Sanders highlights, Deeba's reasoning also performs ideology criticism by turning Althusser's classic example for the unescapable interpellation of the social subject whose identity is prefabricated by institutions, ideological state apparati, and discourses "hailing" them into social interactions inside out (293). Deeba's wording hints at the possibility of relocating ourselves in alternative, new, shifting subjectivities defined along the lines of dysgeographia, a readiness to stray off prescribed paths, to deviate, to wander, and to dare to get lost in a variety of inventive ways. "Like … if someone shouts 'Hey you!' at someone in the street, but someone else turns around. The words misbehaved. They didn't call the person they were meant to" (297). Fluid subjectivities, unstable nonsensical meaning, and disorienting topographies fuse to map the leitmotif of the novel. We are also reminded of Henri Lefebvre's famous argument about how "every language is located in a space; every discourse says something about a space; and every discourse is emitted from a space" and how, as a result, space becomes a "language that can be employed to articulate social relationships, with realms of multiple discourses, and fluctuating centres, mirroring the stages of identity formation" (132).

The illusorily homogenized bourgeois mode of subjectivity is challenged by new sets of unsettling subjectivities imagined for words, books, things, and even buildings. Un Lun Dun is a nonsensical mirror version of London, inhabited by twisted versions of the objects typical of the London city space, like double decker buses rolling on caterpillar treads, leaping on enormous lizard legs or coasting like hovercrafts, karate fighting warrior dustbins called binjas, friendly milk cartons and broken umbrellas recruited into an army. Miéville's affective psycho-geographical agenda recycles commonplaces about the British capital to shed a new light on the habitual environment and to reveal the ordinary as curious and exceptional. Part of the enchanting quality of the Un Lun Dunian city space comes from the defamiliarizing effect that strikes the interpreter of literary nonsense or the grotesque aesthetics alike, the ability to recognize the unmarked original beneath the spectacularly distorted new version's bizarre palimpsest.

This bifocal multi-perspectivism capable of grasping the complexity of the cityscape characterizes the girl adventurers, when Deeba spots a "bridge like two huge crocodile heads, snout-to-snout" and starts humming a tune *"Dum dum dum dum dum, deee dum,"* the theme song to the TV programme *EastEnders,* which starts with an aerial shot of the Thames. Zanna snorts with laughter and joins in, and they sing together looking down at the water below, while passengers look at them as if they were mad (71). The apparently nonsensical lyrics not only signal a rebellious act violating social expectations regarding politely restrained feminine behaviour in the public space, but also reimagine the city as an always already fictionalized terrain, a site and source of endless stories to be told and retold. Via a strange *trompe l'oeil* affect, Un Lun Dun seems both familiar and unfamiliar, very real and genuinely fantastic to the heroines. As Miéville explains in an interview, he seeks to express the immediacy of the urban experience by fictionalizing the bewilderment of a man looking for a post box in a foreign city; a completely everyday thing may seem unrecognizable via "a very low-level of alienation" (Manaugh 2011). As Un Lun Dun mirrors London, the curiosity of the quotidian and the mundaneness of the magical overlap.

Un Lun Dun is also very much a living city, full of organic architectural constructs (Yorick Cavea, for example, inhabits a human body with a bird cage in place of its head with the little bird inside controlling the anthropomorphic mechanism). The bustling city space blurs boundaries between buildings, vehicles, and inhabitants which mimic each other's metamorphic flux to endlessly amaze visitors. Miéville projects onto the unrestrained dynamism of the urban sphere the fabular (il)logic he associates with the imaginative frenzy of children's literature where a sense of wonder can overwhelm cognitive estrangement.

> The two girls stared [...]
> The streets were mostly red brick, like London terraces, but considerably more ramshackle, spindly and convoluted. Houses leaned into each other, and stories piled up at complicated angles. Slate roofs lurched in all directions.

Here and there where a house should be was something else instead.

There was a fat, low tree, with open-fronted bedrooms, bathrooms, and kitchens perched in its branches. People were clearly visible in each chamber, brushing their teeth or kicking back their covers. Obaday took them past a house-sized fist, carved out of stone, with windows in its knuckles; and then the shell of a huge turtle, with a door in the neck hole, and a chimney poking out of its mottled top. (56)

"I know that look," he said to Zanna, smiling. "Astonished, bewildered, excited, frightened ... awed. That's the taste of the first few days in UnLondon." (59)

If the built environment is – as Leslie Kane Weisman suggests – a "cultural artifact shaped by [socio-historically specific] human intention and intervention, a living archeology through which we can extract the priorities" of decision makers, standards of normative behaviour, as well as ways in which we build our own self-image (Rendell et al. 1), the dizzying space of the living, organic, self-(de)composing "city in flux" offers an adequate spatial metaphor, an architectural icon for the heterogeneous, post-human, postmodern "subject in process/on trial" (Kristeva in Moi 91). The city is defined in terms of the psychic, affective reactions of its observers, mostly a unanimous amazement shared by the two girls.

But unlike Carroll's Alice, these heroines yearn to get back home, and instead of forgetfully enjoying timeless wandering, they are troubled by how many days can pass before their families forget them. Hence, each new beautiful view produces affective dissonance by combining awestruckness with homesickness. Miéville produces some truly poetic passages for how the city's built environment can literally be read along the lines of emotional belongings. When they pass "a stepped pyramid, a corkscrew-shaped minaret, a building like an enormous U," Deeba whispers "I wish my mum was here [...] And my dad. Even my brother Hass." and Zanna shares her longing (90). The materiality of the letter takes an architectural form here, as the U-shaped building reminds one of the homonymous second person singular personal pronoun "you" and picture postcards of fabulous landscapes featuring the cliché line "I wish you were here," placing lack, some sort of psychic insufficiency in the heart of the sublime aesthetic experience. This is a perfect example of one's emotional involvement with places, and of affective geography's understanding of feelings in terms of their socio-spatial mediation and articulation rather than just entirely interiorized, isolated subjective mental states (Bondi et al 3).

However, most prominently, in line with the environmentalist message of the novel, Un Lun Dun constitutes the negation of productive urban space in so far as it is an uncanny double, a fantastical city entirely built on discarded waste and powered by the MOIL technology, an acronym for "Mildly Obsolete In London." Whatever is thrown away declared obsolete, in London – "an old computer, a broken radio, or whatever left on the streets – It's there for a few days, and then it's just gone. ... It seeps into unLondon." and "sprouts like mushrooms in the streets" of the undercity where "people find other uses for it" (37). London above is portrayed as a hegemonic power structure blinded by capitalist consumerism, contributing to environmental damage, discharging pollutants, chemicals, smoke from factories, power stations, and chimneys which take the monstrous embodiment of the arch-enemy Smog that threatens "lesser," imperceptible territories outside the home of the privileged few who are also responsible for circumscribing the realm of visibility. Cities in our reality are mirrored in a skewed fashion across the trans-dimensional barrier known as the Odd, creating Abcities like Parisn't, No York, Helsunki, Lost Angeles, Sans Francisco, Hong Gone, Romeless, or Un Lun Dun.

Both the Abcities' attempt to fight environmental catastrophe by recycling waste (creating odd buildings, vehicles, clothes from trash) and the UnGun's way of fighting the Smog by growing plants can be identified as feats of green urbanism. This is a fictional warning against the idea of cities being "parasites" on the natural and domesticated environment, since they make no food, clean no air, and purify only a limited amount of water to reuse (see Odum). Un Lun Dun is a green city in many respects: apart from its zero-waste urban planning, its amazing variety of non-motorized transport reduces carbon emission and facilitates a more sustainable, healthful lifestyle; odd buildings – like the house with a whole jungle inside – evoke inner-city gardens and green roofs' capacity to purify air, absorb CO_2, to maximize the resilience of the eco-system through urban landscape, and most importantly, the connectedness of London and Un Lun Dun guarantees the acknowledgment of the connections and impacts on other cities, communities, and the larger planet, and hence, the recognition of the necessity to live within one's ecological limits. Un Lun Dun as a living, breathing, changing city makes these nearly spontaneous moves to reduce its ecological footprint; hence the adjustment of the relationship between the natural and urban environment seems feasible, yet far from utopian idealism.

4 In Place of a Conclusion: Playable Cities

The imaginativeness with which Miéville describes his fictional city is appealing because it resonates with a fashionable idea in contemporary urban planning. The notion of the playable city toys with temporary experiments – of an interdisciplinary, architectural, design, and performance nature – which interrupt the cold anonymity and utilitarian efficiency of the metropolitan environment. It encourages collective public interactions that actively bring joy, and build a community of *homo ludens* who, by playing in the city, can also embark on a creative adventure thinking about what makes us human, and how we can reimagine a happier, more cohesive urban future for ourselves.

Playable cities can be associated with the need for "an affectionate reappropriation of public places" to redeem city-life from isolation and to facilitate a collective ludic interaction with our spatial surrounding "reinvested with meaning, history, and narratives" (Marinho in Baggini). Many of Miéville's fantastic architectural structures demand a creative attitude from the city dwellers, who will have to find their own ways in/to the building. The edifice of Manifest Station is perforated in several places "with what looked like random holes, and bursting from them were railway lines [springing] in different directions: horizontal; up like a roller coaster; corkscrewing down. A few hundred meters from the great building, they plunge(d) into holes in the street, and down into darkness" (66). Pons Absconditus is an evasive bridge that connects somewhere to somewhere but it depends on the pedestrians' feelings about their destinations where it will eventually take them; while Wraithtown is kaleidoscopically surrounded by ghosts of earlier forms, just to mention a few examples.

Surprisingly, many of Miéville's strange ideas have real-life equivalents realized by creative gambits of contemporary urban design striving to create playable cities. Many playable city projects offer low budget means to reimagine public spaces: installing pianos on streets to invite passersby to fill the city with melodies ("Play Me, I'm Yours" projects), growing fruit and vegetables in public spaces for everyone to share ("Incredible edible cities"), turning avenues into crowdfunded "park and slide" urban water slides (Jerram), or organizing city-wide flash mobs from zombie chase games to mass pillow fights. The idea is to recuperate the long-lost experience of the whole city being a child's playground with the aim to "make cities new and renewed with landscape (urban memories), texture (human scale) and affection (place appropriation)" (Marinho in Baggini). Hence fictional and actual spaces converge as loci of communal (be)longing.

During the writing of this essay the author was supported by the János Bolyai Research Scholarship of the Hungarian Academy of Sciences.

Works Cited

Baggini, Julia. "Playable Cities. The City that plays together stays together." *The Guardian*. 4 Sept 2014. http://www.theguardian.com/cities/2014/sep/04/playable-cities-the-city-that-plays-together-stays-together.

Beer, Gillian. "Alice in Dialogue." *Alice Through the Ages: The 150th Anniversary of Alice in Wonderland* Conference. Cambridge University. 2015.

Bondi, Liz, Joyce Davidson and Mick Smith. "Introduction. The Emotional Turn in Geography." *Emotional Geographies*. Eds. Liz Bondi et al. Burlington: Ashgate, 2007. pp. 1–19.

Braidotti, Rosi. *Nomadic Subjects: Embodiment and Sexual Difference in Contemporary Feminist Theory*. New York: Columbia UP, 1994.

Bucher, Ulrike and Maros Finka. *The Electronic City*. Berlin: Verlag, 2008.

Carroll, Lewis. (1865, 1871) *The Annotated Alice. The Definitive Edition*. including *Alice's Adventures in Wonderland* and *Through the Looking-Glass, and What Alice Found There*. Ed. Martin Gardner. London: Penguin, 2001.

Cixous, Hélène and Marie Maclean. "Introduction to Lewis Carroll's *Through the Looking-Glass* and *The Hunting of the Snark*." Trans. Marie Maclean. *New Literary History* vol. 13, no. 2. (Winter 1982): 231–251.

Clute, John and John Grant, eds. *Encyclopedia of Fantasy*. New York: St Martin's Press, 1997.

Debord, Guy. "Theory of the Dérive." Trans. Ken Knabb. *Les Lèvres Nues*. 9 (November 1956) reprinted in *Internationale Situationniste* #2 (December 1958) *Situationist International Online*. http://www.cddc.vt.edu/sionline/si/theory.html.

Derrida, Jacques. "The Animal That Therefore I Am (More to Follow)." Trans. David Wills. *Critical Inquiry* vol. 28, no. 2. (Winter 2002): 369–418.

Deleuze, Gilles. *Essays Critical and Clinical*. Trans. Daniel Smith and Michael Greco. New York: Verso, 1998.

Dewsbury, John David. "The Deleuze-Guattarian Assemblage: Plastic Habits." *Area* vol. 43, no. 2. (2011): 148–153.

DuPlessis, Rachel Blau. *Writing Beyond the Ending*: *Narrative Strategies of Twentieth-Century Women Writers*. Bloomington: Indiana UP, 1985.

Haraway, Donna. "Situated Knowledges: The Science Question in Feminism and The Privilege of Partial Perspective." *Feminist Studies* vol. 14, no. 3. (Autumn 1988): 575–599.

Irvine, Alexander C. "Urban Fantasy." *The Cambridge Companion to Fantasy Literature*. Eds. Edward James and Farah Mendlesohn. Cambridge: Cambridge UP, 2012. pp. 200–213.

Iveson, Kurt. "Cities within the City. Do-It-Yourself Urbanims and the Right to the City." *International Journal of Urban and Regional Research* vol. 37, no. 3. (May 2013): 941–956.

Jerram, Luke. *Urban Slide Project*. Bristol, 2014. http://www.lukejerram.com/urban_slide/.

Laboratory of Architectural Experiments. "Urbanimals Project." *LAX Portfolio*. 2014. http://lax.com.pl/portfolio_page/urbanimals/.

Lefebvre, Henri. *The Production of Space*. Oxford: Blackwell, 1991.
Manaugh, Geoff. "Unsolving the City. An Interview with China Miéville." *Buildingblog*. 2011. 03. http://www.bldgblog.com/2011/03/unsolving-the-city-an-interview-with-china-mieville/.
McDonough, Tom. *Guy Debord and the Situationist International: Texts and Documents*. Cambridge: MIT Press, 2002.
Mickenberg, Julia and Philip Nel, eds. *Tales for Little Rebels: A Collection of Radical Children's Literature*. New York: New York UP, 2008.
Miéville, China. "Fabular Logic." *Locus. The Magazine of Sci Fi and Fantasy Lit*. Nov. 2006.
Miéville, China. *Un Lun Dun*. London: Macmillan, 2007.
Moi, Toril. *The Kristeva Reader*. New York: Columbia UP, 1986.
Odum, Howard. *Environment, Power, and Society*. London: Wiley-Interscience, 1971.
Rendell, Jane, Barbara Penner and Iain Borden, eds. *Gender Space Architecture. An Interdisciplinary Introduction*. New York: Routledge, 2009.
Rose, Gillian. *Feminism & Geography. The Limits of Geographical Knowledge*. Cambridge: Polity, 2007.
Sigler, Carolyn, ed. *Alternative Alices: Visions and Revisions of Lewis Carroll's Alice Books*. Kentucky: The UP of Kentucky, 1997.
Sutliff Sanders, Joe. "Reinventing Subjectivity: China Miéville's *Un Lun Dun* and the Child Reader." *Extrapolation* vol. 50, no. 2. (2009): 293–307.
Watershed. *The Playable City Award*. 2015. http://www.watershed.co.uk/playablecity.
Weisman, Leslie Kanes. "Prologue." *Gender Space Architecture*. Jane Rendell et al. eds. New York: Routledge, 2009. pp. 1–6.
Woolf, Virginia. *Three Guineas*. London: Hogarth, 1938.
Zipes, Jack. *Victorian Fairy Tales: The Revolt of the Fairies and Elves*. New York: Methuen, 1987.

CHAPTER 10

Translocations of Desire: Urban Topographies of Love in Chimamanda Adichie's *Americanah*

Jennifer Leetsch

Abstract

Composed of seven sections, Chimamanda Ngozi Adichie's 2013 novel *Americanah* opens and closes as a love story between its two protagonists – this love story, however, is not static. It travels and migrates; it is made of movements and counter-movements. This chapter will examine how narratives of dis-placement and re-placement, of arrival and return, are woven into the love story which lies at the novel's centre. Through exploring the romance between Ifemelu and Obinze, this chapter argues that *Americanah* generatively redraws the boundaries of transnational writing – thereby troubling postcolonial narratives of migration and permanent, successful settlement elsewhere.

The emotional geography explored in this chapter shows that the novel's treatment of various metropolitan spaces both conceals and lays bare other relational structures of contact. Emotions do not appear as mere background for the imaginative geography the novel builds but are indispensable for its world- and identity-making. After their more-or-less failed residences in various cities in both Europe and the United States, Lagos, Nigeria becomes Ifemelu's and Obinze's final space: by returning to their African homeland, both migrant protagonists generate for themselves a new old home, a productive and affective space "where boundaries [become] blurred" (*Americanah* 483).

1   Introduction: Spatial Relations

Conceptions of place and space as related to notions of stasis, permanence, and limitation have long come to be found futile. Rather, they now appear as dynamic and fluid, as the product of processes that extend well beyond the confines of a particular locus. Space and place have been recognised as social constructions and as such have impact on identity formations and social development.[1] Our sense of being placed influences and shapes national discourses

---

[1] For a more in-depth discussion of how the field of cultural geography developed its terminology, see Massey (*Space, Place, and Gender*) and Anderson.

of belonging. While spatiality as a more abstract concept defies categorisation and representation, it is possible to access its configurations and meanings via concrete places (cf. Soja). Place as a social construct can no longer be seen as container or reservoir; it is not static or monotone but a social, cultural, imaginative and collective process – executed through means of perception, appropriation, experience, and engagement. This is reflected by feminist geographer Doreen Massey's conceptualisations of locality as always inherently relational:

> [W]hat gives place its specificity is not some long internalized history but the fact that it is constructed out of a particular constellation of relations, articulated together at a particular locus. [...] The uniqueness of a place, or a locality, in other words is constructed out of particular interactions and mutual articulations of social relations, social processes, experiences and understandings, in a situation of co-presence.
> MASSEY, "Power-Geometry" 66

Massey here proposes structures of the side-by-side and of global interconnectedness. Places are not necessarily bound by borders or closed off from the world. Instead, they are exactly that which Stuart Hall proclaims identity to be: not already accomplished, but always implicated in a process of "becoming"[2] (222), of coming into existence through movements of negotiation, positioning, and localisation, "through interrelations rather than through the imposition of boundaries" (Massey, *Space, Place, and Gender* 7).

One of the places where this incessant relationality becomes abundantly clear is the metropolitan space of the city. Here, communities, neighbourhoods, and homes figure as markers of an urban topography that has at its heart the twin concepts of alienation and belonging – and especially those who have to move by nature, namely the migrant and the diasporic, take the city as a creative scaffold to continuously conciliate their troubled sense of belonging. As Homi Bhabha contends:

> It is to the city that the migrants, the minorities, the diasporic come to change the history of the nation. [...] It is the city which provides the space in which emergent identifications and new social movements of the people are played out. It is there that, in our time, the perplexity of the living is most acutely experienced. (243)

---

2   Hall here draws on the Deleuzian concept of "becoming", found not only in his earlier work but especially in his later collaboration with Guattari, where they describe its creative and transformative potential (cf. *A Thousand Plateaus*, 232–309).

This perplexity results in a constant mediation of positionalities and affiliations, revealing what Paul Gilroy has called "the tension between roots and routes [...], where movement, relocation, displacement, and restlessness are the norms rather than the exceptions" (133).[3] Migrants thus need to engage in an act of constantly re-negotiating traditional, conventional ideas of home, neighbourhood, and nation – a negotiation which can be oppressive at times, empowering at others. It is the aim of this chapter to trace both the empowering and the oppressive engagement with the global metropolitan space of the city in Nigerian writer Chimamanda Ngozi Adichie's latest novel, *Americanah*, published in 2013. I endeavour to shed light on how the love story at the heart of *Americanah* depends on and facilitates constructions of place. Since the affective turn in the 1990s, cultural geography has established that the way we produce, co-produce, inhabit, and stage (city) spaces is a deeply affective one, through tactics of moving, feeling, loving.[4] Emotions and senses are implicated in the production of place and spatial, political practices. This relation results in situated knowledges which are able to reclaim and re-politicise, re-map and re-connect territories. As Smith et al. have noted in *Emotion, Place and Culture*, "[e]motions are then intimately and inescapably caught up in the current re-writing of the earth, the production of new, transformed, geographies, and New World orders, that affect us all, albeit in very different ways" (3).

This chapter, then, wants to illuminate how the intimate and affective relationship between the two lovers in Adichie's *Americanah* manages to re-write their transnational world. As Massey has argued, "[t]he identities of place are always unfixed, contested, and multiple," they are "open and porous" (*Space, Place, and Gender* 5). This multiplicity and openness is mirrored in the way Ifemelu and Obinze continually move across the globe and exchange continents (Africa, America, Europe), countries and states (Nigeria, New England, England), and cities (Lagos, Nsukka, New York, Princeton, Philadelphia, Baltimore, London) with each other. Constructing an affective map of their places of belonging does not remain a mere geographical act of travelling or of

---

3   Such tension have of course been some of the most vital animating forces of the postcolonial imagination: literary works that discuss both positive and negative aspects of global migration, transnational relocation and arrival in new spaces abound, and most of them engage in complex discussions of both the anxieties and negative affects as well as the positive potential inherent in such migratory practices. For in-depth discussions about these transnational entanglements in postcolonial literature, cf. Adele Parker and Stephenie Young's volume on *Transnationalism and Resistance: Experience and Experiment in Women's Writing* (2013) and John McLeod's essay on "Sounding Silence: Transculturation and its Thresholds" (2011).
4   See Patricia Clough and Jean Halley, *The Affective Turn* (2007) and Carolyn Pedwell and Anne Whitehead, "Affecting Feminism" in *Feminist Theory* 13.2 (2012).

home-making. It also means that their romantic and sexual relationship produces encounters which open up possibilities to rethink ossified structures. These encounters enable the novel to give way to meaning-making processes of interpretation and transmission. As a consequence, the novel continuously moves in-between the tension of longing and belonging, creating a translocal text that writes desire anew. Thus, figurations of love and notions of place can usefully be brought to bear upon one another to interrogate constructions of (trans)national and diasporic identities. To examine the reciprocity of place and love as offered up by Adichie's novel and specifically its representation of urban spatiality is the purpose of the following discussions.

At the time of writing this chapter, the scholarship on Adichie had focused mainly on her first two novels: *Purple Hibiscus* (2003) catapulted her into national and international limelight, while for her second novel, *Half of a Yellow Sun* (2006), and its sensitive exploration of the Nigerian Biafran war, she was hailed as the new Chinua Achebe.[5] Academic engagement with *Americanah*, however, remained surprisingly sparse, not counting the numerous and often extremely insightful commentaries in the blogosphere and in feuilleton columns of newspapers.[6] The existing journal articles concentrate mainly on the novel's exploration of migrancy and processes of globalization.[7] Whereas critics touch upon the sexual and romantic dynamic between the two protagonists only briefly,[8] I think it lies at the very heart of the text: the love story between Ifemelu and Obinze and their romantic, sexual connection acts as wiggle room for all sorts of political, emotional, and cultural discussions. The main argument this chapter wants to make, then, is that through writing and performing the love story between Ifemelu and Obinze, *Americanah* redraws the boundaries of transnational writing as well as expands the peculiar linkage

---

5   For a perceptive engagement with Adichie's earlier works see Marta Sofia Lopez' "Creating Daughterlands: Dangaremba, Adichie, and Vera" (2007), Anita Harris Satkunananthan's "Textual Transgressions and Consuming the Self in the Fiction of Helen Oyeyemi and Chimamanda Ngozi Adichie" (2011), or Madhu Krishnan's *Contemporary African Literature in English* (2014).
6   See for example Kathryn Schulz's astute review of *Americanah* in the *New York Magazine* (2013).
7   See Patrycja Kozieł's "Narrative Strategy in Chimamanda Ngozi Adichie's Novel *Americanah*: The Manifestation of Migrant Identity" (2015); Caroline Levine's " 'The strange familiar': Structure, Infrastructure, and Adichie's *Americanah*" (2015); Camille Isaacs' "Mediating women's globalized existence through social media in the work of Adichie and Bulawayo" (2016).
8   Such as Jessamy Calkin's "Love in the Time of Cornrows: Chimamanda Ngozi Adichie on Her New Novel" (*The Telegraph*, 2013) or Radhika Jones' "Love in the Time of Globalization: A New Novel Follows Two Lovers Over Three Continents" in *Time International* (2013).

between love and space. To show this, I will draw on Laurent Berlant and Sara Ahmed's conceptualisations of place and emotion as well as on the work of social and cultural geographers such as Doreen Massey, Michel de Certeau and Marc Augé.

2 Moving Desires

Composed of seven sections, *Americanah* opens and closes as a love story between the two protagonists, Ifemelu and Obinze. This love story, however, is not static. It travels, and migrates, it is made of movements and counter-movements. The chapters alternate in describing first the lovers' childhoods in Nigeria and then their adult lives in America (Ifemelu) and Great Britain (Obinze), respectively. The reader stays closer to Ifemelu; her story takes up most of the novel, engulfing other stories but never subordinating them. Adichie posits contemporary Nigeria and the realities of its inhabitants against its colonial pasts and postcolonial futures. Narratives of dis-placement and re-placement, of constructions of blackness, of border-crossings and borderlessness are woven into the love story, which lies at the novel's centre. Roots and routes are superimposed on each other and that which was once supposed to be clear-cut and well organised is now called into question: "Notions of homeland as authentic origin or as a return destination in an essentialized cultural context have been superseded by more dynamic conceptions of abiding diasporic movements and identities" (Munkelt et al., xvii). Ifemelu and Obinze's unsettled romantic and sexual relationship serves both as frame and catalyst for the events recounted.

In its opening paragraphs, *Americanah* circumscribes the urban spaces of Princeton, New Haven, Philadelphia, Baltimore, and Brooklyn, but in the subsequent pages pans out from America to London, Lagos, Nsukka, Newcastle. It navigates localities and manoeuvres passages between different worlds. These transitions and processes of settling down, of travelling and making home, are always connected to affects and emotions. Adichie not only writes her characters into a migrant space but simultaneously also writes this migrant space through the feelings and relations of her characters. The following discussion focuses on the two protagonists of the novel, Ifemelu and Obinze, and their movements through cities, countries, and across oceans – movements which consist not only of simple back and forths, but of active and productive re-inscriptions of their dwelling and transitory spaces. What functions as a link gluing together these trajectories is the relational principle of love and desire. Ifemelu and Obinze, who fall in love during their teenage years in Nigeria, break up and move to different parts of the world. Their romance is deeply entrenched in acts of urban place building, and the aim of my reading is to trace this development.

3 Ifemelu's (In)Visible, (Un)Spoken Cities

> Princeton, in the summer, smelled of nothing, and although Ifemelu liked the tranquil greenness of the many trees, the clean streets and stately homes, the delicately overpriced shops, and the quiet, abiding air of earned grace, it was this, the lack of smell, that most appealed to her, perhaps because the other American cities she knew well had all smelled distinctly. Philadelphia had the musty scent of history. New Haven smelt of neglect. Baltimore smelled of brine, and Brooklyn of sun-warmed garbage. But Princeton had no smell.
> *Americanah* 3

When we first meet Ifemelu, the female protagonist and main narrator of *Americanah*, she is a resident of Princeton, on a scholarship, in an ostensibly stable relationship, a successful and Afropolitan Nigerian immigrant integrated into an America in which she describes herself as "someone adorned with certainty" (3). This certainty, however, is closely interwoven with a sense of lack, or emptiness. Acting more as an outside spectator to the on-goings of her and others' lives and not as someone actively telling her own story, this almost ghostly existence of pretence offers an ambivalent starting point for evaluating Ifemelu's "stations", the architecture of her (hi)story. The city Princeton is the final place she moves to in America and stands for her having finally arrived and settled, but also for having arrived at a dead end. Seemingly having completed a "successful story" of immigration and integration, she has also become immobile, emotionally as well as geographically. The troubling tension inherent to this paradox is exemplified by her visit to Trenton (a suburb of Princeton) to get her hair braided, a procedure which is inherently linked to her Nigerian identity, and something Princeton cannot offer. The hair salon, a locus of African-ness and especially African womanhood, thus, is relegated to the periphery, and she needs to leave Princeton and enter a state of transit to get there (4). The distance from Princeton to Trenton is not a long way to travel to get her hair braided, but on closer look this braiding process takes much longer – in this case, almost six hundred pages. To be able to trace her movements through and across America, the following analysis will go back in history and reach for some of the places and sites that have come to constitute Ifemelu's (be)longing, dwelling, and "becoming".

Americanah produces highly complex interrelations between its characters and the spaces they inhabit and imbue with meaning. When Ifemelu first comes to America as a teenager – alone and without Obinze but full of hope and naivety – Brooklyn, her first stop in the following chronology of American cities, is connected to the affective relational structure of family. As quoted in the epigraph above, its smell of sun-warmed garbage evokes the long hot summer Ifemelu spends in New York with her aunt Uju and cousin Dike – suspended, not yet having begun her life in America. When she then moves to Philadelphia to start college, she lives in a small dingy flat with three almost identical looking American girls (Jackie, Elena, Allison) – and just as Ifemelu describes it years later as having the musty scent of his*tory*, Philadelphia is indeed the place where her story starts. This starting point of Ifemelu's American history, however, is one that is deeply ambiguous and problematic:

> She was standing at the periphery of her own life, sharing a fridge and a toilet, a shallow intimacy, with people she did not know at all. People who lived in exclamation points. [...] People who did not scrub in the shower: their shampoos and conditioners and gels were cluttered in the bathroom, but there was not a single sponge, and this, the absence of a sponge, made them seem unreachably alien to her. (156)

This interplay of intimacy/alienation with the other girls' American corporeality denotes processes of *girling*[9] she is not part of – the interior space of the bathroom which metonymically stands for her first station in America is a girly room that is not her own, as the cultural codes and politics of hygiene remain separate from her. She cannot gain entry into that room and is excluded from these girling processes.

She feels estranged, foreign to herself, and thus Philadelphia is put in stark contrast to her life in Nigeria and especially her connection to Obinze. This connection is severed by her, however, when she undergoes a deeply traumatising experience: desperately searching for a job, for a way to be able to pay her expenses and send money back home, she takes on a different name to work

---

9 Sara Ahmed has described these *girling* processes with reference to Judith Butler as follows: "A gender assignment can be a room, and not all of us feel at home in the rooms we have been given. We might feel more or less at home at different times. Judith Butler taught us to think of 'girling' as a social mechanism. A baby is born: we might say 'it's a girl!' And of course 'girling' moments do not stop happening, even after we are pronounced girls" (Ahmed n.p.).

under a false security card: "At first, Ifemelu forgot that she was someone else" (159), but then she gets better and better at living invisibly, hiding her name, revoking her true identity. When all her search and attempts remain unfruitful, however, she responds to a newspaper advertisement looking for a *"female personal assistant for busy sports coach in Ardmore, communication and interpersonal skills required"* (176) – she ends up "helping him relax" by letting him touch her while he masturbates (177). Ardmore and her experience there initiate a silence, a deep and all-evoking silence that swallows her trauma, makes her hate her body and disrupt her and Obinze's communication:

> She wanted to shower, to scrub herself, but she could not bear the thought of touching her own body, and so she put on her nightdress, gingerly, to touch as little of herself as possible. [...] That night, it snowed, her first snow, and in the morning, she watched the world outside her window, the parked cars made lumpy, misshapen, by layered snow. She was bloodless, detached, floating in a world where darkness descended too soon and everyone walked around burdened by coats, and flattened by the absence of light. [...] She felt herself sinking, sinking quickly, and unable to pull herself up. [...] Between her and what she should feel, there was a gap. [...] She no longer went to class. Her days were stilled by silence and snow. (190)

This silence (the unutterable that belongs to sexual and bodily violation) and the depression that follows is deeply inscribed into Ifemelu's American space. It is the inherent nature of trauma to remain unspeakable, to cause disjunction and dissociation. But especially with regard to literature, textual production, and language, more recent scholarship in connection to affect theory and ethics has shown that reparative work through language and narrative has to be done to *un-swallow* trauma, to retch it up and bring it back into the open.[10] Ifemelu's inability to put into words what has happened to her (marked by her denial of any form of communication with Obinze) is mirrored by her handling of place. Instead of engaging in processes of relationality and an open and productive meaning making (as propositioned by Massey), she shuts herself off from any form of placed or localised attachment – this is marked by her refusal to go outside and interact with the wintery city that sinks into snow. She is "detached" and "bloodless" and Philadelphia becomes a non-place; a place of

---

10   This has been argued for example by Sonya Andermahr and Silvia Pellicer-Ortín in *Trauma Narratives and Herstory* (2013), or Dolores Herrero and Sonia Baelo-Allué in *The Splintered Glass: Facets of Trauma in the Post-Colony and Beyond* (2011).

no "relation, only solitude" as the anthropologist Marc Augé has argued in *Non-Places: Introduction to an Anthropology of Supermodernism* (103).

Slowly, however, Ifemelu not only learns to negotiate the silence caused by her traumatising experience, but she also learns to negotiate the non-place of Philadelphia. While she struggles to carve out her belonging in this American metropolitan space, it becomes clear that Philadelphia is paradoxically also the site demarcating her initiation into America. This undoing of the non-place is marked when she begins "knowing" her surroundings and the place she has found herself in:

> She hungered to understand everything about America, to wear a new, knowing skin right away: to support a team at the Super Bowl, understand what a Twinkie was and what sports 'lockouts' meant, measure in ounces and square feet, order a 'muffin' without thinking that it really was a cake, and say 'I 'scored' a deal' without feeling silly.
> *Americanah* 166

In playing through different variations of voice and voiceless-ness, place and placeless-ness, Ifemelu begins understanding, knowing, and expressing herself: "New words were falling out of her mouth. Columns of mist were dispersing" (167). Having lost the connection to Nigeria and simultaneously to her lover Obinze, Ifemelu is faced with a new, foreign place – one where she is not at home but also one which offers her the possibility to forge a new home, a new sense of belonging, a new identity. As Neil Leach has argued, "understandings of 'belonging' should be inscribed within a context of 'non-belonging'. The very notion of 'belonging' contains within itself a certain sense of initial alienation" (11). The side-by-side of desire for "home" and the process of "homing" points towards how Ifemelu builds up friendship and affiliation through practices of place-making; how she produces an affective rewriting/re-inhabiting of her cities, undergoing developments that are deeply inscribed into personal, romantic, emotional, and erotic matters.

A few years later, when Ifemelu has moved to Baltimore and lives with one of her American boyfriends, she is suddenly brought back into contact with her past, with both Nigeria and Obinze whom she had cut out of her life. She meets a childhood friend, Kayode, in the mall (a prototypical American space) and takes this meeting as a cue to reach out to Obinze: she sends him an email, opening up a digital route to him (278, 293).[11] This reaching out, this desire for contact, is the instance which transports the text of *Americanah* spatially from

---

11 A discussion of the importance of online spaces and digital routes/roots in *Americanah*

America to England, leaving Ifemelu in Baltimore and moving to Obinze in London. This change of place not only signals a change of focalisation and narrative voice, but also a structural and meta-textual shift: Ifemelu's desire (her reaching out, her sending out a message) mirrors what is deeply ingrained into the structure of every love story: a desire for resolution, for overcoming obstacles. The empty space between the lovers needs to be filled up: desire exists in the web of the text, it's "tissue" (Barthes 64) and in the white spaces between the threads. Love and desire, thus, mark not only spatial translocations but also textual ones, producing a story and spinning a discursive yarn.

4   Obinze's Lonely London

> The wind blowing across the British Isles was odorous with fear of asylum seekers, infecting everybody with the panic of impending doom, and so articles were written and read, simply and stridently, as though the writers lived in a world in which the present was unconnected to the past, and they had never considered this to be the normal course of history: the influx into Britain of black and brown people from countries created by Britain. Yet he understood. It had to be comforting, this denial of history.
> *Americanah* 320

As the text takes the meeting between Ifemelu and Kayode as a turning point to leave Ifemelu's story and venture into Obinze's life, in the following I similarly want to concentrate on the spatial counterpart to Ifemelu's America, Obinze's England, as well as the migrational practices of his often-ambivalent place-making in London.

At the beginning of their relationship, when Ifemelu has just left for America, Obinze desperately tries to follow her but is denied a visa. After Ifemelu stops replying to his calls, letters and text messages, Obinze decides to move to England. Obinze's England is a cold one, and his precarious status

---

(which can be traced through the emails Ifemelu and Obinze send each other, and through the blog Ifemelu starts in America, called *Raceteenth or Various Observations About American Blacks (Those Formerly Known as Negroes) by a Non-American Black*) would go beyond the scope of this chapter. Cf. Serena Guarracino's "Writing «so raw and true»: Blogging in Chimamanda Ngozi Adichie's *Americanah*" (2014) and Camille Isaacs' "Mediating Women's Globalized Existence Through Social Media in the Work of Adichie and Bulawayo" (2016).

as an illegal immigrant is mirrored by his spatial tactics there: he is always on the move, shifting places, drifting from one tube station to another, constantly on the train, walking the streets of London, or driving for a delivery warehouse in West Thurrock. These continuous movements underline the helplessness and purposelessness of his life in England. Especially the tube station as an inherently urban space signifies one important spatial aspect of London, the former heart of the Empire in its bustle and thrumming transitory nature: the London underground with its labyrinthine branches and colourful lines transports close-crammed bodies in and out of the city, it carries identities and bridges the different suburbs with their various ethnic make-ups – at once stained with old empire and containing new multitudes. It is almost always tube stations that figure as important turning points in Obinze's story: "It was at a tube station that he met the Angolans who would arrange his marriage" (281), "He met the girl, Cleotilde, a few days later at a shopping centre, in a McDonald's whose windows looked out onto the dank entrance of a tube station" (282) and it is also at a tube station that he realises that he might develop feelings for this strange woman whom he is supposed to marry (285). The stations serve as meeting points between different cultures, races and hopes; they seem almost like dreary, damp and grey versions of Ahdaf Soueif's mezzaterrae or Mary Louise Pratt's contact zones[12] – signifying points of contact but also the sheer vastness and arbitrariness of the city and its inhabitants' lives.

These zones are only accessible to Obinze in a restricted, shadowy way. His life in London much more resembles a closed-off cage in which he has to deal with his anxieties and hardships alone: "He would walk fast on the pavement, turned tightly into himself, hands deep in the coat his cousin had lent him, a grey wool coat whose sleeves nearly swallowed his fingers. [...] [A]nd he would think: *You can work, you are legal, you are visible, and you don't even know how fortunate you are*" (281). His invisibility plays out in different realms: one is the official and legal one, connected to the loss of his name as he – like Ifemelu at the beginning – has to take on a false name and

---

[12] In her essay collection *Mezzaterra: Fragments from the Common Ground* (2005), Ahdaf Soueif describes the construct of mezzaterra as a space of cross-cultural understanding, "a meeting-point for many cultures or traditions" (6) – a space similar to what Pratt has defined her contact zones to be: "social places where disparate cultures meet, clash and grapple with each other, often in highly asymmetrical relations of domination and subordination [...]; the term 'contact zone', which I use to refer to the space of colonial encounters, the space in which peoples geographically and historically separated come into contact with each other" (4).

the social security card of someone else to be able to find work. In order to insert himself into the legitimate grid of work and productivity in London, he has to be(come) someone else. The other, more abstract realm is a logical correlation to the first one: with the loss of a name comes the loss of identity. Obinze corporeally, materially lives in London, but he does so "invisibly, his existence like an erased pencil sketch" (318), a faint trace of himself without being seen or recognized. These processes of *becoming* un-named and de-mobilised (restricted in movement and speech) as an illegal immigrant, mirror Sara Ahmed's idea of race as a restrictive room which stifles "non-white people who inhabit white spaces" (n.p.). Obinze experiences the loss of place, he has "no room to be" (n.p.). Ahmed calls this absence a "not" (a nod to Augé's non-places): "This is how a 'not' can be so tight that it too feels like the loss of wiggle room (we might think a 'not' is quite roomy, perhaps we can make it so, when we embrace this 'not,' willingly and wilfully)" (n.p.). Obinze's geographical, corporeal, and psychological "not" can be traced in the way he moves through urban space: he is "turned tightly into himself", "nearly swallowed" by his surroundings (*Americanah* 317). As Ahmed argues, "you might experience becoming tighter in response to a world that does not accommodate you. You have less room. Sometimes a world can be so tight that it is hard to breathe" (n.p.). The only place which seems to give Obinze room to breathe, at least for a short time, is a book store – where he could "become Obinze again" (*Americanah* 317) and where he finds a small and temporary home in the un-homely city as he reaches out to others.

The tension between home and not-belonging is again and again played out in the paradigmatic metropolitan space, the London underground: "He sat on the stained seat of the noisy train, opposite a woman reading the evening paper. *Speak English at home, Blunkett tells immigrants.* [...] The wind blowing across the British Isles was odorous with fear of asylum seekers" (320). The medical (and sensory, olfactory) discourse ("odorous", "infecting") employed by this nationalistic rhetoric against a supposed reversed colonisation here evokes the deeply panicked, racial anxieties of colonial England in the 17th and 18th century when Britain tried to establish itself as a global power, as a Britannia that had and always would rule the waves. The idea of migrancy as a movement "gone wrong" which turns given structures upside down is deeply entrenched in the utterances of then Home Secretary David Blunkett, which Adichie uses to underline Obinze's troubled existence below legal citizenship.

When Obinze's scam marriage is broken up by the police, he is to be "removed", deported back to Nigeria via a holding cell in Manchester and the deportation centre in Dover: " 'Removed.' That word made Obinze feel inanimate. A thing to be removed. A thing without breath and mind.

A thing" (345). His status as a thing, an unwanted undesirable object to be removed, completes Obinze's failed pursuit to carve out a place for himself in London and now also materially puts him into the restricted, restricting cage of deviance:

> In detention, he felt raw, skinned, the outer layers of himself stripped off. [...] Obinze had read about Dover in a newspaper. A former prison. It felt surreal, to be driven past the electronic gates, the high walls, the wires. His cell was smaller, colder, than the cell in Manchester [...] He could not eat; he felt his body slackening, his flesh disappearing. (347)

The psychological trauma of forceful displacement is transported onto a bodily level, as he can feel himself shrink and literally, corporeally disappear – up until the moment he is welcomed by his mother at the airport in Lagos where he slowly begins to recover.

In pinning Obinze's failed journey against Ifemelu's story of supposed American success and in constantly mirroring these narratives against each other, Adichie draws attention to the contradictions and traumas inherent to migratory movement. Hers is a diasporic transnational writing that challenges compliance and complacence and questions class and privilege. Obinze's traumatic experience of being lost, of being one of the invisible ones cleaning toilets in a foreign country conforms to the classical structure of being made unrecognisably other (of thus becoming other), but it is not a story one as a reader suspects to happen to him after following around Ifemelu through her cities and relationships. Both Obinze and Ifemelu eventually return to Nigeria, to the city of Lagos – one of them because he couldn't build a successful life elsewhere and the other because her successful life elsewhere felt empty. Upon returning, both become "Americanah,"[13] an identity description that in its hybridity points to Adichie's project of offering not a monolithic single story of Africa, but multi-faceted smaller ones. As the text knots together Ifemelu's and

---

13 The first time this term appears in the novel is when Ifemelu and her childhood friends make fun of another girl for pretending to no longer understand Yoruba and adding a slurred *r* to every English word after having returned from an American holiday: "They roared with laughter, at that word 'Americanah', wreathed in glee, the fourth syllable extended" (78). The word play and its linguistic markers and nuances is again used to point to hybrid and ambiguous identity structures, when upon Ifemelu's return to Nigeria years later, her friend Ranyinudo teases her because of her missing American accent: "The problem is that you are not even a real Americanah" (476) and later "You're no longer behaving like an Americanah" (488). These claims mark Ifemelu's final reintegration into her Nigerian space.

Obinze's storylines once again, it moves to Lagos, the final city to be discussed in this chapter.

5   Lagos Is for Lovers

> At first, Lagos assaulted her; the sun-dazed haste, the yellow buses full of squashed limbs, the swearing hawkers racing after cars, the advertisements on hulking billboards (others scrawled on walls – PLUMBER CALL 080177777) and the heaps of rubbish that rose on the roadside like a taunt. Commerce thrummed too defiantly. And the air was dense with exaggeration, conversations full of overprotestations. [...] Here, she felt, anything could happen. And so she had the dizzying sensation of falling, falling into the new person she had become, falling into the strange familiar. (475)

In the following, I will focus on the city of Lagos as both ending and starting point to Ifemelu and Obinze's love story. When Obinze returns to Lagos after his disastrous stay in London, he reinserts himself into his old life. He gradually learns how to engage with the bustle of the city, and turns into an extremely successful businessman, married to a beautiful wife he does not love. When Ifemelu returns to Lagos, she has to re-learn and re-orient herself. She is being "assaulted" by this new city. It is loud, noisy, hot, crammed and dirty, and she describes the bustle as defiant; here, she feels, "anything could happen" (475). In comparison to the clean quietness of Princeton and the grey coldness of London, there is definitely an opposition between Western space (cold, orderly, calm) and African space (chaotic, hot, turbulent) opened up by the novel. This simplistic binary is dissolved, however, when city text and romance text become entangled.

While Obinze's engagement with Lagos is marked by the stability of his job as an estate agent and property owner, Ifemelu's space making is expressed in terms of reading and making sense: "She had grown up knowing all the bus stops and the side streets, understanding the cryptic codes of conductors and the body language of street hawkers. Now, she struggled to grasp the unspoken" (475). Ifemelu has lost the sense of being able to name or map and needs to re-familiarize herself with the language of the city, how its streets are spelled. The text shows Ifemelu engaging in a process of spelling out anew the grammar of her city and thus also of herself: "Ifemelu stared out of the window, half listening, thinking how unpretty Lagos was, roads infested with potholes, houses springing up unplanned like weeds. Of her jumble of feelings, she recognized only confusion" (477). Reading this experience through a lens coloured by Michel de Certeau's spatial theories of the city, the walker – in opposition to the panoptic voyeur – confusedly follows chaotic paths through a metropolitan thicket. But s/he nevertheless produces pedestrian speech acts, a "wandering of the semantic" that makes some parts of the city disappear and exaggerate others, distorting and fragmenting it, diverting it from its immobile order (101). In moving through the city, the walker produces a text that may act as a powerful tactic of re-appropriating territory. Short cuts, turns and detours create disorder and anarchy; walking functions as an interruption: it "slips into the clear text of the planned and readable city" (93) and thus produces "multiform resistance, tricky, stubborn procedures that elude discipline" (96). After a while, Ifemelu has "the dizzying sensation of falling, falling into the new person she had become, falling into the strange familiar" (*Americanah* 475). The notion of the "strange familiar" disrupts any clear-cut binaries the reader would have drawn between Europe or America and Africa as all the city spaces in each country need to be deciphered and made intelligible.

When Ifemelu and Obinze finally meet again, they both start inhabiting the space of the city in different ways, propelled by their desire for each other. They meet in bookshops, cafés and bars, they drive through the city in cabs or Obinze's car, telling each other their secrets. In moving through the urban space and through their pasts, they weave the text of their love story: "They had a history, a connection thick as twine" (538). The lovers' spatial and affective speech acts are deeply intertwined, a fact which is mirrored in their intimate interactions: "He felt familiar and unfamiliar at the same time" (541), "their bodies remembered and did not remember" (551). The erosion of borders and obstacles which features so prevalently in the narrative, a structural convention of telling love stories, is transported onto the corporeal level of love making: "she felt boneless against him" (542), "there was, between them, a weightless, seamless desire" (551) and "there was an awakening even in her nails, in those parts of her body that had always been numb" (551). In her essay "A Properly Political Concept of Love," Lauren Berlant states that "if love is force, though, it is a mess-making force, as its aim is to dissolve toxic sureties" (685). I argue that Ifemelu and Obinze's love story dissolves sureties – and *sure* is here equated with the *toxic*. This stresses the potentially destructive nature of love but also its reparative un-toxifying potential to create and proliferate meaning, linking to how Massey describes place as always relational, dynamic, and engendering interpretation. In construing an affective map of Lagos (geographically) and of each other's bodies (affectively), both Ifemelu and Obinze construct a meaningful sense of belonging. Lagos, in contrast to London or Princeton, becomes an open urban space which enables the productive, if messy, reformulation of transnational identity, "inviting us to map new itineraries of migration and resistance" (Goyal xviii).[14]

Of particular significance for this entanglement of space and affect are the very last words of the novel, when Ifemelu and Obinze finally, ultimately (after seven months in Lagos) enact their happy ending. These words are "Come in" (*Americanah* 588). In their inclusiveness and inward-movement, they stand for integration and synthesis. "Come in" is not only meant in the spatial sense (please enter this flat) but also in an affective, emotive and sensual sense (please come to me, join me). The emotional geographies explored throughout this chapter have shown that the various cities inhabited by the two protagonists (London, Princeton, Philadelphia, New York, Baltimore, Lagos) conceal and lay bare other relational structures of contact, border-crossing and transitory liminal states: love, desire, romance. Emotions do not appear as mere background for the imaginative geography the novel builds, but are indispensable for its world and identity making. After their sometimes more, sometimes less unsuccessful and fraught residences in various cities in both Europe and the United States, Nigeria's Lagos becomes Ifemelu's and Obinze's final space: by returning to their African homeland, both migrant protagonists generate for themselves a new old home, a productive and affective space – one in which all the place building tactics employed prior culminate: "And this was Nigeria, where boundaries were blurred" (483). Lagos as a chaotic but homely place facilitates, enacts, and performs the lovers' translocal identities: they had, finally, spun themselves "fully into being" (586).

Works Cited

Adichie, Chimamanda Ngozi. *Americanah: A Novel*. New York: Anchor Books, 2013.

Ahmed, Sara. "Wiggle Room." *Feminist Killjoy*. September 28, 2014. Accessed June 11, 2016, http://feministkilljoys.com/2014/09/28/wiggle-room/.

Andermahr, Sonya and Silvia Pellicer-Ortín, eds. *Trauma Narratives and Herstory*. Basingstoke: Palgrave Macmillan, 2013.

Anderson, Jon. *Understanding Cultural Geography: Places and Traces*. New York: Routledge, 2010.

---

14 With this portrayal of Lagos as inherently productive and open, Adichie challenges other literary portraits of Nigeria's metropolitan spaces as irreparably stuck in political corruption and other gridlocks, such as in Cyprian Ekwensi's *People of the City* (1954) and Chinua Achebe's *No Longer at Ease* (1960) or, more recently, Teju Cole's depictions of Lagos in *Every Day is for the Thief* (2007) (cf. Habila).

Augé, Marc. *Non-Places: Introduction to an Anthropology of Supermodernism*. Transl. John Howe. London and New York: Verso, 1995.

Barthes, Roland. *The Pleasure of the Text*. New York: Hill and Wang, 1975.

Berlant, Lauren. "A Properly Political Concept of Love: Three Approaches in Ten Pages." *Cultural Anthropology*, vol. 2, 2011: 683–91.

Bhabha, Homi K. *The Location of Culture*. London/New York: Routledge, 1994.

Butler, Judith. *Bodies That Matter: On the Discursive Limits of 'Sex'*. New York: Routledge, 1993.

Calkin, Jessamy. "Love in the Time of Cornrows: Chimamanda Ngozi Adichie on Her New Novel." *The Telegraph*. April 6, 2013. Accessed August 28, 2016. http://www.telegraph.co.uk/culture/books/authorinterviews/9968921/Love-in-the-time-of-cornrows-Chimamanda-Ngozi-Adichie-on-her-new-novel.html.

Certeau, Michel de. "Walking in the City." *The Practice of Everyday Life*. Berkeley: U of California P, 1984, pp. 91–110.

Clough Ticineto, Patricia and Jean Halley, eds. *The Affective Turn: Theorizing the Social*. Durham, NC: Duke UP, 2007.

Deleuze, Gilles and Felix Guattari. *A Thousand Plateaus: Capitalism and Schizophrenia*. Transl. Brian Massumi. Minneapolis, MN: U of Minnesota P, 1987.

Gilroy, Paul. *The Black Atlantic. Modernity and Double-Consciousness*. Harvard: Harvard UP, 1995.

Goyal, Yogita. "Introduction: Africa and the Black Atlantic." *Research in African Literatures*, vol. 45, no. 3, 2014: v–xxv.

Guarracino, Serena. "Writing «so raw and true»: Blogging in Chimamanda Ngozi Adichie's *Americanah*." *Between*, vol. IV, no. 8, 2014: 1–27.

Habila, Helon. "Sense of the City: Lagos." *BBC: The World Today*. July 31, 2003. Accessed March 7, 2018. http://news.bbc.co.uk/2/hi/africa/3110929.stm.

Hall, Stuart. "Cultural Identity and Diaspora." *Colonial Discourse & Postcolonial Theory: A Reader*, edited by Patrick Williams and Laura Chrisman, London/New York: Harvester Wheatsheaf, 1993. pp. 222–37.

Herrero, Dolores and Sonia Baelo-Allué, eds. *The Splintered Glass: Facets of Trauma in the Post-Colony and Beyond*. Amsterdam and New York: Rodopi, 2011.

Isaacs, Camille. "Mediating Women's Globalized Existence Through Social Media in the Work of Adichie and Bulawayo." *Safundi: The Journal of South African and American Studies*, vol. 17, no. 2, 2016: 174–88.

Jones, Radhika. "Love in the Time of Globalization: A New Novel Follows Two Lovers Over Three Continents." *Time International*. May 13, 2013. Accessed August 28, 2016. http://content.time.com/ time/magazine/article/0,9171,2142502,00.html.

Kozieł, Patrycja. "Narrative Strategy in Chimamanda Ngozi Adichie's Novel *Americanah*: The Manifestation of Migrant Identity." *Studies of the Department of African Languages and Cultures*, vol. 49, 2015: 96–113.

Krishnan, Madhu. *Contemporary African Literature in English: Global Locations, Postcolonial Identifications.* Basingstoke: Palgrave Macmillan, 2014.

Leach, Neil. "Belonging." *London: Postcolonial City. AA Files*, vol. 49, 2003: 76–82.

Levine, Caroline. " 'The strange familiar': Structure, Infrastructure, and Adichie's *Americanah*." *MFS Modern Fiction Studies*, vol. 61, no. 4, 2015: 587–605.

Lopez, Marta Sofia. "Creating Daughterlands: Dangaremba, Adichie, and Vera." *Journal of the African Literature Association*, vol. 2, no. 1, 2007: 83–97.

Massey, Doreen. "Power-Geometry and a Progressive Sense of Place." *Mapping the Futures: Local Cultures, Global Change*, edited by John Bird et al., London/New York: Routledge, 1993. pp. 59–69.

Massey, Doreen. *Space, Place, and Gender*. Minneapolis, MN: U of Minnesota P, 1994.

McLeod, John. "Sounding Silence: Transculturation and its Thresholds." *Transnational Literature*, vol. 4, no. 1, 2011: 1–13.

Munkelt, Marga, Markus Schmitz, Silke Stroh and Mark Stein, eds. *Postcolonial Translocations: Cultural Representation and Critical Spatial Thinking. ASNEL Papers 17. Cross/Cultures Series*. Amsterdam/New York: Rodopi, 2013.

Parker, Adele and Stephenie Young, eds. *Transnationalism and Resistance: Experience and Experiment in Women's Writing*. Amsterdam and New York: Brill, 2013.

Pedwell, Carolyn and Anne Whitehead. "Affecting Feminism: Questions of Feeling in Feminist Theory." *Feminist Theory*, vol. 13, no. 2, 2012: 115–29.

Pratt, Mary Louise. *Imperial Eyes: Travel Writing and Transculturation*. London/New York: Routledge, 1992.

Satkunananthan, Anita Harris. "Textual Transgressions and Consuming the Self in the Fiction of Helen Oyeyemi and Chimamanda Ngozi Adichie." *Hecate*, vol. 37, no. 2, 2011: 41–69.

Schulz, Kathryn. "Review of *Americanah* by Chimamanda Ngozi Adichie." *New York Magazine*, 3 June 2013.

Smith, Mick, Joyce Davidson, Laura Cameron and Liz Bondi, eds. "Geography and Emotion – Emerging Constellations." *Emotion, Place and Culture*, Farnham and Burlington: Ashgate, 2009. pp. 1–20.

Soja, Edward. "Foreword." *Postcolonial Spaces: The Politics of Place in Contemporary Culture*, edited by Andrew Teverson and Sara Upstone, Basingstoke: Palgrave, 2011. pp. ix–xiii.

Soueif, Ahdaf. *Mezzaterra: Fragments from the Common Ground*. London: Anchor Books, 2005.

PART 5

Criminal Affects: Crime and the City

∴

CHAPTER 11

Criminal Affects: Hard-boiled Discourse and the New Cultures of Fear in Patrick Neate's *City of Tiny Lights*

Tamás Bényei

Abstract

This chapter reads Patrick Neate's novel *City of Tiny Lights* (2005) as a text that uses the noir discourse to map the multi-ethnic metropolis after 9/11. Noir is a crucial discourse of the (Western) city, concerned with the containability of crime, enabling a 'normal' urban life. *City of Tiny Lights* is a noir thriller morphing into what seems like a multicultural noir or even a post-9/11 noir. Introducing Black British war veteran (ex-Mujahedin and ex-CIA agent) Tommy Akhtar as private detective, Neate's novel stages the disintegration of the noir plot through a twofold redrawing of the city's cartography: Akhtar's past and his "soldier identity" transform the city into a war zone; while simultaneously the international geopolitical conditions – involving arms deals and terrorism – that generate the plot question the relevance of noir investigative methods and the competence of the private eye, while the morphology of the city is altered beyond the authority of Akhtar and of the noir genre.

> In times of terror, when everyone is something of a conspirator, everybody will be in the position of having to play detective.
> WALTER BENJAMIN: *The Paris of the Second Empire in Baudelaire*, 72

∴

Some of the most radical and original recent literary re-mappings of the post-imperial, multi-ethnic city arguably take place in what is known as genre fiction. In the British context, one may think of J. G. Ballard and Michael Moorcock, as well as cyberpunk novels like Jeff Noon's *Vurt* (1993) or steampunk fiction such as Miéville's *Perdido Street Station* (2000), or even some of the comic fantasies by Terry Pratchett set in Discworld capital

Ankh-Morpork (such as the 1989 *Guards, Guards!*), as poignant re-thinkings of the politics of a multi-ethnic city. Crime fiction has also played its part in the literary remapping of the city, from China Miéville's urban fantasy *The City and the City* (2009) and Ben Aaronovitch's noir urban fantasy sequence (*Rivers of London*, from 2011) to the gritty crime novels of black British authors: Mike Phillips's Sam Dean novels (starting with the 1989 *Blood Rights*), Victor Headley's Yardie novels (starting with the 1992 *Yardie*) and the novels of the other X Press writers (cf. Horsley 230), or, most recently, A. A. Dhand's Bradford series featuring Sikh police detective Harry Virdee (*Streets of Darkness*, 2016). The most original black British reworking of the hard-boiled tradition is probably Diran Adebayo's *My Once Upon a Time* (2000), set in a futuristic London where race relations have altered following some unidentified cataclysmic events, and mixing the Jamaican patois of private eye Boy with several other linguistic and cultural registers, including Yoruba mythology which supplies the context for the surreal climax. (On recent ethnic crime fiction, cf. Horsley 199–241, Sauerberg 162–80.)

Patrick Neate's 2005 hard-boiled novel *City of Tiny Lights* might be seen as part of this trend, even though Neate is not a crime writer. He, however, recognised the possibilities in the genre which, "with its tradition of reflecting all the potentially significant elements of a banal and trivial everyday world for the solution of crimes," as Lars Ole Sauerberg writes, "records stirrings in the body politic like a seismograph" (Sauerberg 162). His turn to the hard-boiled genre is part of his ongoing fictional project of mapping the legacy of colonialism and imperial Britain in a variety of genres, from postmodern historical blockbuster (*Jerusalem* [2009]) to fantastic satire (*The London Pigeon War* [2013]). Seen in this context, *City of Tiny Lights* is a conscious attempt to probe the discourse of the hard-boiled genre, which Neate's text follows to the point of parody in a post-9/11 multicultural context. This effect is reinforced by the fact that the publication of the novel eerily coincided with the 7/7 2005 London bombings – eerily, as one of the novel's central events (several bombs going off at the same time in various parts of the capital) recalls what actually did happen in London (cf. Eckstein, Korte, Pirker, "Introduction" 14).

With its "idiosyncratic mix" (Falkenhayner 154) of popular fiction and Asian-British second-generation multi-cultural fiction of the 1990s such as Hanif Kureishi's *Buddha of Suburbia* (1990) and Zadie Smith's *White Teeth* (2000), *City of Tiny Lights* maps out the transformation of the cosmopolitan urban environment into a space where both the private eye and the hard-boiled genre itself are revealed to be inadequate in the face of post-9/11 threats as the affect of (physical) fear which dominates the hard-boiled and noir worlds is replaced by terror. If the private detective, a flâneur, a figure of urban angst, traditionally remains more or less in control of his environment, Neate's novel suggests that this is no longer the case. This chapter will address the self-reflexive strategies whereby *City of Tiny Lights* explores the (in)adequacy of hard-boiled discourse (with its narrative conventions, urban topographies, vision of masculinity and affective mappings of the urban scene) in its mapping of the post-imperial city. I shall argue that the limitations of the relevance or viability of hard-boiled discourse are shown on several levels to be limitations of larger import, and that the reasons for this inadequacy have to do with the transformation of urban spaces as well as with what has been called the new cultures of fear. The breakdown of the noir plot indicates a general inadequacy of certain kinds of urban mappings and knowledges, as well as a radical redrawing of the affective map of the city. Neate's novel achieves this through repeated juxtapositions of the local and the global, juxtapositions that are represented as inseparable from questions of affect.

In Neate's novel, most rules of the genre are scrupulously observed as long as they can be observed: the narrator-protagonist private eye speaks the streetwise, epigrammatic language of Marlowe; the trivial case grows into something unpredictably large which the detective feels obliged to tackle; sleaze and politics at the highest level are involved. The client, a black prostitute called Melody Chase, who is usually referred to by her online profile name "exoticmelody," is a version of the obligatory femme fatale, and she of course fails to tell Akhtar everything he might need to know to solve the case. She wants him to find her missing flatmate, a Russian prostitute (Natasha or "sexyrussian"), who left with a client and then disappeared. The client, an MP called Bailey, is found dead the next day in a hotel room, but there is no trace of Natasha. Akhtar tracks Natasha down in a small seaside resort, where Natasha tells him that she was not in the hotel room when Bailey was killed: having gone down to the local store to buy drinks, only to find Bailey dead on her return. She stole his wallet and phone and made her escape. At this point, the original case – as in *The Big Sleep* and many other hard-boiled novels – is closed, though we are not yet halfway through the text. Akhtar, however, in the spirit of Philip Marlowe, perseveres in his investigation, trying to find out as much as he can about the murder of the politician, and this is when things go seriously wrong.

1   "My Immigrant Friend"

In most postcolonial crime fiction, as Patricia Plummer claims, "the actual murder investigation becomes a prop in a plot which is more concerned with issues of gender, ethnicity and migration, the global vs. the local, and how these forces impact on and shape individual identities" (256). Such fiction tends to engage with political issues through the figure of the socially-politically alert and responsible investigator protagonist – this is what happens, for instance, in the novels of Mike Phillips, where Sam Dean, a street-wise Caribbean-born freelance journalist living in North London, operates with a constant awareness of his blackness, driven by a sense of social responsibility.

While the voice of a Black private eye – as in Walter Mosley and a great deal of other Afro-American crime fiction – often serves to establish an authentic Black voice (Horsley 202), Neate pursues different aims, even though Tommy Akhtar's postcolonial credentials are impeccable to the point of travesty; he is the ultimate multicultural detective with an "English-Ugandan-Indian core" (8), flaunting his multi-hyphenated identity: "After all, I'm a Paki-immigrant-Ugandan-Indian Englishman myself" (122). Driven out of Uganda by Idi Amin in 1972, his GP father Farzad opened a corner shop in Chiswick, naming his sons in tribute to his complicated postcolonial identity: the younger son was named after Indian cricketer Gundappa Viswanath, while Tommy after British comedian and stage magician Tommy Cooper, who often sported an Oriental(ist) accessory – an Egyptian red fez – during his shows.[1]

This bit of imperial cross-dressing seems appropriate as there is in fact something decidedly stagey, even histrionic in Akhtar's self-fashioning. For instance, in a self-conscious display of certain postcolonial tropes, he describes himself variously in terms of mimicry and the abject. He literally becomes the embodiment of the cultural abject whenever he uses public transport rather than one of his brother's minicabs. At one point, he passes out on the tube after getting drunk. "When I woke up, I found I'd dribbled down on my shirt-front and my section of the carriage had been taken over by half a dozen toffs evening-dressed for a night out who-knows-where. They were laughing at me" (Neate 80–1). Akhtar begins to eye one of the girls in a provocative manner, but her boyfriend (who has been jeering at him) backs out. "The English ruling classes that Farzad so admires (and there's so much potential therapy in that statement) don't exist no more. Once they ran the world. Now they don't even

---

[1] There is no space here to discuss the other strain of the novel's self-conscious postcoloniality. Akhtar's father is also an amateur artist whose style was formed by Gaugain and the Tanzanian artist Eduardo Tingatinga (125) – he even met Tingatinga in Dar es Salaam in the 60s (126). He keeps painting murals in his home, including a Frida Kahlo one and one of his dead wife in Tingatinga style as a Shetani (a spirit in East African mythology). It could be argued that Neate's novel follows the bricoleur strategies of Tingatinga art, constructed out of available cheap materials (Tingatinga used masonite boards and bicycle paint) as well as its cultural politics: as Farzad explains, "Tingatinga knew there was no such thing as authentic culture, son. Paul Gaugain was the same." (126).

run a drunk Paki (excuse my shorthand) off a train. They make me ashamed to be English, for real" (81). Abjection culminates in the scene when he leaves the hospital, sill rather worse for wear, with a metal plate in his skull. He takes the bus, where he is duly mocked by a group of youngsters: "On the bus, some thug-lites decided to take the piss and impress their groupies with a chorus of 'Frankenstein is a w – er'. I was too knackered to correct the literary reference. Because I wasn't the deranged genius trying to control life itself, was I? I was the monster dreaming of humanity rebuilt from its constituent parts" (215).

What deserves particular attention in this complex act of self-definition is the motif of control. The passage is typical inasmuch as control is indeed something that Tommy repeatedly disclaims, or rather, his professional successes are the result of a self-conscious display of his lack of control: mimicry. Whenever he is performing the usual noir detective stunts (assuming fake identities, etc.), Akhtar's mimicry includes ethnic elements – overdoing the "Paki thing". When he illegally ventures into the scene of the crime, he once again resorts to the guileless Paki impersonation, putting on the "obsequious Paki grin" (53) when talking to the policemen guarding the area. The mimicry is also invariably a conscious subaltern strategy based on his foreknowledge of how his ethnicity will be viewed by others. Unlike Marlowe and other hard-boiled detectives, he does not want to dominate the verbal battles, but controls situations indirectly by conceding mastery to his interlocutor (even provoking them into verbal or physical violence) and observing them in the process, taking advantage of his disadvantage in order to achieve his – admittedly modest – aims. In all his dealings with others, a certain (subaltern) lack of control is taken for granted. "I reckon – he muses – Jews and Muslims have a whole lot of things in common. Most important among these is that they don't think they're in control, at the heart of it all" (148–9). He makes use of the fact that his ethnic identity might also entail a certain kind of experiential knowledge of the multicultural city unavailable to white British investigators, based as it is on the experience of discrimination and deprivation, much of it invisible to white detectives.[2]

Although his awareness of racial discrimination is acute (as is clear from what he tells us about his schooldays), because of the complex mimicry of his

---

2   The novel is careful, though, not to romanticize this experience into some kind of solidarity-community of the deprived. On the other hand, there is a sense in which prostitutes are Akhtar's doubles, not only because they are also flâneurs/euses, but also because both are marginalised, as indicated by the description of Natasha's boudoir, which, like Akhtar's place, is "both home and office" (77), and by Akhtar's uncharacteristic moment of empathy with the girl while he is going through her belongings and discovers a collection of soft toys (78–9).

voice (hard-boiled tough talk, Tommy Cooper-style wisecrack comedy, overdone ethnic vernacular, a self-deprecating, somewhat histrionic rhetoric), there is here no trace of the heroism of Chandler's private eye: "Down these mean streets a man must go, who is not himself mean, who is neither tarnished nor afraid [...] He must be, to use a weathered phrase, a man of honor [...] he must be the best man in his world" (4). Neither is there any trace of an attempted authenticity, or of what Stephen Knight calls the "recovery of a voice for the dispossessed" (22); we are not even offered an insight into the life of an ethnic community, as Akhtar seems to share his father's view: "There is no authentic culture, Tommy boy" (127). Apart from the Khan family, no character is part of a recognisable, more or less homogeneous ethnic group: they are all loners, coming from all over the place.³ For all his self-conscious post-colonial playacting, Tommy is not a politically responsible agent,⁴ modelled as he is on the original hard-boiled detectives. "As its homophone 'private I' suggests, the figure of the hard-boiled detective is grounded firmly in the individualist ethos of the United States" (Athanasourelis 70). When he looks in the mirror, "I see a lonely, lowlife investigator with a dangerous taste for alcohol and an even more dangerous penchant for rumination. I'm the latest in a long line of Marlowe wannabes" (192). He is a world-weary, cynical private eye in an atomised urban world, who insists on being "small-time" (29–30), and whose job description includes lack of affect as well as lack of involvement: "I'm not in the judgement business" (109).⁵ He has a streak of the death-wish, a daredevil self-destructiveness, complicated by unfounded guilt for the death of his mother; there is a sense of him simply marking time with the help of drink and cigarettes. In retrospect, the hard-boiled private eye becomes a prefiguration of the ethnic subject drifting in post-imperial London, while the metaphysical anxiety of the noir ambience is translated into something culturally specific. In *City of Tiny Lights*, the multicultural condition might be seen as the extension or intensification of something that had always been an aspect of the noir city, "the anonymous dark city, where all, by definition, are strangers in a strange land. Noir characters find themselves embroiled in narratives that unfold in transient spaces that, like city streets, are open to everyone, yet no community,

---

3 These people do not include middle-class or upper middle-class British people – the only such character, perhaps not incidentally, is MP Bailey, who is bludgeoned to death.
4 Patrick Neate's short story ("The Little Book of Tommy: Another Tommy Akhtar Investigation") addresses racism in a bleaker, more direct manner.
5 His attitude to morality is typically ambiguous. On the one hand, he pays lip-service to the expected blasé attitude of private eyes ("I find morality tiring" [69]), while, on the other hand, he insists on a certain standard: "the dirtier your business, the more important your morals become" (127).

no system of values that might reflect or produce consensus, emerges to direct either their desires or their movements" (Palmer 189).

The novel's title, borrowed from a Frank Zappa song and appearing halfway through the text, reinforces this vaguely existentialist streak: the phrase "city of tiny lights" alerts Akhtar to the vulnerability of the city, to the ease with which each of the tiny lights could be extinguished (122). Later, the tiny lights also suggest a kind of mysterious beauty (221–2). This is not unrelated to what Kelly Oliver and Benigno Trigo call "[t]he free-floating existential anxiety of film noir," identifying it as "an anxiety over ambiguous spaces. Its heroes are homeless, directionless, wandering travellers who unsuccessfully try to escape their past and find themselves caught between a rock and a hard place with nowhere to turn and nowhere to go" (217). This is illustrated when Akhtar is crashing out in his Irish policeman friend Donnelly's place (Donnelly keeps calling him "My immigrant friend"), and, browsing a high society magazine, he notes that the people in the magazine

> did not live in any England I knew. They were Hollywood English just like Jones and Paradowski were Hollywood secret agents. They existed only in a mythologized world of stately homes, tea at the Ritz and boxes at the Ascot when in reality, of course, stately homes are the domain of the voracious Japanese, the Ritz is booked out with fat Americans and Ascot boxes are reserved for Arab oil. (278)

For Akhtar, England is, after all, his 'home' of sorts, but as a kind of dream rather than any experiential anchor for his identity. In fact, England is a dream of his father's rather than his own. He has no real anchor: the genre-specific homelessness and unattachment of the hard-boiled hero become, as it were, culturally motivated. One could say that – being a hard-boiled detective and an almost parodistically multicultural hybrid figure – Tommy Akhtar becomes an allegorical condensation of contemporary metropolitan experience which is dutifully explored in Neate's novel (the pastiche of noir fiction in itself makes the text transnational, Akhtar's language Americanising the multi-ethnic city). The investigation plot offers ample opportunity to explore multicultural, cosmopolitan London, often in a humorous way, for instance when Akhtar goes through the junk mail of the two prostitutes, most of which is addressed to previous occupants, indicating that most inhabitants (with non-English sounding names) are only passing through:

> a posturepedic mattress catalogue for Mrs Schiliro, an air-miles statement for Mr Mahmoud, Mrs M. A. Kuntz was offered twenty pounds off

a mixed case from the UK's largest direct wine suppliers. Mrs Frances Siame was pre-approved for a platinum visa with 0 per cent credit transfer. This is the nature of the western world. You accumulate junk whether you're there or not. (71–2)

Tommy's younger brother Gundappa – another nice postcolonial touch – is running a cab company called Phoenecia. The unexpected name, which is simply the result of the fact that the sign could be bought cheaply from a bankrupt Greek restaurant, begins to resonate in the multi-ethnic world of the novel, reimagining London as an international trading centre, a kind of "Mediterranean," but the allusion, like so many other elements in the novel, begins to expand and becomes bitterly ironic as London is revealed to be precisely that: a trading place for arms deals. The drivers employed by Phoenecia represent a heady sample of multicultural chaos, where even names cease to function as reliable ethnic markers, or, when they do, they do so only in unpredictable and oblique ways: Swiss Chris is a big West African, Big John is a tiny Pole whose real name proves to be too much of a mouthful for everybody else (14), while "Irish" is the name of a new young Jamaican called Patrick (101).

This is what Paul Gilroy called "convivial" multiculturalism (Gilroy, *Postcolonial* xv), "an ordinary, demotic multiculturalism" which emerges from "the processes of cohabitation and Interaction". This emphatically 'localised' multiculturalism is something that Akhtar, who – like most hard-boiled detectives – is very much part of his locality, can take in his stride. Although the novel relishes this to a certain extent, it is nevertheless precisely the multicultural and global nature of the city that he is eventually unable to handle, with the case spiralling out of control. The original case is itself also 'multicultural' from the start, and the farther it expands, the more multicultural and international it becomes: apart from Tommy's client Melody Chase, it involves Russian prostitute Natasha, Nigerian coke pusher Tunde ("I heard his voice and had his number" – 134), half-Italian pimp Tony Simone, Russian arms dealer Nikolay Gaileov (in fact CIA agent Chip Paradowski), and the Saudi-British terrorist Azmat Al-Dubayan – the only character who remains absent throughout but has more influence over the events than anybody else.

2 "Scoping the Geography"

As is obvious from the above, Akhtar's competence or lack thereof is inseparable both from the novel's treatment of spatiality and its reworking of the hard-boiled genre. Ever since its inception, hard-boiled fiction has had a significant role in the remapping of the modern city. In fact, as Walter Benjamin claims in his book on Baudelaire's Paris (but he could have used Dickens's London, too), the natural affinity between urban experience and criminality was obvious even before the appearance of the genre (71–2). As soon as the city appears as a mysterious place which somehow exceeds the individuals and institutions living and working in it (as early as in Dickens and Sue), crime becomes the obvious narrative device of conceiving and exploring the mysteriousness of the city itself, and the flâneur-like private eye, situated in the grey zone between legal and illegal, is an obvious protagonist that can explore the diverse and disparate zones within the city. No matter what traces the flâneur may follow, every one of them will lead him to a crime (Benjamin 72).

In the hard-boiled genre, crime is metaphorized spatially as a spreading stain, a network that turns out to include much of officialdom as well as the criminal underworld, thus, most of what actually happens in the city (this is obvious in Hammett's novels, notably *Red Harvest*): the normal life of the city is not something that unfolds independently of crime but is run by organised networks of crime, the two turning out to be coterminous. Thus, noir became a crucial discourse of the city, concerned with and about the containability of crime (stopping the stain, or removing the always-already-there stain, enabling a 'normal' urban life). The hard-boiled detective is normally able, if not to remove the stain, at least to stop its spreading and to remove it locally. *City of Tiny Lights* tests the efficiency of the hard-boiled detective in a contemporary post-imperial and post-9/11 metropolitan environment – thus, the stake is the conflict between the global and the local in the discourse of hard-boiled crime, as well as the very definition of crime.

As Phil Cohen has noted, there seems to be "a growing division in urban studies between those who continue to accord primacy to the spatial economy of cities and the processes of their globalisation, and those who argue for the strategic importance of cultural and political geographies in which the local, however problematically, still holds its explanatory place" (71). This is precisely where Neate's novel is situated, and the gradual disintegration of the authority of the hard-boiled discourse in *City of Tiny Lights* might be seen in this context. Two aspects of the spatiality of the hard-boiled genre deserve special attention for our purposes. First, space in hard-boiled crime fiction is not geometrical-analytical but primarily embodied, phenomenological: the city is not just a place where one reads clues, but also the space where, as Benjamin argues (69), one inevitably leaves traces oneself, where one acts, feels, is in danger. Thus, the noir city is not so much the scene of what happened (as in the analytical detective story) as the scene of what might happen. The hard-boiled genre was innovative in mapping the affective and political landscapes of the modern city, suggesting a spatiality that is in the broadest sense phenomenological: the subject and her world come into existence in constant interaction and interdependence, in a process of worlding. German sociologist Georg Simmel identified the city as the par-excellence phenomenological space already in 1903, when he claimed that

> the most significant characteristic of the metropolis is a functional extension beyond its physical boundaries. And this efficacy reacts in turn and gives weight, importance, and responsibility to metropolitan life. Man does not end with the limits of his body or the area comprising his immediate activity. Rather is the range of the person constituted by the sum of effects emanating from him temporally and spatially. In the same way, a city consists of its total effects which extend beyond its immediate confines. (182)

That is also why an affective component, or *Stimmung*, is an inevitable component of spatial awareness in noir, with the gaze of the hard-boiled detective necessarily, and often vicariously, anamorphotic. In the Embassy, Akhtar is trying to reimagine the encounter between Bailey and Natasha: "I scoped the geography. I tried to figure how this would have looked to sexyrussian [Natasha], exoticmelody and pre-mortem Bailey" (133). Scoping the geography is like reading the cultural semantics of the restaurant – as it would have seemed to a teenage Russian prostitute.

The second key aspect of the hard-boiled treatment of spatiality has to do with the private eye's competence: Neate's novel is a typical representative of the genre inasmuch as its central concern is with the protagonist's mastery over his fate and profession (this is the central argument of John T. Irwin's book about the genre), and Akhtar is a typical hard-boiled detective insofar as this control depends on his being knowledgeable about the city, the local area and its inhabitants: these sections are full of pithy anthropological observation (36) delivered with utter confidence: "Let me tell you something about hookers" (8). In a rare rhetorical flourish, which follows his musings on simulacrum England, Akhtar describes his experiential England:

> The England I knew was a cheek-by-jowl kind of place where seemingly polar opposites were wedded by nation, frustration and location, location, location: stroppy Pakis to small-town racists [...] thug-lites to petrified pensioners, suburban swingers to pregnant pubescents, coke-addled hookers to coke-addled media whores, aspirant Africans to resigned Rastas, loaded gym freaks to obese benefit junkies, entrepreneurs to

economic migrants, organized crime to chaotic bureaucracy, politicians to terrorists, hopeless to hopeful. (278)

For all its apparent randomness, this passage is all about knowledge and control. Akhtar insists that his knowledge is that of location, of the local, and in the alliterative list, which could be continued indefinitely, somewhat like Borges's Chinese encyclopaedia of animals, each contrast creates a new way of distinguishing people, where race is simply one among the factors. Akhtar's success as a private eye depends on such local knowledge, knowledge of location. His ethnic mimicry, the ability to exploit his racial identity is part and parcel of his strategy of turning to advantage his ineluctable locatedness, in more philosophically charged terms, his facticity (Sartre) or *Geworfenheit* (Heidegger).

A crucial test of his (spatial) authority is staged in terms of the contrast and conflation between the local and the global. This is the episode of revisiting the scene of the crime (the murder of Bailey and the disappearance of Natasha), the Holiday Inn Express hotel in one of the anonymous suburbs of the city. The hotel is one of several instances of what Marc Augé calls "non-places" in Neate's novel. Non-places, which Augé considers to be a feature of supermodernity, and contrasts to dwelling places, "cannot be defined as relational, or historical, or concerned with identity" (77–8).

In this scene, the key to Tommy's success is clearly his "spatial" expertise. When talking about the hotel, he recalls a girl he met once in a Chiswick restaurant who was designing fabrics (including those of the seats in the new Ford Focus); looking at the patterns of the restaurant, she said that it "looks in-house to me" (48). That is, it was designed expressly for this place: local design as opposed to the global designs of car seats and hotel chains. The carpet design of the hotel immediately reminds Akhtar of this woman. "I wondered if she'd designed the intricate swirling patterns of greens and greys that hid the dirt and branded the chain all at once. Or maybe it was designed in-house. I wondered how you tell" (48). The ability to distinguish between the global and the local design seems to acquire some allegorical significance for Akhtar, as if the correctness of his verdict were the measure of his control. He decides that the pattern is global ("Now a bird's paid to design corporate homogeny" [48–9]), and, at this stage, he remains in full control both of his own identity (playing the cartoon Paki in the hotel, taking advantage the generic invisibility of Pakistanis) as well as of the spaces and people around him, for instance, when making sure that the CCTV cameras of the lobby are just for show. At night, he easily sneaks into the hotel room which is the scene of the crime.

Rather than a Sherlock Holmes-like mastery of a "neutral" physical space as a set of clues, Akhtar's control of the hotel space stems from a knowledge of the specific kinds of spaces he encounters, with all their cultural features and sedimentations. His survey of the crime scene has a touch of "Rue Morgue" and "The Purloined Letter" inasmuch as he is exploring a place after the police have been through it. He, however, expects to find no new (forensic) evidence but hopes to be able to reconstruct the murder (his hypothesis is that the girl was not there when Bailey was killed): "I didn't expect to find anything but I needed to see nonetheless. I wanted to build a picture" (55). That is, a picture of the possible intersubjective trajectories that might have unfolded in the space of the hotel room containing those two persons. At this point, his spatial expertise is superior to the police's practice of turning crime scenes into forensic space; his knowledge is less technical, based on "lived life" experience.

In the morning, he saunters out to the local area around the hotel, once again with his casual but knowledgeable attitude: "I didn't know what I was looking for but I knew there was something to see" (58). He finds the place where the hotel's wheelie-bins are usually kept, surmising, correctly, that the police are going through their contents right now. "I guessed they'd have no joy and were most likely *looking for the wrong thing in the wrong place anyway.* No imagination, coppers" (58 – emphasis added). Akhtar finds what he wants outside a forlorn parade of shops fifty yards away. "Outside of the shops, there was a pair of dustbins. This was where the Old Bill should have been looking. I pulled on my gloves, I pulled a face, I poked around. Don't call it instinct, call it experience" (59). The crucial piece of evidence is duly found in the bin, suggesting that, in this sequence, it is clearly Tommy's familiarity with spaces and especially their "cultural" uses (he reckons, for instance, and rightly so, that no one is serving at the hotel bar during the night) that enables him to learn more than the police. Akhtar is here what Walter Benjamin calls an "urban physiognomist." Benjamin states that "living means leaving traces" (169), and these traces left behind by the modern city dweller must be carefully preserved by the urban physiognomist, and their meaning deciphered. As Graeme Gilloch says in his recapitulation of Benjamin's urban theory, "[t]he metropolis constitutes a frame or theatre for activity. The buildings of the city, and its interior setting in particular, form casings for action in which, or on which, human subjects leave 'traces', signs of their passing, markers or clues to their mode of existence" (20).

Akhtar's mastery consists in his ability to read the specific *local* environment of one item of a *global* hotel chain (catering mainly for businessmen on the move, part of the global financial circuit). He is in his element as long as he is working on the original case, that of the missing prostitute, a job which involves dealing with the local spaces and people. He loses ground (and becomes presumptuous, slipping into fatal mistakes) when he takes on the unformulated larger case, not realising that the original case is not the opposite of the global case of terrorism and international arms trade but only its tiny, local fragment which, however, cannot be delimited as a local case. By progressively deconstructing the hard-boiled plot, Neate's novel suggests – like Zygmunt Bauman – that the separation of global networks and local places is no longer possible (Bauman 16–7).

Akhtar's overreaching and loss of control are marked by an uncharacteristic misreading of urban space that leaves him physically exposed: he is attacked from behind and nearly killed. He himself resorts to a spatial metaphor when discussing this slip-up: "Everyone has a comfort zone but I knew that mine was shrinking. That thought made me uncomfortable, which was a start." (91) The expansion of the case is accompanied by the shrinking of his comfort zone (his zone of privacy, of efficient operation) as he is caught up in global affairs: it turns out that the MI5 and CIA have files on him, with all the details of his life.

In fact, he should not be surprised by this at all, for there is one aspect of his "worlding" which he keeps downplaying throughout. This, the most important and sinister effect of Akhtar's presence on his life-world is, however, unintended and largely unconscious. Although he seems to fancy himself as streetwise small-time local joker-detective, it is primarily as a war veteran that he affects his environment, bringing war with himself (his war stories from his own past are evoked at key moments of the plot). Tortured by guilt after his mother's death, Tommy went through a period of mental health problems and religious zeal, joined the mujahedin in Afghanistan, fighting the Russians in a "just war" where killing "wasn't an act of politics or religion but belonging" (41). While still in Afghanistan, he became a driver for an American CIA agent who was later blown to pieces. Losing his religion, Akhtar returned to the UK, "slept in West End doorways with Falkland vets" (43), then stayed with Farzad for three years before moving into the Chiswick flat to start a very small business as a small-time private eye. Akhtar's 'emanation' is that of his suppressed soldier-identity: even if he is unaware of this, his mere presence transforms the city into a war zone, making him not the opposite but the uncanny counterpart of the global processes of which he becomes the victim. He is like a fragment of the Deleuzian war machine let loose in the city, becoming a nomad, only to painfully recognise himself in the sinister global processes.

In hard-boiled fiction, the noir city is often conceived in contrast to war, where the latter is seen as the positive pole, with its unwritten rules and codes of masculine heroism, and especially because of its allocation of clear identities: friends and enemies are easily recognisable. In contrast, the noir city is seen as a place where identities are ambiguous, where no code is entirely valid: hard-boiled fiction and film noir "constructed a locus of entrapment, dislocation, anomie, and sexual uncertainty whose most signal quality was the dreadful solitude of its persecuted protagonists, a state of being in stark opposition to wartime notions of solidarity and civic connection" (Palmer 187). In the novel, Farzad follows this logic, arguing that terrorism is simply an intensification of this permanent lawlessness and threat, and thus the opposite of rule-bound war (159).

In *City of Tiny Lights*, war is the most pervasive spatial and affective metaphor, connected to all characters, even Melody, once seen wearing "full combat gear" (79) for the delectation of a client who, Tommy speculates, might be "army fetishist" (80); even contemplative Farzad's artistic mentor was a Zimbabwean artist called Hondo, apparently meaning "war".[6] It is of course the bombings that reinforce the war situation, which expands beyond its metaphorical relevance to include the former hard-boiled plot as well: as the female MI5 agent Jones says, "We are in a war situation" (294), suggesting a global condition of anomie with no outside or local pockets of refuge. Zygmunt Bauman's metaphor of metropolitan existence is similarly warlike: "Contemporary cities are the battlegrounds on which global powers and stubbornly local meanings and identities meet, clash, struggle and seek a satisfactory, or just bearable, settlement" (21). The hard-boiled detective, expert of local matters, finds himself at the intersection of various global processes and networks: global capitalism and its shadow version (illegal arms trade), terrorism and its counterpart, the war against terror, based on "inter-agency skills initiative" (296). The geography of terror is revealed as the geography of terrorism (283) in the sense that both are geographies of what Akhtar repeatedly calls "homogeny" with no privileged points of impact.

The local, however, is not the only opposite of war in the novel: the rivalling global counterpart of the war metaphor is that of cricket. A lifelong cricket fan, Akhtar's father believes that cricket is much more than a game, using it as a frame of reference with universal appeal. Farzad "thinks all life can be explained through cricket" (15); "Farzad always says, 'You can learn everything you need to know from the game of cricket" (4). Tommy seems to have embraced his father's enthusiasm: his narrative is peppered with cricketing metaphors ("you don't know the value of your runs until the opposition bats" [83]) and analogies (97, 98, 113, 214, 222, 258, 303–4). Significantly, he uses his cricket gloves at the scene of crime and when he is rootling in the dustbin, that is, in solving the original case (55).

---

6 The word in fact means war in Shona, although I have found no trace of an artist by that name.

The relevance of cricket, however, is radically questioned – also on the level of the plot, since Akhtar's fatal decision to pursue the larger case is also inspired by a cricketing metaphor (113). Although Akhtar claims he owes his father his "uncanny ability to address problems armed with no more than a cricketing metaphor and a quote from Churchill" (124), this frame of reference fails to resonate outside the sphere of the family and a few close friends: nobody else is familiar with or interested in cricket (or nobody else believes in the universal applicability of any set of rules, sporting or moral). The juxtaposition of war and cricket contrasts two kinds of "global" relevance: cricket allusions introduce the "postimperial global," a tarnished Britishness which has no chance in a confrontation with the more menacing kind of globalism that involves trade in arms and drugs, prostitution, terrorism, and intelligence deals.

The gradual triumph of the global context, which serves "ultimately to collapse the geopolitical and everyday as separate spheres of life" (Pain and Smith xv), also entails a shift of affect in the process of worlding. Affect as such is inherently problematic in the hard-boiled genre with its masculine insistence on keeping cool, and, as is obvious from a few awkward, "emotionally retarded English male moments" (220, 216), *City of Tiny Lights* is no exception, especially in view of its comic tone: in the very first paragraph, Akhtar calls the narrative "a cartoon story" (3). A cartoon world – like late capitalism as it was famously defined by Fredric Jameson – would seem to entail a lack of affect, a flattened world with two-dimensional characters moving about in it.[7] The cartoon metaphor, however, might also be an evasive ploy. At one point Akhtar says that he returned from Afghanistan "half-way mad with post-traumatics" (154). We learn nothing about the three years spent in his father's house or the time spent as a vagrant: PTSD is as good a guess as any, exacerbated by powerful self-inflicted guilt for his mother's death: "But guilt? I can't get enough of it" (201). It seems that any strong emotion is to be avoided by Tommy – whether pity for waif-like Natasha (100), love for Melody or close friendship with Connelly.[8] All such things amount to wasteful "emotional luxury" (100) that threatens the hard-fought balance and impassiveness.

For all his stinted or suppressed emotional life, there is genuine affective charge emanating both from Tommy Akhtar and his client: Tommy is hired because Melody is worried about her flatmate; both live in constant fear and

---

7   It seems that the only possibilities for emotion here are either to be flattened or to become perversions – like the weapon fetishism of Melody's client.
8   His eventual human failure – on one level – is also caused by mismanagement of affect, his inability not to feel paternal about Av, not not show off before him and involve him in his investigation (thus, the failure is the result of the ubiquity of global schemes as well as his own emotional numbness).

have developed a system of checking the other's clients (9–10). The affect of fear seems to be the only constant. Discussing his relationship with his brother, Akhtar claims that

> in the absence of trust, fear is a solid basis for a relationship. Ask any world leader from the dark continent to the White House: keep the people scared and you'll keep them in check. And keeping them scared of you is the simplest thing but keeping them scared of an idea (Communism, Islam or whatever) is the height of progress. There you go: pop political theory, free, gratis and for nothing. (103)

In the above piece of freely offered wisdom, Akhtar already expands the relevance of fear from the intersubjective sphere into global politics, but it is during his interrogation by the intelligence agents that fear comes into its own. In a racist diatribe that seems to be rehearsed, CIA agent Chip Paradowski talks about fear in the context of the British policy of the defence of the realm (207). The Latin form of the expression (Regnum Defende) was adopted as the motto of MI5, indicating that the intelligence service operates in a permanent condition of war, since The Defence of the Realm act was passed by the British Parliament right after Britain's entry into the Great War, giving the government wide-ranging powers. In the USA, it is linked to the "military order" issued by President Bush on 13 November 2001, authorizing "indefinite detention" and "trial by military commission" of noncitizens suspected of involvement in terrorist activities (Agamben 3).

In a later conversation, when British agent Jones declares that they are in a „war situation" (294), Akhtar questions this, arguing that government agencies are generating fear on purpose.

> 'Everyone should be scared.
> "Scared? No. We want people to go about their daily business as normal. All we hope for is heightened awareness of the threat from the PWA and similar fundamentalist groups. All we hope for is to protect our way of life."
> [...] I thought about her definition of the word 'scared' and her professed desire for 'people to go about their daily business.' I remembered Afghanistan. People (including a certain Tommy Akhtar) went about their daily business in a state of permanent terror. It sounded to me like she wanted people to be scared. [...] I wondered if she even understood what she was saying. I thought about 'our way of life,' hers and mine. I wondered if we shared one. I thought about my way of life as, variously,

a Ugandan-Indian, a Paki, an immigrant, a Londoner, an Englishman. I wondered if it was worth protecting. (295)

The auxiliary in Jones's sentence ("Everyone should be scared") indicates the ambiguity of terror. On the one hand, terror is a metaphor of fear (a constant of the hard-boiled genre). Fear becomes terror when it is no longer just an affective state aroused by one object but a prescribed condition that legitimizes extreme measures and policies on the part of the powers that be. Ulli Linke and Danielle Taana Smith argue, the

> emergent cultural system of fear cannot be understood solely as a by-product of violence or as an inevitable symptom of war. Forms of terror are artifacts of history, society, and global politics. Cultures of fear and states of terror are affective tools of government that come into being as a modus of population management deployed by military, political, and administrative actors. (5)

The authors insist that these cultures can only be comprehended on a global level. In a more theoretical vein, we could say that the hard-boiled detective loses control when he finds himself in a state of exception, of the radical suspension of the law by the sovereign (Agamben 2). This suspension of law is also referred to as terror.

It is precisely this affective shift from fear and anxiety to terror that is chronicled by the novel: from the physical fear (or metaphysical anxiety) of the hard-boiled genre, a 'literary' condition or affect, always surmountable by the detective, to terror that proves to be unsurmountable. When, following interrogation and torture, Akhtar is released into the city, the affective state of London after the bombings seems to resonate with his condition. The city, like Akhtar, is scared (297). There is a reciprocity which is prefigured by a sentence that describes the arrival of the armed police into the tube carriage: "the geezer [the policeman] looked so scared that he scared me back" (286). In the new state of terror, fear works like an effect of facing mirrors, endlessly reflected and reciprocated, its origin lost in infinite regress.[9] After his release, Akhtar takes a cab in which yesterday's *Standard* is spread on the dashboard with the headline "Terror Threat Strangles Capital" (298). He re-enters a London that is different

---

9   For a detailed analysis of the dramatization of the effects of fear and the role of the media in disseminating the lexicon of fear in Neate's novel, see Yvonne Rosenberg's essay. Michael C. Frank discusses *City of Tiny Lights* as one of the handful of novels that forge a counter-discourse to the prevalent public discourse of terrorism (62–3).

because differently imagined by its inhabitants (303). In this new condition, "[t]hey were all on the same side. London was scared" (303). In the war on terror that does away with multicultural society, diversity becomes a source of danger, bringing weakness, chaos, confusion (Gilroy, *After Empire* 1–2).

In this condition of terror, the tough guy credentials of masculinity (Akhtar's war past) are useless – just like the ambiguous morality of the hard-boiled discourse. With the translation of fear into terror, the kind of city in which the private eye can operate is a thing of the past. Global capitalism and the global civil war (terror and terrorism, the new culture of fear) are revealed to be intimately related in the novel through the gradual breakdown of the hard-boiled mode. In the new world of terror, Tommy Akhtar, by scrupulously following the rules of the game as specified in the hard-boiled manuals, causes the hospitalisation of his teenage associate and the death of his father's best friend. The hard-boiled detective who takes on really global forces, who is trying to tackle terror(ism) as well as fear, is not simply incompetent: his incompetence proves to be outright damaging.

Works Cited

Adebayo, Diran. *My Once Upon a Time* [2000]. London: Abacus, 2001.
Agamben, Giorgio. *State of Exception*. Trans. Kevin Attell. Chicago: U of Chicago P, 2005.
Athanasourelis, John Paul. *Raymond Chandler's Philip Marlowe: The Hard-Boiled Detective Transformed*. Jefferson, NC: McFarland, 2012.
Augé, Marc. *Non-Places: Introduction to an Anthropology of Supermodernity*. Trans. John Howe. London: Verso, 1997.
Bauman, Zygmunt. *City of Fears, City of Hopes*. London: Goldsmith College, 2003.
Benjamin, Walter. "The Paris of the Second Empire in Baudelaire." Trans. Harry Zohn. *The Writer of Modern Life: Essays on Charles Baudelaire*. Cambridge, MA: The Belknap Press of Harvard UP, 2006. 46–133.
Chandler, Raymond. "The Simple Art of Murder". *The Simple Art of Murder*. NY: Vintage, 1988. 3–8.
Cohen, Phil. "Out of the Melting Pot into the Fire Next Time: Imagining the East End as City, Body, Text". *Imagining Cities: Scripts, Signs, Memory*. Ed. Sallie Westwood and John Williams. London: Routledge, 2005. 71–84.
Falkenhayner, Nicole. "An Unlikely Hero for the War-on-Terror Decade". *Heroes and Heroism in British Fiction since 1800*. Ed. Barbara Korte and Stefanie Lethbridge. Basingstoke: Palgrave Macmillan, 2017. 151–68.
Frank, Michael C. "'A Contradiction in Terms': Patrick Neate's *City of Tiny Lights* as a Literary Intervention into Post-9/11 Discourse". *Terrorism and Narrative Practice*.

Ed. Thomas Austenfeld, Dimitri Daphinoff and Jens Herlth. Münster: LIT Verlag, 2011. 61–79.

Gilloch, Graeme. *Myth and Metropolis: Walter Benjamin and the City*. Cambridge: Polity, 1996.

Gilroy, Paul. *After Empire*. London: Routledge, 2005.

Gilroy, Paul. *Postcolonial Melancholia*. New York: Columbia UP, 2004.

Irwin, John T. *Unless the Threat of Death Is Behind Them: Hard-Boiled Fiction and Film Noir*. Baltimore: Johns Hopkins UP, 2008.

Horsley, Lee. *Twentieth-Century Crime Fiction*. Oxford: Oxford UP, 2005.

Knight, Stephen: "Crimes Domestic and Crimes Colonial: The Role of Crime Fiction in Developing Postcolonial Consciousness." Mühleisen and Matzke 17–34.

Linke, Ulli and Danielle Taana Smith, ed. *Cultures of Fear: A Critical Reader*. London: Pluto, 2009.

Mühleisen, Susanne and Christine Matzke, ed. *Postcolonial Postmortems: Crime Fiction from a Transcultural Perspective*. Amsterdam: Rodopi, 2006.

Neate, Patrick. *City of Tiny Lights* [2005]. Harmondsworth: Penguin, 2006.

Neate, Patrick. "The Little Book of Tommy: Another Tommy Akhtar Investigation". *Multi-Ethnic Britain 2000+: New Perspectives in Literature, Film and the Arts*. Ed. Lars Eckstein, Barbara Korte, Eva Ulrike Pirker. Amsterdam. Rodopi, 2008. 25–32.

Oliver, Kelly and Benigno Trigo. *Noir Anxiety*. Minneapolis: U of Minnesota Press, 1997.

Pain, Rachel and Susan J. Smith, ed. *Fear: Critical Geopolitics and Everyday Life*. Aldershot: Ashgate, 2008.

Plummer, Patricia. "Transcultural British Crime Fiction: Mike Phillips's Sam Dean Novels". *Postcolonial Postmortems: Crime Fiction from a Transcultural Perspective*. Ed. Susanne Mühleisen and Christine Matzke. Amsterdam. Rodopi, 2006. 255–88.

Rosenberg, Yvonne. " 'Stop Thinking like an Englishman', or: Writing Against a Fixed Lexicon of Terrorism in Patrick Neate's *City of Tiny Lights* (2005)". *Multi-Ethnic Britain 2000+: New Perspectives in Literature, Film and the Arts*. Ed. Lars Eckstein, Barbara Korte, Eva Ulrike Pirker. Amsterdam. Rodopi, 2008. 356–68.

Sauerberg, Lars Ole. *Intercultural Voices in Contemporary British Literature*. Basingstoke: Palgrave Macmillan, 2002.

Simmel, Georg. "The Metropolis and Mental Life". Trans. Kurt H. Wolff. *Simmel on Culture*. Ed. David Frisby and Mike Featherstone. London: Edward Arnold, 1997. 174–186.

CHAPTER 12

Inventing History: Katalin Baráth's Hungarian Middlebrow Detective Series

Brigitta Hudácskó

Abstract

The chapter discusses the historical detective series by Hungarian author Katalin Baráth, set in early 20th century Hungary, with a heroine, bookshop-keeper, feminist journalist, and busybody amateur detective Veron Dávid, who is strongly reminiscent of a younger, albeit none the less meddlesome and sharp-witted Miss Marple. Veron's physical and emotional journey of negotiating her identity, both as an accidental detective and an ambitious young woman, takes her all over the Austro-Hungarian Monarchy, finally returning to and making peace with her rural hometown, Ókanizsa. In the series Baráth attempts to lay down the foundations for the heretofore mostly missing Hungarian middlebrow fiction, while integrating it to the Hungarian literary tradition and to the Hungarian landscape and testing the limits of the classic crime genre's adaptability.

In *Feminist Popular Fiction*, Merja Makinen contests the widely accepted critical view that detective fiction "is a male-based genre because of its ratiocinating puzzle-solving element, and that it is an inherently conservative genre because its resolution involves the reinstatement of a hierarchical status quo" (92). She argues that if we but observe the history of the genre, the abundance of female writers becomes instantly obvious; and while the question whether or not detective fiction is indeed a conservative genre, as is frequently claimed, as a whole it "is much more variable and particularly open to exploring the individual in relation to the social and legal matrix" (93). Thus, even though the setup of the classic crime story is bound to be formulaic, it still allows for a great deal of individuality, and very often, even for transgressive ideas and characters. Middlebrow crime fiction seems to bear the weight of the aforementioned assumptions particularly heavily, and it is only recent criticism – including the work of Makinen – that calls attention to the previously overlooked progressive attitudes and ideas inherent to this stratum of the crime genre.[1] Inspired by these recent advances, this paper sets out to examine, first, this progressive history of the (feminist) middlebrow and its absence from the Hungarian literary canon, and second, a Hungarian representative of the genre, Katalin Baráth, who has continued the legacy of Agatha Christie and her contemporaries. Baráth can be compared to such authors as the British Sophie Hannah, Andrew Wilson and Catriona McPherson, or the Australian Kerry Greenwood, all writing historical Golden Age detective fiction in the 21st century, almost a century after the heyday of the genre, generally considered to be predominant in the 1920s and 1930s.

1 A Very British Murder Abroad

Middlebrow detective fiction is an immensely popular yet paradoxical genre: while its place of origin is unquestionably early twentieth-century Britain, the genre's most popular and probably most prolific author, Agatha Christie, has become familiar even in cultures that lack both the middlebrow tradition entirely and an extensive backlist of crime writers. Hungary is arguably one of those cultures: even if we cannot claim that the country's literary tradition has no middlebrow stratum[2] at all or the crime genre itself. Nonetheless, for a multitude of social and historical reasons, twentieth-century Hungary did not provide the ideal circumstances to cultivate this genre. This absence is at once curious and intriguing: curious, because as Robert A. Rushing also notes, crime fiction is, by default, formulaic and, as such, should be easy to reproduce in different settings: "Reader, sidekick, detective, criminal – all of them return again and again to precisely the same scenarios, the same rooms with dead bodies locked from the inside in classic detective fiction, the same dangerous dames in the hardboiled novel, the same grinding, unsatisfying labor in the police procedural" (9). That is, the formula can, in theory, be applied in different

---

1   One of the most recent and probably most spectacular examples of the new wave in crime fiction criticism is *Queering Agatha Christie: Revisiting The Golden Age of Detective Fiction* by J. C. Bernthal, who provides the first comprehensive reading of Christie's work based on queer theory and uncovers a playful and subversive social commentary which may seem surprising in the face of previous conservative interpretations.
2   While we cannot designate a distinct layer of Hungarian fiction as middlebrow, there have arguably been authors in the 20th century whose work could be classified as such, for instance, the widely translated and popular Lajos Zilahy and Endre Fejős. Nevertheless, I argue that the low number of such writers does not suggest that there is an identifiable, significant middlebrow segment in Hungarian literature.

circumstances to the same effect, but, for a number of political and cultural reasons – among them the hostility towards Western influences and the political-ideological conviction that, under socialism, crime will disappear –, the establishment of Hungarian middlebrow crime fiction never took place.[3]

Despite – or maybe even due to – the politically hostile atmosphere, Agatha Christie has remained a mostly unchallenged queen of crime fiction in Hungary as well as a lasting favourite with readers even decades after the publication of her last novel (*Sleeping Murder*, published posthumously in 1975). Given readers' long-standing interest in Golden Age detective fiction, the appearance in 2010 of a Hungarian crime series written in the middlebrow tradition, and featuring a detective reminiscent of already familiar characters from classic works met with considerable enthusiasm and an overwhelmingly positive reception from readers. The detective in this fiction, Veron Dávid, has so far been featured in four novels and two short stories written by Katalin Baráth, whose historical narratives take place in the Austro-Hungarian Monarchy, during the years leading up to World War I. While Baráth undeniably honours the legacy of the Golden Age crime writers, especially that of Agatha Christie, she also presents the social and cultural reality of pre-war Hungary, particularly small-town Hungary, without merely being a slave to the classic whodunit model when reconstructing it in a different environment. The *Veron* series offers an interesting case study which illustrates how the typically middlebrow genre of the classic detective story can be (retrospectively) planted into a location that generally breeds different literary genres and different crimes altogether, and what this development may mean both for the concept of crime and for the person of the detective. In this chapter I am going to explore the social dynamics of the microcosm the detective – Veron Dávid, an amateur sleuth belonging to the classic tradition of Female Gentlemen – comes from and engineers with her activity, and the social, affective and topographical journey she has to take on her quest to carve out a place for herself as a woman and a detective.

Classic crime fiction has been more extensively researched, and international Agatha Christie scholarship has also become more prolific in recent

---

[3] The Hungarian publishing industry was also under very strict and direct political influence after World War II, with directives detailing not only which authors and which books could be published by specific houses, but also how much paper was allocated to each house. The Publishing Directorate encouraged the publication of Soviet literature and that of other socialist countries, while works produced by the imperialistic West were merely suffered as the sales of such works – such as that of bestselling crime fiction – subsidized the production of the commercially unsuccessful but politically supported books. I discuss this at length in *The Ageless Agatha Christie: Essays on the Mysteries and the Legacy*, ed. J. C. Bernthal.

years – with the first collection of essays devoted solely to the discussion of Christie's work being published as late as 2016 –, but Baráth has not yet been widely discussed in Hungarian academia. Due to the above-mentioned similarities I consider it both appropriate and timely to contemplate these writers together, or at least to discuss Baráth in a context where Agatha Christie and her contemporaries provide the most important points of reference.[4] This study also aims to explore the potential limitations of the transferability of the classic crime story formula and the character of the detective: since Baráth's stories do more than merely transplant a classically inspired nosey spinster from one monarchy to another; they also highlight some of the cultural obstacles emerging in the course of such a move.

2 The Mysterious Affair of Style

Before I attempt further analysis of Baráth's novels, a note on the term "middlebrow" itself is due: Melissa Schaub links the birth of the middlebrow to the detective genre, with this intermediary category being a point where "high and low were most likely to mingle and become middlebrow" (viii). As Schaub explains, the hierarchical layering of (British) literature goes back to the 19th century, when sophisticated, high literature separated itself from the low; and then

> [m]odernist writers began to see themselves as set apart from society; and as alienated even from many readers whom Victorians would have considered cultured. So the term 'middlebrow' was coined, to designate, often pejoratively, any serious writer whose work was accessible to a wider audience than the avant-garde. (viii)

Many of those writers who managed to reach this wider audience were crime writers, who were especially active from the 1920s up to the 1950s, when certain cultural tectonic shifts caused the focus of the genre to move away from

---

4   When Baráth's series was first introduced, the marketing materials – and in the subsequent volumes, the blurbs in the books – also tried to appeal to the interest of Agatha Christie fans. It is also true that most crime novels that bear the slightest resemblance to classic detective fiction (such as the books of Elizabeth George), are marketed with references to Christie in Hungary, thus the mere suggestion of a connection between the given author and Christie is not necessarily proof of an actual connection. In the case of Katalin Baráth, however, I argue that the reference is more than a mere marketing stunt.

what we today regard as classic crime fiction to the hard-boiled, popularized by such authors as Raymond Chandler and Dashiell Hammett. Some of the most beloved writers of the Golden Age were women, among them Agatha Christie being the most widely read and remembered. But Dorothy L. Sayers, Marjorie Allingham, Gladys Mitchell, and Ngaio Marsh were also counted among their numbers. While they created several popular detective characters, the one relevant to the present discussion is probably not the most memorable figure, yet still highly significant: Schaub calls this character the "Female Gentleman," a figure that "unites old ideas about class with new ideas about gender" (2) by democratizing and neutralizing gentlemanliness. This character can be observed, for example, in Christie's "Tommy and Tuppence" novels, such as *The Secret Adversary* (1922) and *N or M* (1941), where Tuppence (Prudence), one half of The Young Adventurers duo, turns adventuring into her livelihood and sets out on a number of dangerous enterprises with her childhood friend and later husband, Tommy Beresford, as an equal and constantly present partner in life and crime-fighting. A perhaps even more relatable Female Gentleman can be found in the novels of Dorothy L. Sayers: the successful crime writer, Harriet Vane is introduced into the series in *Strong Poison* (1930), where she stands accused of having poisoned her lover, whom she lived together with but never married. Harriet's innocence is eventually proven by Lord Peter Wimsey, who goes on to marry Harriet and solve crimes with her. Veron's fate often takes similar turns to that of Harriet Vane, with the exception of commercial writing success and an ending that is both romantic and professionally fulfilling in equal measure.

The decades which are generally regarded as the Golden Age of British crime fiction were spent in a radically different political and cultural climate in Hungary, a country still reeling from the traumas of World War I and its consequences, and experiencing an increasing move to the right. Therefore, it is little wonder that this historical atmosphere bred different heroes in Hungary than the openly misanthropic yet lovable Miss Marple, the eccentric Hercule Poirot, or the independent and adventurous Tuppence Beresford. In general, Hungary's cultural microcosm produced an insignificant number of literary detectives up until recent years.[5] I still argue that Baráth's heroine, Veron Dávid, belongs to the class of Female Gentlemen, despite the fact that in the

---

5   Quite a few of these writers published their detective novels under English-sounding pseudonyms – such as the renowned translator, Dezső Tandori, alias Nat Roid –, so this gesture indicates more of an intent to try and join an already existing tradition instead of localizing it to the Hungarian literary landscape.

original tradition these characters ceased to appear in new stories after the 1950s, because, as Schaub explains,

> The Female Gentleman existed during the trough between 'waves' of feminism [...]. Young women of the 1930s revised their mothers' ideals, but in a direction we have since abandoned. [...] During the rising tide of fascism in the 1930s (which Sayers, Christie, and Marsh explicitly denounced), an emphasis on individual choice and perfect honor in personal relations was a form of resistance; our era needs the ideal of honor as a corrective in the same way. (38)

Similarly, in Baráth's novels, Veron has to retrospectively negotiate the changing class and gender roles almost in the same historical period when her British counterparts did, while facing the unique challenges presented by her social and cultural environment. Veron is thrust into a time when her home town and its inhabitants are very much stuck in the past: the hierarchy dividing the local moneyed classes and intelligentsia from the labourers and peasantry is still intact, and quietly respected by most. Gender and social expectations also seem to be unchanging, which are a constant source of internal and external conflict for Veron who, being unmarried in her early twenties, is pitied and often disrespected while trying to negotiate her social and cultural path in uncharted territory.

The novels can, therefore, also facilitate a much needed discussion about femininity and gender in general in a troubled period of Hungarian history, whose memory is charged with emotion even today, and with that, they relate to Golden Age crime fiction even more, because as Bright and Mills point out, "underneath the twists and turns of their plots, novels of the Golden Age often reveal a deep unease about interpersonal relationships, societal structures, and senses of self" (32). The transgressions inherent in the genre are not limited to transgressions against person and property, but "there is an implicit idea of further transgression, against cultural and spiritual rituals" (32). Schaub also notes that novels featuring the character of the Female Gentleman were not overly optimistic about the accessibility of the modern female ideals they prescribed and presented – very likely because reaching those ideals often required transgressive behaviour –, but typically one character per book managed to achieve this vision (19). As we shall see, the *Veron* novels present their own internal conflicts on this front, and giving an unambiguously optimistic reading of Veron's fate would not be realistic under the historical circumstances, which fact may reflect upon the limited abilities of the Female Gentleman to move across cultures.

3 A Hungarian Adventure

In the first book, *The Black Piano*,[6] Baráth's heroine, Veron Dávid is a young woman living in the fictional town of Ókanizsa (in Bács-Bodrog Country, today's Serbia), where she works in the stationery and book shop. In this small town, reminiscent of classic detective story settings, she takes it upon herself to introduce the well-meaning, albeit rather conservative, locals to the wonders of modern(ist) literature and encourage cultural progress in the community. Her attempts, however, garner mixed reactions ranging from mild bemusement to straightforward hostility and criticism, and so does her lifestyle: as a single, educated, bicycle-riding, romance-writing young woman, who, for all her progressive ideas, comes from a traditional peasant family, she often provides topics for the local rumour mill. Veron's – and her mother's – hopes regarding respectability seem to be all but lost by the end of the first volume, after an embarrassing incident, where Veron is found in rather incriminating circumstances: in the company of an unconscious murderer, wearing only a bed sheet. While in later volumes Veron is constantly preoccupied with trying to live down her perceived shame, she still keeps finding herself chasing unsuitable men, even if in the capacity of the detective, thus keeping local gossips busy with her actual or fictitious adventures.

Veron's education, career choices and adventurous nature already qualify her to be counted among the number of fictional Female Gentlemen, even before she embarks on solving criminal cases. Although the middlebrow genre, and Agatha Christie especially, is often considered to be conservative – and their innocent, non-aggressive conservatism is regarded to be one of their main selling points –, recent criticism claims that they are anything but. J. C. Bernthal argues that even though Christie's "books appear profoundly conventional, formulaic and the opposite of subversive, they are constantly making fun of the conventions to which they appeal" (83). With a similar gesture, Baráth's novels highlight the limitations of the very genre they represent, and, at the same time, also attempt to subvert conventional sensibilities gently and with humour, but they also realise there are certain limits to this endeavour.

One of the frequent concerns of middlebrow detective fiction seems to be class struggle as it discusses the possibility of social advancement and the

---

6 At the time of writing, four books have been published in the series, and since they have not been translated to English, the titles and all subsequent quotes are given in my translation. The instalments of the *Veron Dávid* series are as follows: *A fekete zongora* (*The Black Piano*, 2010), *A türkizkék hegedű* (*The Turquoise Violin*, 2011), *A borostyán hárfa* (*The Amber Lyre*, 2012), and *Az arany cimbalom* (*The Golden Dulcimer*, 2014).

impossibility of achieving certain standards and characteristics that need to be acquired at birth, and the devaluation of certain qualities – such as gentlemanliness, for example – that seem to be tainted when they become available to the lower classes. Schaub quotes David Castronovo when she explains that even though the advancing middle class wanted to make gentlemanliness a moral – and thus achievable – category, "no amount of moralizing ever really destroys the magic component of pedigree" or the "fantasy connected with blood" (Castronovo qtd. in Schaub 8). Veron herself has to face these problems as well, although she is trying to rise from a peasant background to the pettiest of bourgeoisie, being a first generation intellectual in her family and breaking out of traditional feminine roles. This transition is neither seamless nor unbroken: as she evolves from shopgirl to journalist to respectable housewife, she experiences several stops and false starts. In *The Black Piano*, she has to realize that education does not necessarily bring her closer to reaching her goals, for even though she has partaken of the highest level of studies available to women in her hometown, the community does not let her shake off her peasant origins and she is still regarded as "Little Veron," whose ambitions are inconsistent with her place in society. In *The Turquoise Violin*, she moves to the capital city and starts working for what she hopes to be a feminist publication, *Woman and Society*; but disappointment awaits her here as well, since the magazine seems to be more preoccupied with beauty and fashion tips than with the burning issues of the times. Veron is constantly frustrated by the fact that she is forced to report on trivial topics, such as a fashionable ice-cream parlour's summer's bonbon selection. Besides the magazine not living up to Veron's journalistic standards and ideals about professional integrity, she has to experience further disappointment as she is often regarded in Pest-Buda as an "ugly, illiterate peasant girl" (*Turquoise* 26),[7] since her way of speech and manners inadvertently give away her humble family origins.

Issues concerning class struggle come to a head when she is kidnapped in *The Golden Dulcimer*: as it turns out, she is not held captive for some dark deed she has committed, nor was she at the wrong place at the wrong time, at least not exactly. The heavily pregnant Veron is kidnapped and held captive *for being the daughter of her father*, more than anything. As it turns out, her father, Szilveszter Dávid, respectable pillar of the community, caused the demise of an outlaw gang decades ago, and the survivors now attempt to take revenge upon him and others who were involved in the incident at the time. An invitation to try out a new coach service is sent addressed to Veron's father, but as he

---

7 "csúf, analfabéta parasztlány" (*Turquoise* 26).

is not keen on such new-fangled innovations and Veron is constantly restless, she takes the opportunity to travel to a neighbouring town on the coach. Although her married name is Mrs Remete and not Dávid at that point, she tends to forget this change in her circumstances, which leads to a life-threatening adventure. To make matters worse, this time she can do little more than figure out the reason for her imprisonment; otherwise she has to wait for her father and husband to come to her rescue as she is reduced by her condition to being a damsel in distress. If we consider the plot of *The Golden Dulcimer*, we find that all the calamities ensue because Veron rarely manages to behave in a gender-appropriate way: she not only forgets her married name and the hand on which she wears her wedding band; her condition – that is, being seven months pregnant – also tends to slip her mind. When, at the beginning of the novel, the coach breaks down and the driver is worried about her condition, Veron interrupts him:

> "What condition?" interrupted Veron with a little more vehemence than intended.
> Haltenberger swallowed and he gingerly pointed his index finger in the direction of Veron's conspicuously round belly. She followed Haltenberger's gesture with her eye.
> "Oh, you mean that," said she and finally realised what he'd been going on about.[8]
> *Golden* 47

Among Veron's gender-related shortcomings, the one that she cannot seem to shake is her attitude towards men, which is at once lacking and provocative, and, as such, transgressive. It is lacking, because – until the fourth volume – she fails to marry at an age that is generally deemed appropriate for young ladies of her standing. While she is no great beauty, as her mother keeps reminding her, and as such should be happy to grasp at any respectable offer that comes her way, she not only rejects István Remete's proposal several times, she also makes little to no effort to make herself more attractive to men (with probably the one exception in *The Black Piano*, where the gentleman catching her eye turns out, regrettably, to be a murderer). At the same time, however, Veron is more than provocative as during all her sleuthing she keeps associating with

---

8 – Miféle állapotban? – szakította félbe Veron, a szándékoltnál valamivel gorombább hangon. Haltenberger nyelt egyet, és mutatóujjával bizonytalanul arrafelé emelte, ahol Veron hasa gömbölyödött feltűnően. Veron követte a tekintetével Haltenberger iránymutatását. – Ja vagy úgy! – fogta föl, hogy mire céloz a másik. (*Golden* 47).

men: some of them are, of course, beyond reproach, such as her godfather and loyal co-conspirator, the local doctor, but in *The Turquoise Violin* and *The Amber Lyre* Veron repeatedly ends up spending significant amounts of time in the company of young, eligible gentlemen during the course of her investigations. She does not remain unpunished for these transgressions, either: just like her predecessor, Harriet Vane, in *The Amber Lyre* Veron is arrested on the suspicions of poisoning somebody: the fiancée of her former beau, István Remete. While eventually she is released and successfully uncovers the actual poisoner, clearing her good name is a more difficult process.

4   Destination Ókanizsa

Beside pushing the limits of her social position, Veron is often testing physical boundaries as well with her free navigation of public places. Her movement is problematic from the very beginning: in *The Black Piano*, she is scolded for riding a bicycle around town – a bicycle she especially asked for after reading about the student protests of 1897 at Cambridge University, which involved the burning of a lady cyclist effigy as the symbol of everything that is wrong with the world, specifically women getting degrees (*Black* 40–1) – and taking the train alone to a nearby town to attend a reading of the scandalous yet popular poet, Endre Ady. In *The Turquoise Violin*, she travels all through the Austro-Hungarian Monarchy chasing a murderer as no decent woman should; in *The Amber Lyre*, she is rumoured to have become a train driver, and in *The Golden Dulcimer*, she is taking a trip on a new-fangled service, a coach – once again, alone and heavily pregnant. It would seem that a majority of the dangerous situations Veron has to face originate from her inability to stay put, as she constantly feels compelled to go and look for trouble. (This characteristic feature, of course, relates her even more to her fellow Female Gentlemen, who are wont to embark on adventures, often on rather unladylike ones.) This is especially problematic and transgressive in her hometown, since the people of Ókanizsa would very much prefer to stay in the place allocated for them to avoid potentially disastrous consequences. In the beginning of the fourth book, one of the elderly gossipmongers laments to Veron's father thus:

> Heed my words, you ought to put it in your last will that your cold mortal remains should forever stay wherever they'd been buried. […] Just imagine the Archangel Gabriel a-coming, blowing his trumpet, and when he looks around, there's nobody there. The heavenly choirs can go on announcing that "the widow Mrs Kökény, née Elizabetta Korbáth from

Korbát is invited to proceed through the Pearly Gates," there won't be anyone to rush forward on their orders. And why? Because I'll be lying in a different cemetery, that's why, but who's going to notify the angels about that, eh? That I was moved on orders from the town council?

Golden 33–4[9]

The local discourse and general sentiments do not favour movement: stagnation is recommended, and with that, being content with one's lot in life. This misgiving regarding motion is illustrated when news about Veron's detective prowess reach Ókanizsa and the local gossips speculate what may have become of her; whether she is an international spy, a train driver, or a tamer of cougars in the circus (*Amber* 24), each possibility connected to constant moving about, and all of them sounding equally exotic and apparently possible for the likes of Veron, who could never be satisfied back at home. In this narrative, the stagnation-loving Ókanizsa is very much positioned as the end of the road. While it is emphatically backwards and provincial, always comparing unfavourably to more advanced and progressive nearby towns like Senta and Subotica, it is, however, not unusually provincial in the sense of being homogenous. Ókanizsa represents a tiny cross-section of the different nationalities of not only the Austro-Hungarian Monarchy but of contemporary Europe as well, with a Croatian landlord, a Serbian police captain, a German prostitute and a French waitress merely being a few of the – mostly – respectable inhabitants of the town, who have all arrived at Ókanizsa at the end of their journey and found their home and community there.

Movement appears to isolate and endanger the individual, both physically and socially: even the most trivial, practical segments of her life are permeated with indicators of Veron's triple status as outsider/defector/intruder. Her appearance, for example, is described as follows:

> She didn't wear a corset, nor did her mother, as opposed to the wives and daughters of doctors, lawyers and notaries. She was the daughter of a peasant working in a petty bourgeois position, and since she had few

---

9 – Én mondom magának, rovassa bele a testámentumába, hogy a kihűlt földi porhüvelye mindörökre ott marad, ahova elásták … […] Képzelje csak, legyön a Gábriel arkangyal, megfújja a harsonát, aztán szétnéz, és sehun senki. Hiába citerázzák az angyali karok, hogy „özvegy Kökényné, született korbáti Korbáth Elizabetta, fáradják be a Paradicsomba!", nem lesz ott senki, aki a parancsukra készséggel felelne. Azért, mert én ippeg egy másik cinterembe feküszök. Csak hát az angyalokat arról ki fogja értesíteni, he? Hogy engem várostanácsi parancsra átköltöztettek?" (*Golden* 33–4).

examples to follow, she wasn't overly confident navigating between urban fashion and traditional peasant clothing. In Ókanizsa, where farmers and gentlemen were forever divided by an ever-present demarcation line of hierarchy that was nearly impossible to cross, Veron, as a woman, stood in the middle of the line completely alone.

Black 40[10]

Veron's transgressions seem all the more serious because her way of managing space angers the elders of Ókanizsa and also defies some social norms on which the community is based, rules and rituals that are being threatened by the Female Gentleman's actions, as Melissa Schaub has pointed out. Breaking the rules regarding clothing appropriate to one's social standing may not carry serious consequences, but the unwritten rules that prescribe how and to what extent certain groups or individuals, such as foreigners or women, can have access to the world at large carry significantly more weight. Historically women's access to public spaces has been severely limited, and this was the case in early twentieth-century Ókanizsa as well: a separate refreshment room for the ladies is offered in the local restaurant where they can partake in drinks and gossip, but the designated space for women still seems to be the home in the novel, This is also the reason why, at the end of the first volume, Veron refuses a marriage offer that would confine her to the domestic sphere. Regarding women's spaces, Elizabeth Stanko argues that

> women's access to public space is restricted by the circulation of narratives of feminine vulnerability. Such narratives are calls for action: they suggest women must always be on guard when outside the home. They not only construct 'the outside' as inherently dangerous, but they also posit home as being safe. So women, if they have access to feminine respectability, must either stay at home (feminine in domestication), or be careful how they move and appear in public (femininity as a constrained mobility). Safety here becomes a question of not inhabiting public space or, more accurately, of not moving through that place alone.
>
> STANKO qtd in AHMED 69

---

10   Fűzőt nem viselt, ahogy az anyja sem, ellentétben az orvos-, ügyvéd-, jegyzőfeleségekkel és lányokkal. Egy parasztgazda lánya volt polgári állásban, és példa híján kevés magabiztossággal lavírozott a városi divat és a hagyományos falusi viselet között. Ókanizsán, ahol a gazdákat és az urakat minden pillanatban tapintható, alig átjárható státuszsáv választotta el egymástól, Veron egyes-egymagában állt ennek a sávnak a közepén mint nő. (*Black* 40).

Veron subverts these narratives by not allowing herself to be confined to one space (or to be confined by restrictive and outdated clothing): instead, she is constantly on the move, in transit, either by public transport or by bicycle, moving within the town or navigating further unknown areas, or even in her imagination: at the beginning of *The Black Piano*, she is working on a romantic novel about the French countess, Joséphine and her knightly suitor, Armand, thus spending time in imaginary Paris instead of among the dusty shelves of the Árkádia stationery shop. We cannot disregard the fact, however, that she is eventually severely punished for this tendency by the fourth novel, which is one of the major reasons why an optimistic reading of her fate is not possible: she does not appear to be one of those Female Gentlemen who manage to realize their feminist destiny against all the discouragement from society at large.

The perpetually moving Veron cannot be singlehandedly blamed for her unnatural tendency of constantly seeking out trouble and crime, as trouble and crime also have a tendency to occur in places where one would not necessarily expect it: in the Árkádia stationery shop, in a movie theatre, in the vicarage, or in fashionable holiday resorts. If these locations remind the reader of classical crime fiction, it is not by accident: as Bright and Mills argue, the presence of the dead body is especially disturbing in Golden Age crime stories because it has a tendency to turn up in places – such as the library, the vicarage, a gentlemen's club, and rural England in general – not associated with death and violence, and which are "considered safe" (35). This is why the corpse is "out of place." This quality of the corpse was noted by W. H. Auden as well, when he wrote for *Harper's Magazine* in 1948: "The corpse must shock not only because it is a corpse but also because, even for a corpse, it is shockingly out of place, as when a dog makes a mess on a drawing room carpet". This tendency can certainly be attributed to the classic tradition,[11] and as such we can observe it in Baráth's detective series as well: most of the crimes occur in a rural environment – three out of the four books take place in Ókanizsa –, and most dead

---

11 In the very same article Auden refers to Raymond Chandler, who "has written that he intends to take the body out of the vicarage garden and give murder back to those who are good at it. If he wishes to write detective stories, *i.e.*, stories where the reader's principal interest is to learn who did it, he could not be more mistaken; for in a society of professional criminals, the only possible motives for desiring to identify the murderer are blackmail or revenge, which both apply to individuals, not to the group as a whole, and can equally well inspire murder" (Harpers.org). In Auden's view, then, it is a misguided endeavour to remove the dead body from its unnatural habitat as that would apparently refute the aims of the genre. Of course, devotees of the classic and the hard-boiled tradition tend to disagree on several accounts apart from the location of the corpse, yet this difference seems crucial to the present argumentation.

bodies pop up in the unexpected locations listed above. Unlike Miss Marple's St. Mary Mead, however, the Hungarian countryside is a less peaceful land: *The Golden Dulcimer* playfully invokes the legendary outlaw, Sándor Rózsa, who is remembered in folk mythology much like Robin Hood: taking from the rich and giving to the poor. The fact remains, however, that the hero of Southern Hungary was definitely a murderer and a thief – a criminal at home in the rural landscape. Now Mrs Kökény's worry about the Archangel Gabriel not finding her in her original burial plot seems more reasonable, given the tendency of the corpses of Ókanizsa to appear "out of place." This disorderly behaviour of corpses then also entails that they may be found by individuals other than those whose profession entails that they must come into contact with death, such as doctors or members of the police – who, at the beginning of the series, have not encountered a murder in ten years, so they are nearly as clueless as Veron herself –, and the corpses are come upon by innocent bystanders: in *The Black Piano*, the first murder victim staggers straight into Árkádia with an Ady poem on his person, so Veron feels almost morally compelled to investigate as the case seems to require her specific area of expertise.

5 Cards on the Table

In conclusion, the detective formerly known as Veron Dávid has, I believe, joined the ranks of Female Gentlemen as an intrepid young lady fighting not only crime but social injustice, short-sightedness and gender inequality. Her success in this endeavour may not be as unequivocal as the success of several other fellow Female Gentlemen, but that is most probably due the difference not only in geographical location but also in historical and cultural circumstances. The *Veron* series, more or less ironically, keeps pointing out that while the classic crime formula, including typical characters, can be uprooted and planted in different settings, there are limits to the success of this endeavour. In the short story "The Belgian" (published in the same volume as *The Black Piano*), the intrepid Veron meets (and proceeds to step on the toes of) Hercule Poirot and the pair attempts to solve a mystery together (with Poirot coming to the wrong conclusion, much to his own and observers' dismay), while in *The Amber Lyre* she is reading a volume of Sherlock Holmes stories and tries to apply Holmes's deductive reasoning on the spot, with very little success. Although both instances are ironic gestures, they playfully point out that the classical investigating methods do not necessarily work in Hungary without being affected by the local circumstances, because, as Veron explains to Poirot, "this is Hungary, monsieur. And everything works differently here" (*Black* 303).

By the same token, the trope of the outsider thrust into the middle of an investigation fails to work in this setting, and it is Veron burdened with an abundance of local knowledge who has a chance to unravel the mystery and identify the criminal element.

In a small town in the middle of Central Europe in the early 20th century, a young woman will always start from a disadvantaged position, but instead of trying to explain away these disadvantages, I would rather call attention to them: it is "the social and legal matrix" mentioned by Makinen (93) and the individual's relationship with it that takes a central place in the crime narratives, as Katalin Baráth has managed to localize the Golden Age crime novel in Hungary not by slavishly recreating every single building block of the original model but by calibrating it to local circumstances, even if this means that the original model – the uncompromisingly successful Female Gentleman – will not be viable in the new environment.

Works Cited

Ahmed, Sara. *The Cultural Politics of Emotion*. Routledge, 2004.
Auden, W. H. "The Guilty Vicarage." *Harper's Magazine* 196, no. 1176 (1948):406–412.
Baráth, Katalin. *A borostyán hárfa* (*The Amber Lyre*). Agave Könyvek, 2012.
Baráth, Katalin. *A fekete zongora* (*The Black Piano*). Agave Könyvek, 2010.
Baráth, Katalin. *A türkizkék hegedű* (*The Turquoise Violin*). Agave Könyvek, 2011.
Baráth, Katalin. *Az arany cimbalom* (*The Golden Dulcimer*). Agave Könyvek, 2014.
Bernthal, J. C. *Queering Agatha Christie: Revisiting the Golden Age of Detective Fiction*. Palgrave Macmillan UK, 2016.
Bernthal, J. C. "'The sumptuous and the alluring.' Poirot's Women, Dragged Up and Dressed Down." J. C. Bernthal, editor. *The Ageless Agatha Christie. Essays on the Mysteries and the Legacy*. McFarland & Co., 2016. pp. 81–97.
Bright, Brittain and Rebecca Mills. "The Revelations of the Corpse. Interpreting the Body in the Golden Age Detective Novel." Casey A. Cothran and Mercy Cannon, editors. *New Perspectives on Detective Fiction. Mystery Magnified*. Routledge, 2016. pp. 32–51.
Hudácskó, Brigitta. "And Then There Were Many: Agatha Christie in Hungarian Translation." J. C. Bernthal, editor. *The Ageless Agatha Christie. Essays on the Mysteries and the Legacy*. McFarland & Co., 2016. pp. 130–144.
Makinen, Merja. *Feminist Popular Fiction*. Palgrave Macmillan UK, 2001.
Rushing, Robert A. *Resisting Arrest. Detective Fiction and Popular Culture*. Other Press, 2007.
Schaub, Melissa. *Middlebrow Feminism in Classic British Detective Fiction*. Palgrave Macmillan UK, 2013.

Index

10:04 11, 22, 25–26, 29

A Piano in Mid Air 91–92
Aaronovitch, Ben 201–202
Adebayo, Diran 201–202
Adichie, Chimamanda Ngozi 13–14, 181
Ady, Endre 81, 229–230
affect 1–3, 4–8, 9–11, 12–15, 21–22, 24, 25–26, 27, 28–29, 30–33, 35–36, 37, 54–55, 57–58, 60–61, 62, 63–67, 101, 103, 106–107, 110–111, 112–113, 114, 119–120, 126–127, 130–131, 137, 140–141, 175, 188–189, 196, 202–203, 205–207, 215–216, 217–218,
   affect and emotion 2–3, 6–7, 11, 24, 25, 97–98, 185–186
   affection 96–97, 99–100, 178
   affective 2–3, 4–6, 9–15, 22, 24, 25–26, 30, 32–33, 55, 57–58, 59, 60–62, 65–66, 74–75, 90–91, 92–93, 94–95, 103–104, 106–107, 112–113, 116, 118, 119–120, 127–128, 132–133, 136, 140, 144–145, 149–151, 152–156, 164–166, 176, 189, 195–196, 209–210, 214, 215–216, 217–218, 222
      affective dissonance 176
      affective distance 74–75
      affective geography 137, 176
      affective investment 94–95, 103–104
      affective map 13, 14–15, 183–184, 195–196, 202–203
      affective milieu 115–116, 119–120
      affective mobility 10–11, 22
      affective psychogeography 163–164, 169–170, 174–175
      affective topography 15, 90–91
      affective turn 136, 183
   impersonal affect 10–11, 25–26, 28–29, 30
   transpersonal affect 10–11
African American literature 13, 131
African diaspora 186, 190
Afshar, Haleh 146–147n1., 147
Agamben, Giorgio 41–42, 43, 44, 59–60, 216, 217
Ahmed, Sarah 6–7, 109–112, 116, 184–185, 187n9, 191–192
Alice in Wonderland 13, 163–164, 169

Alighieri, Dante 62–63
Allingham, Marjorie 223–224
Altieri, Charles 61–62, 66
Americanah 13–14, 181
Andermahr, Sonya 188–189n10
Anderson, Jon 5–6, 128–129, 133, 135–136, 137
Anima Rerum– The Soul of Things (Anima Rerum – A Dolgok Lelke) 37, 38–39, 45–46
Antal, Nimród 73
Anzaldúa, Gloria 140–141
Appadurai, Arjun 3–5, 7
archive 54, 59, 66–67
Arias, Santa 76
Assmann, Aleida 36, 37–38, 40
Athanasourelis, John Paul 205–207
Auden, W. H. 232–233, 232–233n1.
Augé, Marc 81–82, 134–135, 184–185, 188–189, 191–192, 211
Auschwitz 10–11, 37, 40, 48
Austro-Hungarian Monarchy 1–2, 14, 222, 229–230

Bacsó, Péter 91–92, 96–97
Baelo-Allué, Sonia 188–189n10
Baggini, Julia 178
Bakay, Eszter 92
Ballard, J. G. 201–202
Baltimore 183–184, 185–186, 189–190, 196
Baráth, Katalin 15, 220–221, 222–223, 222–223n3, 224–225, 226, 232–233, 234
Barcan, Ruth 114
Barker, Chris 9–10
Barthes, Roland 189–190
Bartov, Omer 2, 7–8
Bates, Timothy 125–126
Baudelaire, Charles 26–27, 54, 64, 208–209
Bauman, Zygmunt 212–213, 214
Beer, Gillian 166–167
belonging 5–6, 75, 112–113, 114–118, 119–120, 129–130, 164, 176, 181–182, 183–184, 189, 192, 195–196
Benjamin, Walter 5–6, 26–27, 40–41, 54, 55, 59–60, 59–60n2, 61, 64, 208–210, 212
Berlant, Lauren 149–151, 195–196

Bernthal, J. C.   220–221n1, 226
Bhabha, Homi   182
Bondi, Liz   6–7, 164–165, 176
Borges, Jorge Luís   211
Bottoni, Stefano   1–2
Boutry, Katherine   130–131
Brah, Avtar   4–5
Braidotti, Rosi   168
Brandstetter, Gabriele   44–45, 47–48
Brennan, Teresa   6–7
Brickell, Katherine   4, 22–23, 127–128
Bright, Brittain   225, 232–233
Brook, Peter   35–36
Brooker, Peter   131
Buck-Morss, Susan   26–27n2.
Budapest   9–10, 11, 12, 14–15, 109–110, 112, 120
Bush, George   216
Butler, Judith   187n9
Byrne, Ted   63

Calkin, Jessamy   184–185n 8
Carlyle, Thomas   60
Carroll, Lewis   13–14, 163–165, 168, 171, 173
Cass, Vivienne   117–118
Castronovo, David   226–227
Central Europe   1–2, 1–2n2, 7, 9–10
Chadwick-Joshua, Jocelyn   126
Chameleon (Kaméleon)   107
Chandler, Raymond   205–207, 223–224
Chaney, Michael A.   142–143, 152–153
Chiswick   204, 211, 213
Christie, Agatha   220–221n1, 221–224, 225, 226
Chute, Hillary   141, 142–143, 145, 158
City of Tiny Lights   14–15, 201
Cixous, Hélene   165–166
cognitive mapping   134–135
Cohen, Phil   209–210
Cole, Teju   11, 22, 24, 25–26, 195–196n14
Colpani, Gianmaria   2
communal living   90–92, 95–98
Connell, R. W.   74–75, 76
Cooppan, Vilashini   24–25
Crang, Mike   5–6, 129
Crawford, Allison   36, 45
Crowley, David   92, 93n4
Császi, Ádám   71–72
Csizmady, Adrienne   92
Cuhorka, Emese   37, 40

Dabashi, Hamid   146–147n1
Dánél, Mónika   85
Darda, Joseph   141–143
Datta, Ayona   4, 22–23, 127–128
Davidson, Ian   59n1
Davidson, Joyce   6–7, 164–165, 176
Davidson, Michael   54–55
de Beauvoir, Simone   145–146, 151–152
de Certeau, Michel   6–7n7, 6–7, 59–60, 62–63, 184–185, 194–195
Debord, Guy   63, 166–167
Debrecen   37, 39, 40
Deleuze, Gilles   11, 24, 25, 54–55, 165–166, 167, 182n2, 213
Delta   12, 71–72, 74–75, 80, 85
dérive   61, 63, 166–167, 168
Derrida, Jacques   59–60, 165–166
Dewsbury, John David   163–164
Dhand, A. A.   201–202
Duff, Cameron   106–107, 110–111, 118, 119–120
DuPlessis, Rachel Blau   172
dysgeographia   13–14, 166–167, 169–170, 174

Eastern Europe   1–2, 1n1, 7, 7–8n10, 9–10, 72–74, 76, 80, 82–83
Eastern European cinema   71–72n1, 72–73, 76, 80–81, 83
Eckhard, Petra   134–135
Eckstein, Lars   202
Egedy, Tamás   89–90n1, 92
Ember, Judit   93–94, 97–98
Embroideries   145–146, 157n2, 158–159
England   183–184, 189–191, 192, 207–208, 210–211, 232–233
entrapment   91–92, 93–94, 101–102, 103–104, 213–214
Europe   3–4, 73, 74, 139–140, 151–152, 155–156, 183–184, 194–195, 196, 230

Fahidi, Éva   10–11, 36, 37, 38–39, 40, 41–42, 43, 44–46
Falkenhayner, Nicole   202–203
Family Nest (Családi tűzfészek)   90–91, 98–99, 101–102
fascination   2–3, 12–13, 125, 128–129, 131–133, 135–136, 137
fear   13, 14–15, 110–111, 114–115, 116, 127, 129, 130, 164, 165, 190, 202–203, 215–218, 217–218n9

Fejős, Endre   221–222n2
Fekete, Ibolya   97
Female Gentleman   222, 223–225, 226, 229–230, 232, 233–234
femininity   12, 13, 14, 58, 91–92, 93–98, 99–100, 102–104, 116, 146–147n1, 148, 165–166, 169–170, 171–172, 173–174, 175, 225, 226–227, 231
Fitch, Andy   53–54
Fitzpatrick, Ryan   54–55, 56, 58–59n1
flaneur   26–27, 28, 60–61n2, 125–126, 168, 202–203, 208–209
flaneuse   13–14, 169–170, 173–174
Foden, Giles   26–27
Foucault, Michel   59–60, 76
Frank, Michael C.   217–218n9
Freitag, Ulrike   22–23
Freud, Sigmund   45, 80–81
Fried, Nico   37
Fučik, Julius   48
fugueur   28
Fusfeld, Daniel R.   125–126

Gáfrik, Róbert   8–9n14
Gallagher, Catherine   30–31
Gaugain, Paul   204n1
Gelencsér, Gábor   75, 98–99
Gilloch, Graeme   212
Gilroy, Paul   183, 208, 217–218
Goda, Krisztina   108–109
Goethe, Johann Wolfgang   59–61
Golden Age detective fiction   220–221, 220–221n1, 222, 223–225, 232–233, 234
Goldman, Marlene   44
Gott, Michael   72–73
Goyal, Yogita   195–196
Grandt, Jurgen E.   130–131
Great Migration   125–126, 131
Greco, Monica   6–7
green city   171
Greenwald Smith, Rachel   22, 24–25, 28–29
Greenwood, Kerry   220–221
Gregg, Melissa   61, 62, 66–67, 126–127, 130–131
Greiner, Clemens   22–23
Griffin, Farah J.   131
Grimm brothers, the   171–172
Grodeczki, Wiktor   109–110n3
Gröning, Oskar   37–38
Grunwalsky, Ferenc   97

Guarracino, Serena   189–190n11
Győri, Zsolt   71–72n1

Habila, Helon   195–196n14
Hacking, Ian   28
Hammett, Dashiel   209, 223–224
Hannah, Sophie   220–221
Haraway, Donna   170–171
hard-boiled fiction   202–203, 205–211, 212–214, 215, 217–218
Hardt, Michael   3–4, 6–7
Harlem   13, 125–126, 127–130, 131–132, 133, 134–136
Hartman, Geoffrey   37–38, 40
Hazlitt, Sarah   63
Headley, Victor   201–202
Heidegger, Martin   211
Herczog, Noémi   40–41
Herrero, Dolores   188–189n10
Herzog, Todd   72–73
Hlibchuk, Geoffrey   54–55
Hodge, Stephen   106
Holocaust   10–11, 36, 37–38, 39, 40–41, 42, 43, 44–47, 49–50
Horsley, Lee   201–202, 204
Horváth, Ádám   107–108n1
Horváth, Sándor   90–91
Hot Men, Cold Dictatorships (*Meleg férfiak, hideg diktatúrák*)   112
housing estate   12, 89–90n1, 91–92, 96–97, 101
Hungarian cinema   12, 71–73, 75, 89–92, 107–108, 116

Irvine, Alexander C.   169
Irwin, John T.   210–211
Isaacs, Camille   184–185n7, 189–190n11
Islamic Revolution   143, 146–147n1
Iveson, Kurt   170–171

Jameson, Fredric   9–10, 215
Jazz   13, 125, 131, 133, 135–136, 137
Jerram, Luke   178
Jobbit, Steve   73
Johnston, Lynda   108–109
Jones, Radhika   184–185n8
Joseph, Maia   54–55, 60–61n2

Kahlo, Frida   204n1
Kalisky, Aurélia   46–47

Kalmár, György 8–9n13, 12
Kálmán C., György 8–9n13
Kékesi, Zoltán 37–38
Kellermann, Peter Felix 47
King, Shannon 127–128, 133
Király, Hajnal 72–73, 80, 81–82, 85
Kisantal, Tamás 45–46
Kiséry, András 8–9n13
Knight, Stephen 205–207
Komandarev, Stephan 86
Konrád, György 92
Kontroll 73
Koolhaas, Rem 57
Korn, Leslie E. 45, 47–48
Korte, Barbara 202
Kovačević, Nataša 1, 1–2n1, 2
Kovács, N. Tímea 94–95
Kozieł, Patrycja 184–185n7
Krishnan, Madhu 184–185n5
Kureishi, Hanif 202–203

LaCapra, Dominick 45–46
Lagos 13–14, 183–184, 185–186, 193–194
Lajkó, Félix 80
Land of Storms (*Viharsarok*) 82
Laub, Dori 36
Leach, Neil 189
Lefebvre, Henri 59–60, 75–76, 90–91, 174
Lerner, Ben 11, 22, 25–26, 29–32
Let Go of My Beard 91–92
Levi, Primo 41–42
Levine, Caroline 184–185n7
Leys, Ruth 44
Ligeti, György 42
Linke, Ulli 217
London 9–10, 13–14, 169, 171–172, 174–175, 176–177, 183–184, 185–186, 189–190, 194, 195–196, 201–202, 205–209, 217–218
Longhurst, Robyn 108–109
Lopez, Marta Sofia 184–185n5
Lord, Christopher 1–2
Lőrincz, Csongor 40–41
lyric poetry 53, 54, 64, 65–66

Makinen, Merja 220–221, 234
Manaugh, Geoff 175
Margalit, Avishai 37–38
Marsh, Ngaio 223–224, 225

masculinity 12, 13–14, 71–75, 76, 77, 85–86, 91–92, 93–95, 97–98, 101–102, 167, 173–174, 202–203, 213–214, 218
Massey, Doreen 5–6n6, 58–59, 83, 96, 181–182, 183–185, 188–189, 195–196
Massumi, Brian 24
McCloud, Scott 141–142
McDonough, Tom 168
McLeod, John 183n3
McPherson, Catriona 220–221
Men in the Nude (*Férfiakt*) 107
memory 28, 36, 37–38, 54, 77–78, 86, 127–128, 132–133, 134, 135, 225
Merkel, Angela 37
Messud, Claire 26–27
middlebrow fiction 14–15, 220–221, 223, 226–227
Miéville, China 13–14, 163–164, 169, 171, 174–176, 178, 201–202
Mignolo, Walter 139–140, 159
migration 22–23, 125–126, 127–128, 151, 183n3, 190, 195–196, 203–204
Mills, Rebecca 225, 232–233
Mishkova, Diana 3–4
Mistletoes (*Fagyöngyök*) 93–94, 97–98
Mitchell, Gladys 223–224
Moi, Toril 176
Moorcock, Michael 201–202
moral witness 37–39, 40, 44–45, 46–47
Moreno, Jacob L. 47
Morrison, Toni 13, 125–126, 127–128, 131, 134–135, 137
Moxley, Jennifer 62
Müller, Péter 44
multiculturalism 159, 202, 204, 205–208
Mundruczó, Kornél 71–72, 80–81, 109
Munkelt, Marga 185
Munt, Sally R. 111
Murai, András 91–92
Myslik, Wayne D. 106–107, 116

Nadar 54
narratives of return 12, 72–73, 80–82, 83, 147, 152–153
Neate, Patrick 14–15, 202–203, 204, 207–208, 210–211, 212–213
Nedbálková, Katarina 114–115, 116
Neelakantan, Gurumurthy 106

Negri, Antonio   3–4
New York   9–10, 11, 25–26, 28–30, 32–33, 125–126, 127–129, 130, 185, 187, 196
Ngai, Sianne   28–29
Nimród, Antal   73
noir   14–15, 201–203, 205–208, 209–210, 213–214
nomadism   23, 168
non-place   79–80, 81–82, 134–135, 188–189, 191–192, 211

Occasional Work and Seven Walks from the Office for Soft Architecture   11, 53–54, 55, 56, 57, 58–61, 62, 65, 66–67
Odum, Howard   177
Oliver, Kelly   207
Open City   11, 22, 25–26, 29–30
Orosz, Dénes   107–108n1

Paddison, Ronan   75–76
Pain, Rachel   215
Pálfi, György   71–72, 77
Paquet-Deyris, Anne-Marie   127
Peacock, Laurel   65–66
Pedwell, Carolyn   6–7, 183n4
Peer, Krisztián   48–49n2
Pellicer-Ortín, Silvia   188–189n10
Perczel, Karola   44–45
Peršak, Nina   108
Persepolis 2: The Story of a Return   139–140, 147, 149, 151–152, 158–159
Persepolis: The Story of a Childhood   139–140, 143–147, 149–151, 157, 158–159
Philadelphia   13–14, 183–184, 185–186, 187–188, 189, 196
Phillips, Mike   201–202, 203–204
Philo, Chris   75–76
picara   166
Pirker, Eva Ulrike   202–203
playable city   177
Plummer, Patricia   203–204
Ponzanesi, Sandra   2
postcolonial   8–9, 8–9n14, 13, 130–131, 183n3, 185, 203–205, 208
Pratchett, Terry   201–202
Prefab People (Panelkapcsolat)   90–91, 97–98, 101, 102–103
Princeton   14, 183–184, 185–187, 194, 195–196

psychogeography   5–6, 63, 163–164, 168
Pucherová, Dobrota   8–9n14

queer place-making   112, 120
queer sexuality   120

Rabinovitz, Lauren   26–27
Ramazani, Jahan   23
Reemtsma, Jan Philipp   44–45
retreat   71–72, 73, 74, 77–78, 79–80, 82–84, 85, 109–110, 115–116
Robertson, Lisa   11, 53–55, 56, 59–61, 62–63, 64–67
romance   13–14, 185–186, 194, 196
Rosenberg, Yvonne   217–218n9
Rousseau, Jean-Jacques   59–60
Routledge, Paul   75–76
Rudy, Susan   55, 56
Rushing, Robert A.   221–222
Ruskin, John   58, 59–60
Russell, Danielle   126

Sacks, Marcy S.   131–132
Sághy, Miklós   73–74
Sahr, Wolf-Dietrich   125–126, 127–129, 133, 135–136, 137
Sakdapolrak, Patrick   22–23
Sartre, Jean-Paul   211
Satkunananthahn, Anita Harris   184–185n5
Satrapi, Marjane   9–10, 13, 139, 141–146, 149, 152–153, 157, 158
Sauerberg, Lars Ole   201–202
Sayers, Dorothy L.   223–224, 225
Scapettone, Jennifer   56
Schaub, Melissa   223–225, 231
Schissel, Wendy   75
Schmid, Heiko   125–126, 127–129, 133, 135–136, 137
Schmidt, Christopher   54–55
Schmitz, Markus   185
Schulz, Kathryn   184–185n6
Sea Lavender, or the Euphoria of Being (Sóvirág – avagy a létezés eufóriája)   11, 36, 37–38, 40–41, 44, 45–48, 49–50
Secret Years (Eltitkolt évek)   117–119
Seigworth, Gregory J.   61, 62, 66–67, 126–127, 130–131

shame 2–3, 12, 35–36, 42, 45, 107, 112–113, 114–115, 120, 152, 204–205, 226
Sharp, Joanne P. 75–76
Shaviro, Steven 73–74, 77–78
Shohat, Ella 159
Simmel, Georg 209–210
Skoulding, Zoë 60–61n2
Sláma, Bohdan 86
Smith, Danielle Taana 217
Smith, Michael Peter 23
Smith, Mick 6–7, 164–165, 176
Smith, Susan J. 215
Smith, Zadie 202–203
Soja, Edward W. 90–91, 181–182
Soueif, Ahdaf 190–191
Spahr, Juliana 62, 66
Spiegelman, Art 45–46
Stanislavski, Konstantin Sergeievich 44–45
Stanko, Elizabeth 231
state socialism 12, 74, 77–78, 83, 91–92, 94–95n5, 103–104, 113–114, 115–116n7, 118, 120
Stein, Mark 185
Stenner, Paul 6–7
Stevenson, Deborah 127
Stewart, Kathleen 65
Stier, Oren Baruch 45–46
Stőhr, Lóránt 110–111
Straus, Erwin 46
Strausz, László 77–78, 79–80
Stroh, Silke 185
Stroschein, Sherill 8
Sulik, Martin 86
Sutliff Sanders, Joe 174
Szabó, Réka 11, 48–49n2
Szelényi, Iván 92
Szeman, Imre 73–74
Szomjas, György 90–91, 97

Takács, Judit 108n2, 115–116, 118n9, 120
Takács, Mária 113–115, 117–119
Tally, Robert T. 9–10
Tamás, Gáspár Miklós 73–74
Tandori, Dezső 224–225n5
Tarr, Béla 80–81, 90–91, 97–100, 101, 102–103
Taxidermia 12, 71–72, 73–75, 77, 80, 85
Tehran 13, 140, 147–148, 151, 152, 153–156, 157
Terada, Rei 24–25
terrorism 83, 208, 210–211, 212–215, 216, 217–218n9, 218
testimony 11, 35–36, 37–39, 41–42, 44, 49–50, 66–67
The Agony of Mr. Boróka (Forró vizet a kopaszra!) 91–92, 96, 98–99
The Amber Lyre (A borostyán hárfa) 228–230, 233–234
The Black Piano (A fekete zongora) 225, 226, 228–230, 232–233
The Euphoria of Being 11
The Golden Dulcimer (Az arany cimbalom) 227–228, 229–230, 232–233
The Turquoise Violin (A türkizkék hegedű) 226–227, 228–230
theatricality 10–11, 35–36, 37, 38, 49
Thelwall, John 63
Thien, Deborah 6–7
This I Wish and Nothing More (Nincsen nekem vágyam semmi) 107
Thoreau, Henry David 59–60
Through the Looking-Glass 165–166
Thüringer, Barbara 38–39
Tingatinga, Eduardo 204n1
Tóth, Eszter Zsófia 91–92, 94–96
translocal subject 127, 128–129, 135–136, 137
translocality 2, 3, 4, 9–11, 12–13, 15, 21–22, 28, 29–30, 53, 127–128, 129, 132–133, 134, 137, 183–184, 196
transnationalism 3, 4–6, 13, 22–23, 127–128, 139–140, 142–143, 145–146, 152, 155–156, 183n3, 183–184, 193–194, 195–196, 207–208
transpersonal community 10–11, 22, 25–26, 29, 30, 32–33
trauma 8, 10–11, 12–13, 35–36, 40–41, 44–46, 47–48, 49, 71–73, 78–79, 80–81, 82, 83–84, 126, 127–128, 132–133, 134, 136, 145, 149–151, 158, 167, 187–189, 193–194, 224–225
Trencsényi, Balázs 3–4
Trigo, Benigno 207
Turda, Marius 8

Un Lun Dun 13, 169, 171
urban experience 10–11, 53, 54–55, 56–57, 58–60, 62, 125–126, 175, 208–209
urban fantasy 168, 171, 201–202
urban subjectivity 126–128, 131, 137
Urry, John 125–126, 127–129, 133, 135–136, 137

utopian   32, 58, 100, 101–102, 103–104, 177
Valassopoulos, Anastasia   152, 158–159
Vancouver   11, 53, 54–55, 56, 59–60, 66
Verdery, Katherine   91–92, 93–94, 94–95n5
Vermeulen, Gert   108
Vermeulen, Pieter   26n1, 28, 29n3
Vienna   9–10, 13, 140, 151–155, 157
Viswanath, Gundappa   208–209
von Oppen, Achim   22–23

Waldenfels, Bernhard   42–43
walking   26, 27–28, 56, 62–63, 64, 66, 169–170, 194–195
Wall Driller (*Falfúró*)   90–91, 97, 98, 101–102
Warf, Barney   76
Weich, Dave   158
Weitz, Eric D.   2, 7–8
Weitzer, Ronald   108

welfare   83, 90–92, 94–95, 102–104
Wharton, Steve   107–108
Williams, Raymond   4–5n4
Wilson, Andrew   220–221
Wilson, Elizabeth   26–27n2
Wolff, Larry   7–8n10
Wood, James   26–27
Woolf, Virginia   72–73, 74, 168
World War I   7–8, 222, 224–225
World War II   1, 7–8, 9–10, 58, 77
Wulf, Christoph   42, 44–46, 48

Yeldho, Joe V.   126

Zappa, Frank   207
Zilahy, Lajos   221–222n2
Zipes, Jack   173
Zsigó, Anna   48–49n2

Printed in the United States
By Bookmasters